The American President

THE
AMERICAN
PRESIDENT

By Sidney Hyman

GREENWOOD PRESS, PUBLISHERS
WESTPORT, CONNECTICUT

Library of Congress Cataloging in Publication Data

Hyman, Sidney.
   The American President.

   Reprint of the ed. published by Harper, New York.
   1. Presidents--United States. I. Title.
[JK516.H9 1974]   353.03'13   73-15166
ISBN 0-8371-7170-9

Originally published in 1954 by Harper & Brothers, New York

Reprinted with the permission of Harper & Row, Publishers, Inc.

Reprinted in 1974 by Greenwood Press,
a division of Williamhouse-Regency Inc.

Library of Congress Catalogue Card Number 73-15166

ISBN 0-8371-7170-9

Printed in the United States of America

To Faye

Contents

I

THE INSTITUTION

1

The President reigns and rules

The entry of the presidency on the American scene – Shadows of the presidency now stretch over the earth – Reflects America's twentieth-century bigness – Prophecies of Alexis de Tocqueville and Thomas Jefferson – President's place at the summit of our domestic life is not due to a constitutional mandate – Or to any seizure of power – It is due to nonlegal factors – The social need met elsewhere by the Crown – Why the Supreme Court or the Congress cannot serve the same need – Dual character of the presidency as an office and as an institution – Dilemma of a President – He reigns and rules – Combines elements that draw us to power and repel us from it.

In advance of George Washington's arrival in New York for his first inauguration, the Senate was agitated by a question of ceremony. Should the new chief executive have a ringing monarchical title, or should he have a republican one a bit more sonorous than "The President of the United States of America"? James Madison eventually put an end to the debate by citing the constitutional declaration in favor of the latter form. But in the interval, there were those on the street whose reaction was expressed in a cartoon. Captioned "The Entry," it showed President-elect George Washington astride an ass and in the arms of his valet, Billy

Humphries. As Humphries sang out with hosannahs and birthday odes, a Devil in the background joined in with this counterpoint:

> The glorious time has come to pass
> When David shall conduct an ass.

The exuberant irreverence which met "The Entry" of the presidency on the American scene did not end with that event. Washington's successors have all been portrayed as self-deluded figures in an empty pageant of state or as dedicated enemies of American freedom. Yet the presidency itself has come to be our leading social invention and our main contribution to democratic government. Today, its impulses circle the earth. This new global role was forecast briefly in the administration of Theodore Roosevelt, the first of the modern Presidents. It lit up the sky again in the days of Woodrow Wilson. It gained fixed form in Franklin D. Roosevelt's third term. It matured in the administration of Harry S. Truman. And by 1952, it appears to have been a crucial factor in General Eisenhower's election. For the first time in American history, a man wholly divorced from domestic affairs nevertheless won the presidency mainly on the grounds that his experience on the international scene gave him superior qualifications for the post.

The vast theater of action on which the President now moves simply reflects the facts of America's twentieth-century bigness. Had we remained a small nation, living in rural isolation with a barnyard economy, the President would either have been spared the need or denied the means to be a generative force on the world scene. That he now seems to be a prime mover of events—or a prime defaulter in the face of events—is intimately connected with our change from a thin web of farms into a complex industrial machine, from a town hall meeting into a republic with obligations imperial in type. With strange historical tact, moreover, these changes reached their climax at a time when other free nations, exhausted by two wars, lacked the material means to check Communist aggression. If these nations are revived in their strength or are released from their fears of the East, it is to be expected that they will reduce both their dependence on the American initiative and the deference they show American spokesmen; there are signs that this process may now be under way. For the indeterminate future, however, we are fated to hold the role of "the first among equals," with consequences for the presidency foreseen by Alexis de Tocqueville more than a century ago.

"It is chiefly in its foreign relations," he wrote in 1835, "that the executive power of a nation finds occasion to exert its skill and strength. If the existence of the Union were perpetually threatened, if its chief interests were in daily connection with those of other powerful nations, the executive department would assume an increased importance in proportion to the measures expected of it and to those which it would execute." Today, as part of the measures expected of him, the President does more than propose the ground rules for American military, diplomatic and economic policies. He makes the same sort of proposals to the other nations in the Western alliance. The President not only is America's chief administrative officer; he also co-ordinates a network of programs shared in by foreign executives. He not only can veto the work of the Congress. The threat of his veto hangs heavy over the heads of foreign assemblies. He is the party leader, the guide and interpreter of public opinion, the keeper of the conscience, the ceremonial head, the disciplinarian and the source of clemency. He is all these things and more, not only for Americans from whom he derives his authority, but for a vast nonvoting world constituency.

The proof of this came in the autumn of 1952 when other peoples were forced to postpone their own domestic decisions until Americans decided who would succeed President Truman. By that act, they confirmed with a vengeance a prophecy made by Thomas Jefferson in December, 1787, before the Constitution was ratified. "The election of a President of America some years hence," Jefferson wrote, "will be much more interesting to certain nations of Europe [and we now add, Asia, the Middle East, Africa, South America and the Pacific], than ever the election of a king of Poland was." And these nations, though they do not cast a single vote, share an equal interest with Americans in everything the President does after his election. When he creaks they groan. When he wobbles they feel unhinged. When he is forced into foreign policy compromises with his domestic enemies— whether of necessity or through timidity—they feel betrayed. And when he speaks and acts with firmness in defense of the Western tradition, they feel uplifted.

To some extent, what Americans expect of a President in the conduct of our external affairs sets the stage for his ascendancy in our domestic life. So that he can better serve our purposes on the world scene, we tend to concentrate the management of the national energy in the hands of this one man. And we do this in proportion to the strength he shows in using what is given to him. Yet his great internal influence cannot wholly be explained in this way. Neither can it be explained by citing a constitutional mandate which presumably gives the President a pre-eminent position in domestic matters. Nor can it be explained by repeating the charge that Presidents have raised themselves to the summit of our internal affairs through the primitive device of "usurping power." For the real source of his supremacy lies outside the law of his office or any willful use of authority beyond the law.

Consider, first, the nature of a President's legal mandate and the extent to which Presidents have respected it. The Constitution does not make the President superior to, stronger or more important than the Congress and the Supreme Court. It gives to each enough strength to do its assigned part in serving a joint purpose stated in the Preamble. But it withholds from each the increment of strength by which it could crush or displace the others.

In this design for what Alexander Hamilton said was a system of "power as the rival of power," conflicts are not only inevitable; they were deliberately invited by the constitutional architects as a condition that would keep the system in balance. Yet when these clashes occur, there is the rending cry that the Constitution has been undermined, while the finger of suspicion generally points to the Executive as the guilty party. It is charged that he has dictatorial ambitions at the particular expense of the Congress; and, since he is only one man, he fits the stereotype image of a dictator. It is the rare voice which suggests that dictatorships can also come in the form of committees; that in a free and easy construction of its own "inherent powers," the Congress may have usurped the authority of the Executive while it shunned its own responsibilities as a legislature.

For the most part, however, it is difficult to charge either

[7]

the Executive or the Congress with a "usurpation of power" when the two collide. If the points at issue between them are viewed coolly, they commonly show up as questions on which any two men can have legitimate differences of opinion. Should the President have a tight or a broad range of administrative discretion that he can use within the four corners of any law Congress enacts? Who should have the right of initiative at those points where the President and the Congress hold overlapping constitutional duties? Who should lead and who should follow in those fields where the Constitution says neither "Thou shalt" nor "Thou shalt not" to any branch of the government? In this same situation, whose "inherent powers" shall take precedence over those claimed by the opposite branch? Which of the President's constitutional powers can be exercised on his own initiative, and which of those powers must remain dormant until the Congress says he can use them? Should the President be bound by the prohibitions or directives Congress expresses in resolutions, when the laws, by contrast, leave him free to use his own discretion? Must the President enforce all laws automatically? When two laws touch on the same topic, is he free to choose one and not the other, or can he reject both while he seeks his solutions by "influence" instead of law? And finally, whose version of an emergency shall serve as the basis of emergency action? These questions are inherent in the Constitution proper. The way in which they are resolved, however, is strongly influenced by the interplay of personal traits among those who govern at any particular moment.

If the Constitution does not place the President on a plane above the Congress, neither does the new work load carried by a President of itself represent an absolute increase in his powers over those of the Congress. This alone can be said. It is self-evident that his work has in fact increased to an inhuman extent. George Washington signed 44 laws and 1 executive order in a representative year. In a similar period, Franklin D. Roosevelt signed 408 laws and 315 executive orders. Washington vetoed only 2 bills in eight years. In his tenure to the close of 1951, Harry S. Truman used the defensive power of his office in the outright veto of 175 bills, and in an additional 66 pocket vetoes. Washington granted 9 pardons and appointed 65 persons to Federal jobs in 1791. In a recent year, President Truman signed 500 civil pardons—plus 9,000 military pardons in 1952—and made 25,000 appointments. Washington prepared the national budget on a single sheet of paper. The average presidential budget today runs over 1.5 million words, or fifteen times the size of this book.

Washington's supervisory role was limited to 9 agencies, of which the Treasury, State and War Departments alone had the status of major departments. Yet in midsummer of 1789, when the presidency was only a few months old, he informed a French diplomat that he had no time to read or answer the dispatches that poured in on him. In June of the next year, he was more specific. "These public meetings," he wrote to his friend, David Stuart, "with reference *to* and *from* different Departments of State—is as much, if not more, than I am able to undergo." With far better reason did Harry Truman complain in October, 1951, about the "oppressive" nature of his office. By a count of the Hoover Commission, he was held responsible in one or another way for the work of 9 major departments, 104 bureaus, 12 sections, 108 services, 51 branches, 460 offices, 631 divisions, 19 administrations, 6 agencies, 16 areas, 40 boards, 6 commands, 20 commissions, 19 corporations, 5 groups, 10 headquarters, 3 authorities and 263 other miscellaneous and often overlapping bits of government machinery. In combination, they employed 1 out of every 62 civilians in the nation, in contrast to 1 out of every 2,000 in Washington's day.

Yet the increased work load of a President does not by itself represent the presence of new organic powers. It can represent a more frequent use of his traditional powers, demanded by the exigencies of the time. Today, for example, the President is heavily engaged as the chief organ of foreign affairs and as the commander in chief of the armed forces. In these two roles he can plunge the nation almost single-handedly into a frightful war. But the decisions of any President have held this same potential since 1790; the cause lies in the functions the Constitution allocates to the presidency. That the danger of a mishap now seems greater than ever before is due to an environment piled high with targets, with trigger-happy friends and enemies, and with a pervasive overlay of explosive materials.

In the same vein, it matters little if the President signs or vetoes one bill or a thousand of them; if he pardons one criminal or five hundred of them. His constitutional power to share in the legislative process, or to grant pardons remains uniform and the proportions apply equally to his power to appoint, to administer and so on. In short, the more frequent use of these traditional powers does not increase their organic nature any more than the inflation of a toy balloon increases its rubber content.

One final point. Much is made of the fact that the power of the presidency has been vastly increased by the "delegation" of power granted it by the Congress. Yet it is questionable whether the word "delegation" is properly used in this connection. Except by an amendment to the Constitution, the Congress cannot, for example, lawfully delegate its taxing power to the President even if it wanted to do that, any more than the President can voluntarily delegate to the Congress his power as a commander in chief. Though the case is admittedly open to a sharp rebuttal, the so-called "delegation" of power by the Congress to the President seems to involve one of two acts. (1) The Congress defines and explicitly states the terms under which the President can exercise the powers vested in his office by the broad language of the Constitution. But it gives him nothing beyond what is latent in his office. (2) The Congress "borrows" the President to act as an Executive for constitutional powers which remain throughout in the hands of the Congress.

I have been suggesting by implication that we must look beyond a legal description of the presidency to account for the place it holds at the summit of our internal life. In a shift of view, we come upon this. The presidency is something more than an office based on law, just as the Papacy is something more than a Vatican ruled by canon law. The presidency is also an institution whose character is deeply rooted in the American mood and culture. The larger a republic—or an empire—grows, the more its people seem to need a common reference point for social effort. Something, somewhere, must serve as a source of unity in diversity, of continuity in change, of order in progress. In the abstract, the Constitution was designed as an American answer to this universal need. Yet the Constitution takes on meaning only through men; not the living alone, but those who moved through its parts to leave bits of themselves as exhibits of what this and that word meant.

Something must total all these bits; must be the outer sign of our race experience; must serve as a kind of cultural apotheosis in which the nation can see an image of its best aims. Among our constitutional bodies, the Supreme Court is too remote and specialized for this work; the Congress is too large and diffuse. In the case of Congress, its own personality is split. Part of it, the House, represents the people directly in proportion to their numbers. The other part, the Senate, represents the states directly on the basis of their legal equality. Taken as a whole, the congressional aura suggests a sum of disconnected local forces, in continuous flux as they vie with each other for short-run ends. Organized for precisely this purpose, the Congress gathers in the mass of rights and demands that pour from the national and the international watershed into the legislative turbine. It meets some of them in full, delays some, compromises others, rejects still others. Over a stretch of time, it generally produces a balanced effect where no one gets all that he wants and no one loses all that he has. Yet for all its great skill in meeting these present day strains—and that skill at times dwarfs the nineteenth-century legislative giants—the Congress has no unitary identity that can serve as the symbol of what Americans as a whole think or wish themselves to be. It has no unitary voice that can state the national aim, and no unitary arm that can nudge everyone forward to points beyond the immediate, ameliorative compromise.

By a process of elimination, the President alone can do what is wanted, provided his antennae are sensitive to the psychological advantages in the place he fills. He is one man, not a committee. He is visible. He lives on a plane of his own outside the Congress and the Court. His policies can be overthrown. But he cannot be overthrown in his person for four years, except by an impeachment. Though he is sharply judged by the memories of his predecessors, his size seems to grow larger and clearer because he stands in their place. When he appears in person on the national stage, his vision of reality can become the national vision, with tremendous consequences for good or evil. From the center of the stage, with all eyes fixed on him, he can advance a theory of cause and effect in which disconnected facts acquire new and related meaning. And most important of all, he can lend his personal style to proud imitation by millions of people in private stations; he can bind the aspiration of the nation to the upward leap of his individual conscience, and infuse his own compassion into the national mind. He is, or can be, the essence of the nation's personality. In him, many things can flower—or decay.

This institutional side of the presidency, with its accompanying color and pageantry, is not unlike the role the Crown plays in a constitutional monarchy. Yet there is a difference of a marked sort, beyond the fact that the American President is elected to dignity while the Crown comes to it through birth. Where there is no Crown, in countries like present-day France, Italy or Germany, one man, with the title of President, is elected to act as if he were the constitutional monarch. The main duty of this one man, like that of his royal counterpart, is to foster a pious attitude toward the nation as a whole, and a will to sacrifice for it. But it is at this point that the difference sets in.

The American President

The American President not only reigns. He also rules. He *is*, and he *does*. Here is a basic cause of tension. He combines the sentimental aura of the Crown with the workaday labors of a unitary prime ministership. He suggests the quality of timelessness. But he is also a force in continuous motion. He sifts, defines, chooses from among alternatives, and he exercises his own will to decide what the national purpose shall be and how it shall be met. And it is because he is exalted in his institutional aspect that he has a greater distance to fall as an Executive. It is felt that if only he will use right reason, he can solve every problem; that if he doesn't solve it, the fault is not in the problem but in his moral failure. It is felt, too, that he actually has a free hand to do what we expect of him at home and abroad; if he doesn't use that hand as we wish him to, the cause, once again, is his moral failure. That he is bound by law and custom to work in a controlled and predictable way; that he does not have God's power to make a crab walk straight; that the pressure of age-old historical forces can narrow the range of his alternatives to a single brittle option all too often are overlooked.

What is expected of him and what he actually does are judged without considering whether the means at his disposal were adequate to the responsibilities piled on his shoulders. Thus it comes about that what the President draws to himself in his boundless institutional character, he can lose in his official character as an Executive, acting in a sphere circumscribed by law. In this he personalizes the eternal clash between the forces that attract us to the seat of power and those which repel us from it; between the conviction that nothing can be done without power, and the opposite conviction that those who wield it are either unworthy of it or invariably misuse it.

In the chapter that follows I shall indicate how this same dualism sets the tone for presidential campaigns.

2

The People's choice

*The grounds for passion in the choice of a President – An abstract of
the natural advantages and disadvantages inherent in three representative candidacies – The mystery of a President of all the people – The
will to accept a decision for its own sake – Exception of the 1860
election – In all other cases, power has been transferred in peace –
True even in 1876 election won by fraud – The nature of our political
parties supports the concept of a President of all the people.*

An American becomes the President, first, by the appraisal
he makes of himself, second, by action of his party nominating convention, third, by a vote of the people as a whole,
and fourth, by a vote of the Electoral College.

To pass the first barrier—to place himself in nomination or
to accept one—he must have a generous measure of spirit.
To pass the second, he must be acceptable to over twelve
hundred party delegates, generally equal to each other in
voting strength, but markedly unequal in the number of
people they represent. To pass the third barrier, he must win
the approval of the qualified in a constituency of 156,000,000
people. As for the fourth barrier, he sometimes needs a
broad measure of luck if the spread of ballots across the land

[*16*]

is to produce the electoral combination that gives him the victory.

The electorate, meanwhile, forms itself into a brotherhood of the guiltless for the purposes of a presidential campaign. The wrongs of the past and present, born of collective negligence and comfortable self-deception, are heaped on one man. The bright promise of the future is centered in one man too. Danger gives a special thrill to the proceedings, for there is little margin for error when the work done in a campaign period cools into its fixed form. What the victor in the presidential contest is authorized to get on Inauguration Day is irrevocable—except for an impeachment—for four years, in peace or war, in boom or bust.

With so many millions to be won over, each with a different vision of reality, hardly any plan for victory is too fatuous to lack its backers. The candidate is told that he can be heard only if he lies, or he can be believed only if he dissembles. He is told to trust the reason of the people, and he is told that the people are children who are to be beguiled by fantasies. Every stir of the wind, every idle statistic, every decimal point, every analogy to previous events which passes without notice under ordinary circumstances, is cited as a portent of his defeat or triumph.

The past of the man is resurrected and a pattern of expectability is discovered in it. He is held to be unique; yet what he will do is forecast on the basis of his resemblance to a stereotype of generals, governors, Senators and the like. All the words he ever spoke or wrote, whether half asleep or wide awake, are exhumed and examined under circumstances to which they may no longer apply. But they are used thereafter as beacons showing the path he will follow in the dark future. All he says during the campaign on any topic, whether great or banal, is examined with concentrated seriousness as if he were a new Adam, the first man who ever thought about anything.

It is said that he commands a small court of self-seekers. It is also said that his election will be to no avail since he will not be able to control his party. In almost all cases, it is observed that he did not ask for power. And it is also observed that he held back and masked his real and driving ambition only because he knew that a premature revelation would of itself organize the forces opposed to him. And so it goes. The virtues of the candidate are drawn on so grand a scale that they scrape the sandals of the heavenly choir. His vices are shown to be so great that they can excite the grudging admiration we often give to a vast catastrophe of nature. Above all, it is claimed that his election to the presidency will bring the nation to at least the suburbs of Utopia, and with a little luck, perhaps to the metropolis itself. To which "the other side" answers that his election will plunge the nation into a howling wilderness from which there can be no rescue.

A leading question cuts across the tumult. Does belonging to the party in power give to a presidential candidate any natural advantages; or do the advantages lie with the candidate from the opposition party? If an answer, true for all times and places is wanted, none can be given. Each campaign is a sum of special tensions and accidents, including the personality of the candidates, the extent to which they are identified with matters at the focus of national attention, the history of their parties, the hopes excited by party names, the quality of lesser candidates down to a township surveyor, a sudden eruption in foreign parts, the nature of the weather over the farms and the cities, the apathetic who stayed home on election day, the people who vote one way because someone they hate votes a different way, an off-the-cuff remark made by someone prominently identified with a candidate's cause. All these elements can stir up a kinetic energy, capable of shoving the electorate and the candidates in directions they had no desire to go. And the victory that is won by any one man takes on the color of inevitability only when all the votes are in.

But if an exact appraisal cannot be made except in terms of specific campaign settings, it is possible to make an abstract of the sort of prospects encountered by three representative candidates. Viewed through the eyes of the main actors, they seem to be as follows:

1. *The President as a candidate to succeed himself.* The man who holds the presidency may suffer by comparison with a Washington or Lincoln. Yet his occupancy of the place they filled begets a certain reverence for him. Solely as a curiosity, he will attract a crowd wherever he does. Those who come to gawk may end up by listening to what he has to say. He does not have to identify himself by exaggerated bellowings so that the electorate will know he is alive. Since he is still the President, he can act as well as speak. He can initiate measures which appear to be a part of the normal work of his office, though they can be timed for their effect on the campaign. He may have muffed a number of problems in his administration. But he automatically draws to his side the support of the many millions who are "used to him" and who prefer his known shortcomings to the untested virtues of his rival.

Above all, no President has been so inept that he cannot take credit for some act or policy that has benefited millions beyond the range of his direct patronage. It is this specific achievement, bearing the stamp of the President's name, that juts out as the rock that can shatter the opponent. Since the opponent generally has had some experience in public affairs, he knows that the rock was not made of pasteboard. It was shaped as an answer to real human needs. But what to do about this achievement is the bedeviling question. He can promise that he will not disturb its essential character but will simply polish its rough administrative edges. He can promise to crush it, hoping thereby to win strength in some other quarter. He can snore with his eyes open and try to act as if the presidential achievement was not a matter of historical record. Yet any of these actions invite trouble.

In promising to continue a particular program, he praises by implication the creative abilities of the President who was responsible for it. He invites the question why the country should change Presidents when the main contenders for the office think alike. And he may offend those of his own supporters who want to end the program. But if he promises to scrap it, he has no assurance that the votes he gains in a second quarter will offset the votes he is bound to lose among those whose pattern of certainty he threatens. If he ignores the program altogether, he can lose the support of those who want a hard and fast reassurance one way or another. In the end he can rupture his cause by his indecisiveness. The pattern lends itself to repetition in a different form when, instead of a solid good for which a President can take credit, there is a hard-core problem that defies an easy answer. What can the rival say that has not already been heard from the White House? If he offers a nostrum, part of the nation may dismiss him as a mountebank. If he ignores the problem altogether, there are those who will say that he has no conception of "the seriousness of the times." If he approves the position the President has taken, he risks the charge of saying, "me too." And all this works to the advantage of the President.

2. *The candidate of the opposition party who runs against a President.* This man often starts with two marked disadvantages, in addition to those just indicated. First, he is burdened by the legislative record of his party; and that record often suggests a policy of chronic obstruction. Second, he carries over into the campaign the wounds inflicted in his fight to win the nomination. His position is not like that of the President who wants another term; there are no comparable forces within the opposition party which compel it to pick a particular man as its standard bearer. The victorious candidate is often severely taxed before he wins his internal triumph; but thereafter, in the campaign proper, he invites the charge of a sell-out when in the name of "party harmony," he embraces the men whom he lately described as enemies of the party and the national interest.

As an offset to these burdens, the candidate who runs against a President can concentrate on getting elected to the exclusion of all other things. No one will censure him for being away from his desk "in these critical times," while he sounds the partisan note. No one will say that he disgraces the office of the presidency by the intensity of his partisanship. He is in the happy position of being able to speak with impunity. In the field of foreign affairs, in particular, he does not have to weigh his words for their effect on a world-wide audience—though by every rule of public decency he should do this. Yet the regrettable fact remains that he is in a position to tune all his remarks to the prejudices of the American voter. His conscience alone fixes the limit of what he says, for he need have no fear that a foreign ambassador may call one hour later on the Secretary of State to demand an explanation or reassurance.

Neither is an opposition candidate burdened by the animosities which cling like static electricity to every President. He is free to exploit the sense that all who wield power are by nature sinful or invincibly ignorant of where the common interest really lies. He can parade himself as the source of a new and transcendent unity—this, in contrast to the divisive activities of the man in the White House. He can say that America would have been spared its many woes if he had been the President all along. He can let his imagination soar as he describes the Kingdom that would automatically Come with his election. And he can do this without inviting the question: "Why didn't you make it Come before this time?"

In short, if the President has an advantage that comes from the fear of change, the candidate in opposition to him is at liberty to exploit the bewitching lure of the future tense. And he is sustained in this by a human will to believe that when the old king dies and the young prince ascends to the throne, by that event alone, everyone will become beautiful and rich.

3. *The candidate who is not the President, but is of the party in power.* This sort of candidacy, an uncommon event, is also the most difficult to negotiate. In the twentieth century, for example, William Howard Taft and Herbert Hoover were the only two who triumphed over its handicaps. The

man cast in this part lacks the aura that surrounds the incumbent in the White House. Yet he also lacks the advantage of appearing as something new, fresh and independent in his own right. Regardless of the circumstances that made him the party standard bearer, he invites the charge that he is the captive of the outgoing President; at the same time, he is not at liberty to disassociate himself sharply from the policies of the President. If he details his errors, he offends against the person and entourage of the President and becomes a witness testifying to the incompetence of his own party. Even if he proposes new policies, the opposition asks why they were not put into effect by the incumbent.

He is restrained at all points by the fact that his party is in power. He cannot single it out as the devil who is to be flayed. Except in cases where the Congress is in the hands of the opposition party, the natural devil in a presidential campaign *is* the party which holds the Executive. Nor can the candidate play the part of an imaginative prophet, portraying the golden age his election will inaugurate. The evidence is at hand that the previous victory of his party did not bring all good things to pass. If his party has been in power for any great length of time, every problem it has failed to solve appears to be due to its inherent corruption and to its passion for a bad spectacle. If a war has occurred in the period of his party's administration, the opposition is quick to say of the candidate that he belongs to a political conspiracy whose presidential leaders are never content unless they can embroil the nation in periodic holocausts. On the other hand, the achievements of a party long in power tend to lose their clamorous, historical background. They come to be accepted as a sort of divine visitation from on high, without travail and hard infighting down here below.

Nevertheless, the candidate is not without some natural advantages, particularly during the early ascendancy of his party. If he is burdened by the President's faults, he benefits from an identity with his virtues. And he can use them in his own cause, as though he was making a bid to succeed himself within the presidency.

It is mystifying enough to decide how, in a specific campaign, the elements of strength and of weakness inherent in different kinds of candidacies ultimately lead one man to victory and another to defeat. Yet the mystery does not end here. The larger challenge is this. How is it that, no matter who is elected and why, the victor is promptly hailed as the President of all the people? In any realistic sense, he cannot possibly be this. He cannot match each vision of America as it is prophesied by the millions who voted for or against him, or didn't vote at all. Yet the nation decrees an act of oblivion on the mischances and partisan claims of the recent past. A decision by a part of the nation is converted into a decision of the sovereign whole, and the new President is accepted in a style suggesting that his triumph was inevitable all along. "Well, we'll go along with it," we say, in that most meaningful of Americanisms. Not through coercion, and not forever, but voluntarily and on a contingent basis. The capacity to say this has been present even when the decision was in express opposition to what a majority of the people actually voted for.

The one exception was the election of Abraham Lincoln in 1860. Why the South chose to use the event as a pretext for secession continues to perplex historians. At few other moments was our system of checks and balances—in politics and in law—better poised to block any rash act in any Federal quarter. While Lincoln's election did represent an unprecedented triumph by the people of one section, acting through a sectional party and program, the effect could have been neutralized—for two years at least—not by secession but by a continuation of the South in the Union. All the Republicans had gained in 1860 was a tenuous hold on the presidency. A quarter of a million more Northerners than Southerners voted against Lincoln, while his national vote was a million short of a majority. Within the Congress, the Republicans lacked thirty seats of having a majority in the House and four in the Senate. Lincoln could pass no laws by himself. He could make no appointments hostile to the South; they would not be confirmed by the Senate. Most of the committee chairmen were Southerners. A large part of the officer corps for the Army was Southern in origin, as was a large part of the administrative bureaucracy and a majority of the Supreme Court. If a war of liberation was unavoidable, it should have been brought on by the Republicans in the act of leading the *North* out of the Union. But secession paid scant respect to logic. When it was the South that left, Southerners forced the proof of what they had feared the most. The Republicans at once became the majority throughout what remained of the amputated government.[1]

[1] Southerners came to change their mind about this minority President. "Without doubt," wrote General James Longstreet in 1885, "the greatest man in rebellion times, the one matchless among 40 millions for the peculiar difficulties of the period, was Abraham Lincoln." With less justice, they had changed their minds much earlier about Jefferson Davis, chosen by a "unanimous" vote to be the President of the Confederacy. Though the place he held was arranged by the Confederate Constitution to "impart stability to the government and withdraw all motive for courting popular

At all other times, however, the American will to accept a decision for its own sake—and to convert it into a decision of all the people—has proved stronger than the active forces of disunion. It was first shown in the election of 1800 when Thomas Jefferson and Aaron Burr tied in the Electoral College, with Jefferson emerging as the victor by a vote of the House of Representatives. It was shown again in 1824 when John Quincy Adams was chosen by a vote of the House, though Andrew Jackson led in the electoral vote, and in what appeared to be the popular vote. In fourteen other elections, men have succeeded peacefully to the presidency though they received a minority of the *total* popular vote that was cast. The list reads: William Henry Harrison, 1840; James K. Polk, 1844; Zachary Taylor, 1848; James Buchanan, 1856; James A. Garfield, 1880; Grover Cleveland, 1884 and 1892; Benjamin Harrison, 1888; William McKinley, 1896 and 1900; William Howard Taft, 1908; Woodrow Wilson, 1912 and 1916; and Harry Truman, 1948. Add the election of Thomas Jefferson, John Quincy Adams and Abraham Lincoln, and there are seventeen cases in which the victor could not realistically be the President of fifty per cent of the people, much less all of them. In an eighteenth case, the

---

favor at the expense of duty," the Civil War had barely begun before the forces of nullification went to work on Davis. In 1862, Thomas R. R. Cobb, one of the leaders of the Confederacy, wrote that "Davis was the embodiment and concentration of cowardly littleness he garnishes over with pharisaical hypocracies." Edward A. Pollard, a leading Southern editor, called Davis "a literary dyspeptic who has more ink than blood in his veins, an intriguer, busy with private enmities." Vice President Alexander Stephens remarked that Davis was "driving the Confederacy into a dictatorship." And so on. All this was a far cry from the mood voiced by Davis not long after he assumed the presidency. "For now we *are* brethren," he said, as though in a marriage vow, "not in name merely, but in fact. Men of one flesh, of one bone, of one interest, of one purpose and of identity in domestic institutions."

election of 1876, a decision was accepted despite the air of fraud it wore.

As the Democratic candidate in 1876, Samuel Tilden led his Republican rival, Rutherford B. Hayes, in the popular vote. He also won a clear majority of the electoral votes, with 184 in his favor, and 165 going to Hayes. Excluded from the count were a total of 20 electoral votes from Florida, South Carolina, Louisiana; also Oregon. These had been cast for Hayes. But in the case of the Southern states, there was a great deal of evidence to show that the popular vote behind the electoral returns had been produced through fraud, intimidation and violence. Nevertheless, if the 20 votes were accepted as lawful, Hayes could emerge as President by one vote.

While the army of occupation stood ready to serve the Republican cause in the South, two unresolved Constitutional questions shoved the same cause along in the legal forum: Who was to count the electoral votes? Who was to count those votes in relation to a state's power to appoint electors?

1. Under the "Twenty-Second Joint Rule," enacted by Republicans in the 1864 Congress, it was agreed that the count should be made by both houses acting separately and not as a joint body. Moreover, the consent of both chambers was required before the votes of any state would be considered. But in 1877 the House was under Democratic control; the Senate, under Republican. If the 1864 rule was re-enacted over Republican opposition, it would allow the Democrats to veto and exclude the votes in dispute. Tilden's victory would be assured.

2. Though the Democrats were strong for states' rights on

other points, they now said that in any count of the electoral votes, the power of the Congress and of the states overlapped; that the Congress had the right to inquire whether the appointment of electors in a state was accompanied by fraud and violence. The Republicans countered by saying that the power of the Congress was limited to its automatic registry of electors formally certified by state election officials. If, in this respect, the parties reversed their traditional views toward the powers of the central government and those of the states, the higher law of convenient circumstances made the flip-flop quite in order. The Republicans controlled the election boards of the states where the electoral returns were in dispute.

The wrangling between the Democratic House and the Republican Senate continued up to one month before Inauguration Day in 1877. To provide a President of some sort who would be on hand to take the oath of office, the Congress agreed to form an Electoral Commission. It was to use the uncertain power of the two chambers in the contested matter, and to define those powers while using them.

Party representation on this eccentric body matched the Congressional majorities. The House agreed on three Democrats and two Republicans; the Senate reversed the order with three Republicans and two Democrats. Five Justices of the Supreme Court were also appointed. Of these, four were identified in the enabling act, the aim being to divide them equally by their presumed party preferences. The fifth Justice, the crucial figure on the Commission, was to be chosen by the other four. It was intended that he should be Justice David Davis of Illinois, whose political views were sufficiently vague to invest his choice with the air of impartiality. Davis, however, balked at picking a President of the United States all by himself. In any case, before he could reconsider this unique opportunity, the Illinois Democrats, with inexplicable timing from the point of view of their national interests, elected Davis to the Senate.

His place eventually went to Justice Joseph P. Bradley of New Jersey. As a Republican, Bradley not only followed the party line, but helped develop it to the point where it was adopted by the Commission on a straight partisan vote of 8 to 7. It was Bradley's view that the two houses of Congress, and hence the Electoral Commission, were limited by the Constitution to the special power of counting electoral votes, authenticated by state election officials. It had no power to go behind the returns and to inquire whether the state authorities were guilty of fraud and misconduct. Thus the disputed Southern votes were admitted; the Oregon vote was admitted on a different ground, and the Republicans won the presidency.

While these events moved to their climax, there were those who cried, "Tilden or Blood!" The more ardent Democrats took their Civil War uniforms out of mothballs and awaited the signal for a march on Washington. But Tilden did not want the presidency handed to him like skewered shishkebab. Neither would he have any part of a plan that the election should be determined by a drawing of lots. "I do not care a snap of my fingers for the Presidency, and will not consent to raffle for it," he said. Even when the Electoral Commission returned its verdict, Tilden kept his peace. "I can retire to private life," he said, "with the consciousness that I shall receive from posterity the credit of having been elected to the highest position in the gift of the people, without any of the cares and responsibilities of the office." The alleged theft of the presidency soon led to his physical breakdown. Yet in giving up what he won without trying to save it by force, he allowed our constitutional morality the time span it needed to restore itself. As the victor, Hayes also took the oath of office as a President of all the people.

The question again intrudes itself: What is it that lies behind our will to accept a decision for its own sake? What is it that sustains a concept of the President of all the people when the obvious facts so often run to the contrary? Part of the answer, at least, is intimately bound up with the nature of our political parties, with which I shall deal in other chapters. Now, however, I want to consider only those party traits which bear directly on the immediate question.

3

Party Government

||||||||||O|||||||||||O||||||||||||O|||||||||||O|||||||||||O|||||||||||O|||||||||||O|||||||||||O||

Portrait of European party man – One-interest parties lead to coalition governments or to dictators – Traits of maturity in American party man – Our parties are not Utopian – Their fundamental points of agreement and disagreement in domestic and foreign affairs – Digression on question of isolationism – The factions within each party – The "boss" as an artist – The politics of net gain – Pragmatic use of ideologies – Our political fluidity – Party contributions to our constitutional morality – Party differences disciplined by four rules of constitutional government – Pragmatic wisdom underlying those rules – Respect for those rules gives a sense of reality to the concept of a President of all the people.

Exclusive of the Englishman, the European party man, who works in a very old physical setting, nevertheless tends to imitate the young man whose down has not yet turned into a beard. A dissenter in his own right, he is impatient of dissent in others. He would have a form of social life built not of odd-shaped pieces used in different ways, but from uniform slabs of matter, each hard, precise and stockpiled. Asked a question, he has no beard he can first stroke, entwine with his fingers, smooth out again, and then give a slow reply of, "Perhaps, and yet—maybe not." His hand flies to his smooth chin and slips off in an abrupt "Yes" or "No." Yet his tragedy is that he cannot shake off a mystical homesickness for the protective authority he knew as a child. And so, proclaiming his liberty, he can annihilate his ego by placing it at the disposal of one man who will rule the discordant mass of the homesick without himself being ruled.

This image of youth applies with special force to French politics. There, a political party tends to speak for one interest as though it alone could claim the sum of truth as a birthright. Each party would build the state in imitation of what it sees when it looks at itself in a mirror. All that doesn't fit the smooth face is shorn off. At this point, however, a difficulty crops up. No single French interest is large enough to be the state or to rule it. And as long as numerical majorities continue to be the source of a party's title to form a government, the one interest is trapped in its own logic. It can form a government only with the aid of others. But where American political parties form their coalitions *before* an election, the French form theirs *afterward*—and in this they refute the assumptions on which they exist. For in combination they report on the fact that the state is something much more complex than the one-interest party makes it out to be.

The inevitable sequel to a coalition government is a "petty drama of personalities" where men either wait for a calamity to happen, or act as though their aim was to win a prize at the end of a game of musical chairs. A rulership of this sort, unless held together by the rivets of war, has no real firmness, no organized outlook on public questions, no courage even to state those questions—all from the unwillingness of any element to be identified as the author of solutions no one really likes.

It develops, however, that even men on a pirate ship want a stable social frame from which they can reach for the exact and the predictable in their private lives. Faced with this universal need, coalition government shapes two solutions to the disorder it fosters. The first finds the real source of authority lodged in the permanent administrators who are responsible to no one except their *esprit,* and who, by the law of simple continuity, enthrone the administrative rule over legislative deliberations. In the second solution, a single party pleads the higher law of crisis. It demands the sole rule of the government, promising that even though it is a minority, it will meet the crucial need of the hour. It will bring order out of chaos. For the burlesque antics of rival parties, it will substitute a politics of principle. For the mass of egos that pull the state apart, it will erect a single supreme ego who will hold all things together, by force if need be.[1]

In contrast, the American party man shows the traits of maturity from within a youthful physical setting. For the mature person generally adjusts his appetite to what his stomach can digest, not to what his eye can see. He guards himself against the extremes of heat and cold; moves be-

---

[1] What this last generally leads to was foretold by Thomas Jefferson in his *Notes on the State of Virginia,* written in 1781–82. Said Jefferson: "It is error alone which needs the support of government. Truth can stand by itself. Subject opinion to coercion; whom will you make your inquisitors? Fallible men: men governed by bad passions, by private as well as public reasons. And why subject it to coercion? To produce uniformity. But is uniformity of opinion desirable? No more than of face and stature. Introduce the bed of Procrustes then, and, as there is danger that the large men may beat the small, make us all of a size, by lopping the former and stretching the latter. . . . What has been the effect of coercion? To make one half of the world fools, and the other half hypocrites. To support roguery and error all over the earth."

tween peaks and plains with a backward glance at how far
he's come from home and with a question whether the road
back is still open. He knows that in his time he has picked
up a few crotchets, but he claims them as a right of age.
Sometimes he enjoys an inward smile at his talent for irrita-
tion, and sometimes he will storm simply to prove that he
still can cause quite a sensation. He has learned that the
world was born long before he came upon it and will go on
long after he leaves it; that he hasn't the strength to will his
way to all that he likes; that what he dislikes he must learn
to "put up with," while hoping at the same time that his
children and their children might know a better life. But
above all, having chased after the truth, he knows its elusive-
ness; knows how often it is reached not by a direct hit, but
either is stumbled on absent-mindedly, or is pinched out by a
union of contradictions; knows too, that if error screws its
way into the mind, it does that by twisting some small truth.

The whole of this portrait of maturity, if it is fairly drawn,
is reflected in American party politics in explicit ways. Despite their campaign vaunts, neither the Republicans nor the
Democrats are really Utopian in aim. Nor, for all their cries
of imminent disaster, do they respond to a leadership which
preaches a doctrine of doom. To both, the good society *is*
attainable, not now, but up the road and over the hill. The
"goodness" of the present good society is that it *shall* progress
up the road, the march to be judged not alone by fixed
standards, but by those that are changed in a pragmatic way
even as progress is made. Moreover, both accept the institution of private property as the source of most though not of
all social effort. The military socialism of wartime excepted,
both parties give the political order the task of maintaining

the frame of liberty in which a separate economic order based on private property can do its work. It is because of their agreement on this fundamental point that our two major parties seem so alike in their other traits.

They may back short-sighted programs which defeat the domestic purposes to which they are committed. But neither of them to date, despite charges to the contrary, has struck a deliberate and calculated blow at the process of free exchange. They may call for a parallel tool like a public power program to work by the side of the private one. They may provide vast sums of socialized credit to private borrowers—with results later to be noted. They may urge a compulsory minimum base for safety, health and wages. They may devise compensatory actions for the government to undertake when the private enterprise system falters. But neither party —not even in the depression of the 1930's—has urged that economic inequalities can be removed by dividing the means of production before they turn their wheels. Both have said that the private property system should be made to work so that of itself it can organize and distribute the abundance our technology can produce.

But if they both operate within the frame of democratic capitalism, they differ on measures that can (1) put more people to work; (2) create a climate that will spur private employers to produce more; (3) give to all hands a fair share of what is produced when the system fails to do that; (4) police that part of the productive plant in which the public has an interest as distinct from the rights of ownership or management; (5) conserve the nation's natural resources for the future while meeting the industrial needs of the present; and (6) distribute fairly the human and material costs of national efforts like defense programs which serve the rich and the poor alike.

In foreign affairs, the lines between the two parties are generally drawn in terms of high tariffs against low tariffs, isolationism against internationalism, a sentimental pacifism against militarism, and a preoccupation with the problems of Europe as against Asia—or the other way around. Yet it is difficult to assign to either party a hard and fast ideological position on any of these topics. The party attitude toward a tariff, to illustrate, is bound up with all the internal divisions in our domestic economy. It is not a high or low tariff as such which becomes the decisive issue, but more often the specific items in a tariff schedule.

The simple question of whether a party is in office or out of it also influences its attitude toward the conduct of foreign affairs; when a transfer of power takes place, the presidential victor frequently pursues the same basic course he formerly attacked. An example of this occurred at the very start of our national life, when the Federalists and the Republicans were sharply opposed in their attitudes toward England and France who were then at war. Though the Republicans, led by Jefferson, assailed the foreign policies of George Washington and John Adams (whose Federalist presidencies favored the English cause), Jefferson as President reversed his outlook when Spain transferred the Louisiana Territory to France. "There is on this globe one single spot, the posessor of which is our natural and habitual enemy," Jefferson declared. "It is New Orleans." If New Orleans remained in French hands, he continued, "we must marry ourselves to the British fleet and nation . . . [to hold] the two continents in sequestration for the common purposes of the united British and American nations."

In a more modern vein, it was not during the Democratic presidency of Harry S. Truman that an American army was first sent to join an allied expeditionary force without express congressional authority. The precedent was established in the Republican presidency of William McKinley at the time of the Boxer Rebellion. Again, our first great intervention in the balance of power between foreign nations did not occur during the Democratic administration of Woodrow Wilson. It occurred during the Republican administration of Theodore Roosevelt at the time of the Russo-Japanese war in 1905. And it was Theodore Roosevelt again, not Wilson, who cried the loudest for intervention in the European War of 1914. It was the Stimson Doctrine, promulgated under Herbert Hoover in 1931, which was developed by Franklin D. Roosevelt in his "quarantine the aggressor" concept of 1937—and applied by President Truman in the Korean War, and it was Mr. Hoover's 1932 concept of American capital exports to backward nations which reached a refined maturity in the Truman "Point Four" program announced in 1949. In these and in similar cases, what was acceptable to a political party when it had the management of our foreign affairs became unacceptable in some party circles when it turned that management over to the rival party. Or what the rival denounced when it was out of power became a leading party doctrine when it assumed power; at the very minimum, it became the doctrine of its victorious presidential candidate after he took the oath of office.

In the past these shifts could be partly explained by the way Americans reacted when our diplomacy touched on the land of their origin. The Irish-American, for example, alive to memories of the Irish struggle for independence, balked at any policy that favored the English. The German-American and the Italo-American, through a not unfounded fear that their assimilation would be interrupted, resisted any foreign policy in which Germany or Italy was identified as an enemy of the United States. Until the Nazi invasion of Norway, the Norwegian-American, conditioned to the traditional neutrality of his homeland, also resisted any American intervention in the conflicts of Europe. Meanwhile, the party that was out of power saw in these restive ethnic groups a potential source of strength through whose agency it could become a majority. It therefore tried to win them over by advancing the notion that America was separate from Europe and had no need to become entangled in its affairs.

This sort of appeal won local successes in areas where a particular ethnic group was predominant. When it was extended to embrace the nativist heirs of the pioneers, traditionally suspicious of all foreign powers, the strength mustered proved sufficient to force a short-run veto on the diplomatic policy of the party in power. But in time of international crisis, this appeal never was able to muster a winning majority across the nation. Three main counter forces seem to account for the failure. (1) For each ethnic group that was gained by the so-called "isolationist" appeal, another group was lost. In the two World Wars, for example, any accretion of isolationist strength in German-American quarters was more than offset by the loss of strength among Americans whose native lands were attacked or conquered by Germany. (2) The largest block in both parties is the

"English vote," formed of some 80,000,000 people who today trace their descent back to the British Isles. Since England has been involved in every international crisis in this century, the English-American, reacting in the exact manner of any ethnic strain, has demanded and won support for the "mother country." (3) On a geographical basis, the English vote coincides with the "Solid South," with its enormous voice in the management of the government. The South, having been by-passed by post-English waves of immigration, has not been distracted by political appeals to any other ethnic group. Moreover, its need of export markets for its cotton crop tends to foster an international view among its political representatives; in any showdown, they are in a position to enforce their will.

The recent rise of a bipartisan foreign policy toward Europe may reflect the awareness among our party leaders that Soviet imperialism has forced a semblance of unity among the various ethnic strains in America—for the first time in our history. Great bitterness still prevails among Americans of Central European origin whose homelands have fallen under Soviet rule. This can bring a political profit to candidates who succeed in blaming the event on a rival party. But there appears to be little profit in trying to build a new majority by playing European ethnic strains against each other, when almost all of them feel that only a vigorous American hand in Europe can save their homelands from a Russian conquest.

As the 1952 campaign demonstrated, it is primarily over Asia that one can now risk a loss or bid for political strength without disturbing our new unity. Since Asia is the homeland for only a handful of Americans, the course of our policy there can be argued on the grounds of "interest," "prestige," "strategy" and the like, without wounding the feelings of any major ethnic strain. As these indefinite terms are tossed around, every American, regardless of his origin, is invited to lament the fact of treachery in high places and to protest his superior devotion to America's world purposes. Moreover, he can do this for the first time in fraternal alliance with the "nativist" American, without inviting the old suspicion that his primary concern is not with America, but with the European land from which he emigrated. In the 1952 campaign, General Eisenhower was the principal beneficiary of this new attitude.

It remains to be said that each party is involved in acute internal rivalries. Each has a "faction of memory" which wants to reconstruct the former era when it gained a major share of the rewards our society has to give. Each has a "limitist faction" which recalls the former era as a time of hardship that had to be overcome before the goods of the present were won. But it fears that any further social change will imperil what is in hand. It would therefore commit everyone to the support of the prevailing balance of forces. And lastly, each party has a "faction of hope." It, too, recalls the past as a period of denial. But its maximum demands have not been fulfilled in the present. So it asks for a new turn of the roulette wheel on the chance that it will gain what it wants.

That political parties generally manage to contain these conflicts is due in no small measure to a special group of party leaders. Though they bear the odious name of "bosses," they are, in a way, a group of artists, absorbed in the problems of selection, proportion and arrangement. They have but slight interest in ideologies and are often amoral in their methods. But like all artists, they ask to be judged primarily on aesthetic grounds—on how effectively they have put together a "winning combination." What they accept, reject, or even ignore in a party stand on any domestic or foreign matter will be ruled by their desire to steady their own ranks, to win over the independents in the nation at large, and to attract the restive elements who appear to be losing the internal fight in the rival party. Their main interest throughout is in a politics of net gain.

They know that if they bid for or reject one group, they automatically repel or attract a second one. But they have no real way of knowing what weight any particular individual will give to his multiple experiences. Will he give greater value to events that affect his domestic status? Or to his feelings about foreign affairs? Will he be most sensitive when his pocket book is bruised? When his religious sentiments are involved? The bosses must nevertheless try to decide on the course that will leave them with the greatest residue of strength for the "winning combination." They will then entrust it to the individual whom they feel best embodies its leading elements. They would prefer to find him within the established leadership of the party. But when this is impossible, they have looked for him on the periphery or even in the neutral zone which separates the two major parties. Thus the phenomenon of the general turned into a presidential candidate. (Except for Andrew Jackson, not one of the military figures cast in this role was a party leader of the first rank at the time of his nomination.) The same principle of selection also led to the nominations of Woodrow Wilson in 1912, Wendell Willkie in 1940, and Adlai Stevenson in 1952.

[*41*]

(Three variations on the foregoing should be noted. (1) When two factions within a party reach a stalemate, they may split off to form separate parties. In 1824, for example, a stalemate in the Republican-Democratic party between limitists led by Henry Clay and John Quincy Adams, and the faction of hope led by Andrew Jackson, led to the formation of a separate National Republican and a separate Democratic party. (2) When the factions within each party reach a simultaneous stand-off, the situation is favorable to the emergence of a new national party. This occurred after 1850. In the Democratic party, the faction of memory composed of Southern slaveholders and the Northern limitist faction led by Stephen A. Douglas were stalemated by the near equality of their strength. Somewhat the same situation prevailed in the Whig party between the Southern limitist faction led by men like Alexander Stephens and the Northern faction of hope led by men like William Seward. In their struggle to get off dead center, both parties were torn apart and the Republican party emerged out of the chaos. (3) When any single faction reaches a position of overpowering command simultaneously in the two major parties, one of the imperiled factions may splinter off in a bid to form a new national party. This occurred in 1924 when the faction of memory gained a decisive upper hand in both the Republican and the Democratic parties. The result was that the faction of hope in both parties joined forces in the La Follette Progressive movement.)

In all of this, it may be useful to speak of a "right," a "center" and a "left," so long as we do not fool ourselves into thinking there is a substantial left-wing opinion, or a right or a center opinion in our major parties in the sense that each is fixed in its place, content, and whirls in its socket in the same way through the same men all the time. A view of this sort can by itself force the polarization of our society as it did on the eve of the Civil War. The word heard at the time, that compromise was impossible, that the lines were drawn, that "the argument was exhausted and all must stand to arms," of itself widened the social breach until it was closed again by brute force.

This does not deny that there are marked patterns in the behavior of various economic elements, as there are among ethnic and religious groups. But the human composition of the groups constantly changes. And the group patterns themselves frequently skid past fixed ideological lines. The economic and political doctrines of Jefferson and Hamilton, for example, have been used interchangeably by every cluster of people in the land. The same is true of the doctrinal views about a strong central government or states' rights, and about a strict or a loose construction of the Constitution. If the process is a rational one, the view each group embraces or rejects at any particular moment is determined by the immediate good it hopes to secure and the evil it hopes to avert. But just as often, it is based on non-rational inducements like nostalgias, nearness to the sources of power, or the yearning for respectability, prestige, recognition and applause. The classical example was provided by the household slaves among the New England Federalists. When they secured their freedom, they voted Federalist with satisfying snobbishness. So will a shoestring businessman today vote against himself, to gain in return a sense of identity with the merchant prince who can snap the shoestring at will.

Even our divisions drawn along regional lines are unstable.

The most graphic proof of this is the transcontinental shift
of sentiment within the Republican party, all in a single
generation. In the 1920's, the conservative Republicans on
the East Coast felt that the progressive Republicans in the
midlands should be read out of the party. Senator George
H. Moses of New Hampshire described them as "Sons of the
Wild Jackass." And James R. Grundy, President of the Pennsylvania Manufacturers Association, was equally tart. Having geared a political machine to yield a high tariff, Mr.
Grundy complained that the Congressional spokesman for
what he called "the backward states"—he included South
Dakota, North Dakota, Montana and Idaho among them—
"threw a monkey wrench into the machinery twenty-four
hours a day." This, he said, was vicious, not only because
they wrecked something they didn't understand, but also
because they gave back nothing of use to the land. In fact,
said Mr. Grundy, if "the volume of voice" of the backward
states were "reduced to the proportion of their tax contributions to the support of the government, some of them would
have to use an amplifier to be heard." And having said this,
he strongly implied that something ought to be done to correct the grave mistake made by the Founders when they
gave each state two votes in the Senate.

Yet in recent years, we have seen the new Sons of the Wild
Jackass take over what was once the new England and
Middle Atlantic temples of orthodoxy, while the heirs to
Senator Moses and Mr. Grundy fill the plains which once
rang to the voices of La Follette, Norris, Borah, Frazier,
Beveridge and Brookhart. During the 1952 Republican con-
vention, for example, it was the leaders of the Taft alliance
between the Midlands and the rotton boroughs of the South

who complained bitterly that the New Dealish coast Republicans had thrown a monkey wrench into the machinery of victory in the three preceding presidential elections. The coast Republicans, said the Taft men, did not know how to win anything. They had pursued a policy indistinguishable from that of the Democratic party, while the only sure way to victory was by a return to a no-compromise Republican stand, even if this meant that the coast Republicans were to be left homeless.

Though the two major parties turn in wild performances from time to time as they deal with domestic and foreign problems, we would fly apart as a nation if it were not for the positive work they also do. It is they who first bring about a tentative agreement among energetic rivals, and who narrow down points of difference so that they can be digested by the formal apparatus of the government. No one can predict whether they will continue this historic work. Their future course will depend largely on how well we preserve our civil liberties, and how well we discriminate between political conspiracies on the one hand, and political heresies on the other. We may eventually decide that to live in a world of menace we should gouge out our eyes, rip out our tongues, burst our eardrums, hack off our hands, and now blind, mute, deaf and unable to share any knowledge even by the use of sign language, make our darkness doubly dark by crawling under leaves in the animal hope that danger will pass us by. To the degree that our political parties prove to be the carriers of this alien and diseased method, their rot will spread outward until the whole of our society will be so corrupted that a probing finger striking it from without will make the hard shell collapse on the rotten center.

Thus far, however, our two major parties have managed to avoid the extremes that lead to social dissolution. At the base level, they give men a sense of place they otherwise might not have had. They give them access to prestige by peaceful instead of violent means. They give them a sense of unity that takes the bite out of personal loneliness. They give them the sense of a nationwide community of interest. For the millions who come to America from foreign lands, and for the other millions who migrate from our farms to our cities, the two parties perform an invaluable community service in humanizing the American leviathan. The methods they have used to do this have not always been lawful. Yet the net effect was a clear proof that somebody was around to lend a helping hand when there was a need for it.

The cynical, of course, may scoff at the President or the presidential aspirant who employs the two thousandth anniversary of the birth of Virgil to note "America's good fortune in having so many sons of Italy who have contributed so richly to our national life." The variants are endless. Yet through the honor paid its hero, each ethnic group in the land is told that it too is worthy; that its past has been an honorable one; that it has an important place in the tidal flow of American life. The cynical may scoff too at the President or the presidential aspirant who is shown greeting a Cotton Queen, or a Cherry Queen, or a Boy Scout and Red Cross leader, or the railroad engineer on a crack train. Yet through acts of this sort, vocation, regional and social service groups are told that their purposes as a group are also worthy; that they also contribute to the vitality of the land.

Party Government

What the party chief does, tens of thousands of party workers do also. All alike are taught to respect every eccentric and main-line interest in the nation, because each person has an equal vote on election day. It does not detract from what the parties do to say that their motive is a selfish desire to win votes. All this one can say. But one should add that in the course of winning votes, the parties and their leaders often gain a larger end which was not part of their conscious plan. They offer themselves as the ever-ready source of *attention* and *service* for all who have something on their mind.

In a larger sense, the aversion both the Republican and Democratic parties have for extremes, and the way they bring into the bloodstream of public action only what has already been filtered through the screen of popular agreement, may not be the cowardice it is commonly called. It may be the better part of constitutional wisdom. If what is sought for in political action is justice for a society—the whole of it, and not just a part of it—then the moderation in policy (though not in speech) our two parties have shown in the past carries an enormous good. For we are not ruled by some airy-fairy device with thistles for wheels and dew-drops for oil. We are ruled by two major political parties— wholly extra-constitutional—who between them indirectly control the formal lawmaking organs. They can make, break or change those organs, and through them the nation.

We all gain when the two parties as they seek their *own* gain, refuse to risk everything on a single throw of the dice; when each party makes sure that its stand on any point, if it proves wrong, will not mean an irrevocable defeat—that whatever the issue, each will still have a regenerating ele-

[47]

ment around which a new majority can be built in a future day. We all gain when the two parties move somewhere between the extremes of the bold and the standpat. Then, through the party mechanism there is spread to the small fibers of our social life the great gift the English gave us—the spirit of the common law with its sense of orderly change from which constitutional government draws its life.

Nowhere is this spirit more active than in the work of the party nominating conventions. (The general theme will be dealt with more fully in a later chapter. But it is in point to offer a passing comment here.) The conventions, in their shortcomings, may appear to speak "only those opinions which seemed to have received the sanction of the general voice"—as a youthful Woodrow Wilson once lamented. They may omit the "mention of every doctrine that might be looked upon as part of a peculiar and original programme." They may seem to disqualify men "whose decisive careers have won them a well-understood place in public life." But if given more than a hasty view, it may become apparent—as it did in 1952—that their concern with "availability" also eliminates the doctrinaire who is identified with a geographical section, an economic group or a single social stratum. As Louis Brownlow has observed, the choice of a candidate is "apt to fall to one who seems tolerant enough to listen to various views and flexible enough to become identified as the leader of many causes; many causes not always contradictory in substance but frequently rivals for priority in prestige."

The steadier view would also inform the onlooker that he is witnessing no ordinary demonstration of self-discipline, despite the smoke, bleatings and buncombe. Here are upward of 1,200 people, dissimilar in local origin and outlook, convoking themselves voluntarily as the principals and the judges in a court of the common law. Here, they reinterpret the present in the light of the past and make a prophecy for the future. Here, they make new decisions, yet seek to show that they are consistent with the precedents established by the great party chieftains who look down at them from the photographs overhead. And with few major exceptions, almost everyone present tries to digest whatever decision is reached, despite the bitter disappointment a good part of the convention has at adjournment time after its champion has been rejected.

From the Democratic and Republican conventions have come overlapping presidential candidates and programs chosen and shaped to the common law rule that party differences must not be so great that they foreclose four great aims: (1) When the party forms the government, it shall govern by consent instead of coercion. (2) It shall itself consent to surrender the government to the direction of a rival party. (3) When this exchange takes place it shall be in a peaceful way. (4) The changes in existing relations and proportions in the whole community shall be of a moderate instead of a drastic sort.

Each of these requirements has a firm support in pragmatic experience. A majority can rule by consent only if the minority is in substantial agreement with it. At least the two must not be so polarized in their views that points in contest cannot be compromised. Again, a party will peacefully surrender the direction of the government to a rival party only if it knows that, when it does, it will not be placed at the mercy of the rival, the undoing of whose acts may require a revolution. Nor can there be a peaceful exchange of power unless the two parties—however much they disagree on the means—still hold in common the great ends of our society. Finally, there can be no order and no continuity in communal life under party government unless each party contains some of the "permissible" elements present in the rival. (I emphasize "permissible" by way of excluding crooks, demagogues, hate-mongers, charlatans and all whose public conduct clearly shows an invincible contempt for the laws of constitutional government.) For this overlap between "permissible" elements offers insurance that when a party forms the government, the interests represented by the outgoing party will still have a "voice" in the new government; also, that before a party forms a government, it will have appraised the kinds of problems and human forces it may have to face when it takes authority.

It is precisely because our major parties have met these specifications on every occasion except the Civil War that a victorious leader can peacefully assume power and can appear to be the President of all the people on the day he is inaugurated. Whether he wins by a majority or a minority of the popular vote, those who opposed him momentarily are reassured about his future intentions by observing the character of his party. They see that it contains many people like themselves, similar in their constitutional outlook and needs. And they feel that if these friends and relatives at court cannot initiate any great good in their common interest, they will at least have enough strength to veto a potential evil.

What happens after power has changed hands is quite a different story.

4

The President as an artist

IIIIIOIIIIIIIIIIIIIIOIIIIIIIIIIIIIOIIIIIIIIIIIIIOIIIIIIIIIIIIIIOIIIIIIIIIIIIIIOIIIIIIIIIIIIIOIIIIIIIIIIIIOIIIIIIIII

The victor in the White House – The conflict between the rule of numbers and the rule of interest – Coalitions must be built from issue to issue – How the people react to this – The way the President is limited in the use of his best abilities – The role of the Congress – the role of the Supreme Court – How the President is affected by the co-existence of two Constitutions – The need for a compilation of presidential usages and precedents – The difficulty a President faces in gauging public opinion – Why the traditional distinction between "strong" and "weak" Presidents has little value – A proposed distinction drawn in terms of how Presidents use public opinion as a source for laws – The artistic faculty involved in this – Analysis of its traits – Example of Lincoln – Example of Jefferson – The Presidents who lacked this artistic faculty – Examples of presidential tragedies that resulted – But any President regardless of his artistry will suffer abuse.

Not long after the victor in any presidential election contest unpacks his bags in the White House for the first time,
the soft haze of his Inauguration Day gives way to a harsh
glare. He receives the light but no clear-cut images of his
place. He reels awkwardly until the conscious learning
process—the "growing in the White House"—changes (if it
ever does) into the poise of the virtuoso whose style seems
untutored. Actions that seemed graceful in a lesser post sud-

[51]

denly become grotesque in the long mirrors of the presidency. The manifestoes which stirred the nation during the campaign acquire the flat thump of a cracked drum when voiced again inside the presidential study. Events that marched in single file when the President viewed them from outside the White House become an oceanic churning from within. When he tries to deal with them, he finds that he is caught and tossed about by two opposite principles of representation.

The first is the *legal* rights of the majority, based on the rule of numbers. It holds that fifty per cent of the people *plus* any fraction of one per cent or more, has the right to shape the policies and to choose the managers of the government. The second principle is the *political* rule of interests. It holds that fifty per cent of the people *less* any fraction of one per cent or more are also entitled to a voice in the government and to a suspensive veto over the legal majority. How can the President move abreast of these cross-currents? If he won less than fifty per cent of the popular vote, by a strict adherence to the rule of numbers he has no real right to form the government or to shape its policies. All he represents is an interest or a union of interests which exceeded numerically the nearest rival. Even if the President received a fraction of one per cent or more over fifty per cent, he knows from his campaign experience that no one interest in the land is big enough or cohesive enough to form a majority all by itself. Many minorities totaled the winning combination.

If the President intends to follow "the will of the people," who expresses that will? His problem would be simplified if the coalition he built for an election-day victory remained stable. But it does nothing of the sort. It is torn apart when one minority gets what it wants, when a second gives up hope, and when all are suddenly lashed by the intrusion of physical events, unforeseen and unprovided for in the campaign formula. To get any kind of measure enacted, the President has to build a special coalition for the immediate object in view. Sometimes he can do this by reshuffling the forces within his party. He can also pick up support from among dissidents in the opposition party, or he can appeal directly to the nation in the hope that its groundswells will override all party lines. But whatever he does, he is never free of the nagging question of whether the real majority is not made up of the shy and silent citizens who can flare like a pillar of phosphorus when they are rubbed the wrong way.

There is more to his worry than this. Is a majority of one per cent, even if it lends itself to a physical count, sufficient to back an act that calls for great sacrifices? A case in point occurred in August, 1941, when the Congress of the United States agreed by one vote to keep the army in being. Was that vote big enough to invigorate President Roosevelt's hand in the field of foreign affairs? Though it passed the test of fifty per cent plus a fraction of one per cent, it clearly was not a sanction for diplomatic and military audacity. By how many degrees, then, must a majority be raised before it can presume to be the legal engine for social effort? The President's question is no easier when he views the minority of one per cent less. It, too, is made up of bits and pieces. How large, then, must the piece be before its claims are recognized as a "legitimate" minority? When a decision is called for, how long should the short-run suspensive veto of a minority interest be respected? When should the majority conquer and yet spare? When should its triumph be made absolute—even if it is won over the minority by no more than a single vote?

The President is not alone in his concern. The Congress also is heavily involved as it shapes its own answers to these questions. But it is the President, up on the high wire and in a strong wind, who holds our main attention. Meanwhile, as we watch him, we do not sit still for very long. On any issue, when we find ourselves on the side of the legal majority, we cannot understand why the President throws his weight to the political minority. On a second issue, when we find ourselves with the political minority, we cannot understand why the President throws his weight on the side of the legal majority. We say that the President lacks conviction; that he has no stability or unity of purpose; that he is just a "cheap politician." It is altogether possible, of course, that his instability may be due, first, to chronic shifts in *our* observation point, and, second, to his efforts to keep some sort of balance between numbers and interests, between what the law allows and what politics demands.

With each new decision he makes, he becomes less and less the President of all the people. If he leads, he is a dictator. If he follows, he is a weakling. If he appoints old friends to high places, he governs by crony. If he gets rid of them when they prove unequal to their new places, he "uses" people. If he speaks directly to the nation, he is a demagogue. If he waits for a proper moment to disclose bits of news, he withholds vital information a free people must have if it is to make wise decisions. And so on. Meanwhile, as the seashells of 156,000,000 humming people raise a din in his ears, all the Presidents who have held his place before him lay a hand on his shoulders. They demand that he enlarge himself beyond his natural talents. They also demand that he tame his rebelliousness. One says, "Thou shalt." The other says, "Thou shalt not." One says, "Be bold." The other says, "Be circumspect." One says, "The scrupulous respect for the law is the highest duty of every officer." The other says, "The higher duty is to save the country when it is in danger."

The President soon finds that he is not wholly free to uphold, defend and protect the Constitution to the best of *his* abilities. What he more often upholds is a concept of "the best" as it is defined by law, by the elaborate cultural pattern grouped around the presidency, by the work of the Congress and the Supreme Court, and by the outcome of rivalries within and between the political parties. By a use of his own best abilities, for example, the President can alert the nation to gathering dangers when their diagnosis is hard and the cure is not too painful. But those who live on a lower plane may deny him the use of his proposed remedy until the diagnosis is simple and the cure is hard. Yet it often happens that the proper sequence of cause and effect is switched, so that woes not of the President's making are traced to him as if the worst of his abilities had willed them into life.

A President, moreover, can be cramped in the use of his best abilities by the manner of his succession. When he follows a President of a rival party, as Franklin D. Roosevelt followed Herbert Hoover, he can blame the predecessor for all that is wrong. But he cannot do this when the succession is within the same party. He must not only respect the sensibilities of the ex-President and all those who were prominent in his administration, he must also portray his party as a fairly ominiscient force throughout its history. Yet in defending the past record, he also revives all the rancors of the past. In the end, they may attach to him, as though he had been at fault all along.

The Constitution tells the President what powers and duties he is to discharge to the best of his abilities. But he finds that it does not tell him how, when, and on what objects he is to discharge them. In large measure, the rule of action must come from the Congress. But because of its inertia, low politics, honest doubts, or merely from the habitual nature of events to be surprising, the Congress does not, nor can it, foresee and deal with every contingency. Much less can the Supreme Court do that. It neither was created to be, nor has it undertaken to be a source of practical wisdom, guiding the day-to-day work of the President or the Congress. It has taken particular care to keep a hands-off policy on executive acts in the military and diplomatic area; acts, which are not contrary to the express laws of the Congress, but rather, are without congressional authority.

The President, both as Commander-in-chief and as the Nation's organ for foreign affairs [the Court declared in a representative opinion] has available intelligence services whose reports are not and ought not to be published to the world. It would be intolerable that courts, without the relevant information, should review and perhaps nullify actions of the Executive taken on information properly held secret. Nor can courts sit *in camera* to be taken into executive confidence.

Nor does the Court presume to tell the President what will win judicial support if and when an act leads to a future legal contest. The rule of abstention was laid down in Washington's day. When he once asked for a norm of conduct, not to be found in the Constitution or in any congressional index, the reply came that the Court was not competent to state it. "We exceedingly regret every event that may cause embarrassment to your administration," Chief Justice John Jay wrote to Washington, "but we derive consolation from the reflection that your judgement will discern what is right, and that your usual prudence, decision and firmness will surmount every obstacle to the preservation of the rights, peace and dignity of the United States."

As a related matter, mention should be made of the Court's reluctance to stir up constitutional questions on the separation of powers. One can argue about how the Court spins the interpretation of laws in ways not intended by the Congress, or how it assumes the role of a proponent of legislation when it forces the Congress to close gaps in the existing legal structure. But the phenomenal fact remains that in all its history up to the time of the fight over President Roosevelt's plan to reorganize the judiciary in 1937, it struck down as *unconstitutional* less than seventy laws among the thousands enacted by the Congress. In that same period, executive acts were virtually untouched. When constitutional questions cannot be side-stepped, as when President Truman seized the steel industry, the general practice of the court is to formulate a constitutional rule no broader than is required by the precise facts to which it is to be applied.

What, then, can a President do when there is no constitutional, congressional or judicial compass, and little prospect of creating one in a swift-breaking emergency? Of necessity, he is forced to turn within himself, seek the rule of "the best" located there, and try to legitimize it by acting upon it.

But the process is an uneasy one. As the child of constitutional government, the President may doubt whether his oath to uphold, protect and defend the Constitution was meant to be a residual source of power for the Executive when all other organs of the government stalled in a crisis. Yet he also knows that the people in general do not put a fine point on legalistic questions when they view the presidential *institution*. They are concerned with pragmatic results; if the President succeeds in meeting an immediate danger, they will generally allow the happy finale to purify the means by which it was achieved. Yet a doubt in the President's mind on the legal powers of his office can make him fatally irresolute in action. When his half measures lead to failure, he is damned for the illegality of the means, and he is denied the consolation that he protected "the spirit of the Constitution"—though he strained the letter. An extreme example of this occurred in the administration of James Buchanan. Despite the clear sign that the South was preparing for war through the seizure of Federal arsenals, forts, post offices and naval facilities, Buchanan maintained that the general government had no power to coerce the rebellious states. All it could do under the Constitution was to "conciliate" them. When the popular clamor to halt the drift to secession was not quieted by this legal opinion, Buchanan ventured to restrain the South through several mercurial acts which betrayed his persistent doubts about the President's power as a commander in chief. The acts overawed nobody, infuriated everybody, and led to the subversion which a Jackson or a Lincoln might have checked by presidential audacity.

In a continuing examination of his place, the President inevitably discovers the coexistence of two Constitutions.

The President as an artist

One, adopted in 1789, states the general principles and structure of a Federal government based on a doctrine of coordinate, separate and interdependent powers. If the Bill of Rights and the two prohibition amendments are excepted, we have a residue of only ten changes in this text throughout 165 years of its history. Four of these enlarge the rights of citizens, and four provide for changes in election mechanics. An added change—the Eleventh Amendment—grants to the states an immunity of sovereignty. The Sixteenth Amendment, dealing with a Federal income tax, is the only constitutional grant to the central government of a power it did not explicitly possess in 1789.

Yet it is clear that we would not have gone very far in our national adventure if the propulsion we needed to get past novel events had been confined to that one grant. What we required we developed in the vast stretches of an "unwritten Constitution." Built pragmatically in a movement from event to event, it is formed of statutes, judicial opinions, administrative interpretations of the law, and of precedents the Presidents have created as if they were common-law judges. Regarding those precedents, it is certainly true that a "use does not make a right." But the political reasons which compel respect for the use itself were succinctly stated by the Supreme Court in the following extract taken from a representative opinion:

Both officers, law-makers and citizens naturally adjust themselves to any long-continued action of the Executive Department—on the presumption that unauthorized acts would not have been allowed to be so often repeated as to crystallize into a regular practice. That presumption is not reasoning in a circle but is the basis of a wise and quieting rule that in determining the meaning of a statute or the existence of a power, weight shall be given to the usage itself—even when the validity of the practice is the subject of investigation.

Though the interaction of the two Constitutions produces great social good, it may also lead to a breach of the peace when the President embarks on a course backed by precedent alone. The eruption has its origin in the want of graphic support for his act. For the unwritten Constitution of which the precedent is a part is located in many places; not only in public records, but also in memories, biographies, letters, speeches and records of conversations which shape the climate of our constitutional morality fully as much as does the formal agreement reached in 1789. Indeed, the latter is simply a declaration of intention to live under constitutional government. It does not by itself create the stuff that makes constitutional government possible. But while the President may draw on this scattered material to sanction his act, his critics sometimes ignore it when they challenge him. They seize the slim text of the written Constitution, always on hand, and they proclaim what is true: that it contains not a single word that gives explicit permission to what the President ventured to do.

If the President has Franklin D. Roosevelt's keen sense of symbolism, whenever he draws on the unwritten Constitution he may use the images of the past to form his defense in historical depth. To President Roosevelt, for example, the first peacetime draft in the history of America was not extraordinary. As he explained it, it was simply a call to the youth of the nation to answer the militia muster. World politics thereupon shrank to an Indian uprising on the American frontier. Battleships became canoes, and tanks became squirrel rifles to be fired in the defense of log cabins. Yet not all our Presidents have had the skill to dress novel events with old names that stir the great memories of the race. Or those who have the talent often lack the time to use it artfully. The story of past actions compiled in haste often merely steadies the inner will of a President battered by swift-breaking events. He thrusts out a decision for the nation to see, without clothing it in memories.

In this naked form, it is swiftly attacked as a constitutional obscenity. The pitch of the attack seems to rise in fury the longer an opposition party has lacked the sobering influence of responsible power. The party either forgets its own past when it controlled the Executive, or it deliberately ignores the fact that Presidents of its own choice helped shape the precedent for the executive act they are now excoriating. Meanwhile, those of the President's party who are new to government or were not forewarned of what was coming do not know what to say or to do. They feel the tug of party loyalty. They feel that they are involved in the President's fate. But the cries of outrage which split the national eardrum make them suspect that he *did* commit an original sin. Torn by doubts, frightened by the opposition's war drums, the President's men are often tempted to desert him, with the frequent result that he faces the massed battalions of the enemy all alone.

Within a few hours, moreover, the whole nation now gets a stereotype showing the man in the White House as a cross between Julius Caesar and the village idiot. The President may try to repair the damage by issuing "clarifying statements." Press and radiomen may amend their first reports when they learn that their story is at least 165 years old;

that the event happened first in Washington's time; that on every like occasion since then, Presidents have acted in the same way. Here and there across the land, private citizens who like to read the minutes of the previous meeting write letters to the editor to the same general effect. In all of this, the attempt is to dissolve the first portrait and to substitute one with more traditional lineaments. But the going is hard. To many people, the first conviction that the President was outrageously wrong comes as a rare note of certainty in an otherwise baffling world. Even if the truth underlying this view has the frailty of a toothpick, these people are not to be blamed too much if they latch onto it as though it were a floating spar in a stormy sea that had just wrecked their ship.

If this is a fair description of what often happens, it might help to gather in one place the unwritten Constitution that bears on the presidency. The codification of this material by a latter-day Justinian could destroy the virtue of elasticity it has in its present state. If, however, it was merely to be collected, it could conceivably brace our constitutional morality in several ways. It would reveal to the President what his predecessors have actually done in like cases. It would tend to ease the pressure on the White House staff, which now flies in many directions to gather in haste the sanctions of the past for an emergency need of the present. It would give to those who deal in public opinion an index to what is really a presidential innovation and what is simply a variation on an old theme. And it would arm the rest of us with a means for judging whether the President or those who attack him are the protectors or subverters of the constitutional order.

But even with a guide of this sort, the President has no real way of knowing where to place his weight in our shifting national currents. There is, of course, a passionate truth to what Alexander Hamilton expressed in the seventy-first *Federalist*. He acknowledged that the republican principle demands that the deliberate sense of the community should govern the conduct of those entrusted with the management of public affairs. "But it does not require an unqualified complaisance to every sudden breeze of passion, or to every transient impulse which the people may receive from the arts of men, who flatter their prejudices to betray their interests." The people, he continued, commonly intend the public good but do not always reason right about the means of promoting it. The wonder is that they err as seldom as they do, "beset, as they are, by the wiles of parasites and sycophants, by the snares of the ambitious, the avaricious, the desperate, by the artifices of men who possess their confidence more than they deserve it, and of those who seek to possess rather than to deserve it." Hamilton laid down the maxim that when occasions arise in which the interests of the people are at variance with their inclinations, "it is the duty of the person whom they have appointed to be the guardians of those interests, to withstand the temporary delusion, in order to give them time and opportunity for more cool and sedate reflection." And he concluded by remarking on the instances in which this sort of behavior saved the people "from the very fatal consequences of their own mistakes, and has produced lasting monuments of their gratitude to the men who had the courage and magnanimity enough to serve them at the peril of their displeasure."

But the Hamiltonian truth has its omissions. It provides no weather vane to distinguish the sudden breeze of passion from a prevailing trade wind of deep conviction. Nor does it state a rule so that those who manage the public business can know in all cases when they are right and the reasoning of the people is wrong, or when the people themselves have the better grasp of reality. What then is a wise defiance of public opinion, or a wise compliance with it? What distinguishes the "bullheadedness" of a President, which is bad, from his "bulldog tenacity," which is good? To what extent can the success won by defiance obscure the fact that it might have been won by other and less costly means? Or can nothing here be known except in hindsight prescience?

These general questions become needle-sharp in the day-to-day work of a President. As he hears a popular outcry, he can believe it to be broadly based. When he humors it, he can find that he pleased the wrong audience and deeply wronged the right one. He can believe, as did Herbert Hoover during the depression, that the outcry comes simply from "partisan politicians" or "agitators" whose fulminations need not be taken too seriously. In this belief, he can continue his performance without revising his lines or the supporting cast until he is driven bodily from the stage. On the other hand, the first to react to any move are often those who see that they stand to lose by it, either in a material way or politically. But since any act of his works to the disadvantage of someone, each new move is met by an outraged chorus. Because the benefits of the act may not become clear until later, those in whose interest it was made take longer to clear their throats for the note of approval. (A case in point was the Social Security Law enacted at a time when the lines were being drawn for the 1936 presidential elections.)

Often too, in the interval before a majority opinion jells in support of the President, public attention is diverted by an outcry against something else he does in a wholly different area. (For example, the Social Security Law was followed in early 1937 by a tumult over the Roosevelt message on the reorganization of the Federal judiciary.) As the new event, with all its dramatic freshness, holds the center of the stage, little notice is given to the belatedly formed majority which backs up the earlier act. It quietly and unobtrusively passes over as an ingredient of the public mood, without a printed registry of its presence. Even the President may not notice it. And as he can come upon evil days by playing from a strength that he does not actually have, he can also damage himself through timidity at a time when he is far stronger than he imagines.

Bearing all this in mind, a grouping of Presidents different from the one that is traditionally made may be ventured. It is the practice of most writers to distinguish between Presidents according to their attitudes about executive power. It is observed that some Presidents have said with Theodore Roosevelt that they could do anything for the people which the Constitution did not expressly prohibit; that others have said with William Howard Taft that they could do nothing beyond what the Constitution expressly demanded. Yet this distinction—despite its stirring overtones regarding Presidents who "seized power" and those who "respected the Constitution"—has no real utility. What Presidents have *said* they could or could not do, and what they have actually done, rarely move along parallel lines. The simple fact is that all our Presidents have obeyed the fundamental concepts of limited government. There have been only a handful of acts, most notably in the exceptional circumstances of Lincoln's presidency, for which some sort of constitutional support could not be found. And even Lincoln either tried to bring any act by fiat under the legal protection of his power as a commander in chief, or had the Congress give retroactive approval to what he had done.

Though we speak of "strong" and "weak" Presidents, it is misleading, I repeat, to state the difference in terms of those who refused to be bound by the letter of the Constitution or those who bowed before it. It is also misleading to state the difference in terms of those who asserted the supremacy of the Executive *over* the Congress and the Court, or the other way around. As constitutional executives, all of them maintained that the presidency was neither inferior nor superior to the other branches of the government; that the three rested on a plane of equality, each strong in its own right, and each invested with powers and duties appropriate to its special sphere of responsibility. The better distinction between "strong" and "weak" Presidents can be drawn in terms of how they managed the slippery imponderables of public opinion. The "strong" ones knew how to weave and guide that opinion into the machinery of the government so that *the work of the presidency could proceed under the sanction of the law.* The "weak" ones, lacking that talent, were limited in their work to what was funneled to them *by the men outside the presidency who actually commanded public opinion, or at least congressional opinion.*

Upon the basis of this distinction, men like Washington, Jefferson, Monroe, Jackson, Polk, Lincoln, Cleveland, McKinley, Theodore Roosevelt, Wilson, Franklin D. Roosevelt, Truman—and, at random stages, Taylor, Hayes, Benjamin Harrison and Taft, form a distinct class of Presidents. They varied in their social outlook. They faced different problems. They knew sharp defeats as well as triumphs. Some of them were right and others were proven wrong in what they did. Yet, to a greater or lesser degree, they shared a common talent in directing public opinion so as ultimately to secure a legal prop for a good part of their programs.

An observation made by Woodrow Wilson, loosely applied, seems to cover them all.

A great nation [he said], is not led by a man who simply repeats the talk of the street-corners or the opinions of the newspapers. A nation is led by a man who hears more than those things; or who, rather, hearing those things, understands them better, unites them, puts them into a common meaning; speaks, not the rumors of the street, but a new principle for a new age; a man [to whom] the voices of the nation . . . unite in a single meaning and reveal to him a single vision, so that he can speak what no man else knows, the common meaning of the common voice. Such is the man who leads a great, free, democratic nation.

Wilson was not necessarily describing someone who was gifted in oratory. He was referring here to Abraham Lincoln, who was heavily overshadowed by the elocutionists of his day. Nor was he describing an administrator. Lincoln was among our more inefficient Presidents when it came to the work of the Executive. Secretary of State William H. Seward complained bitterly about this man who kept his files inside the sweatbands of his stove-pipe hat. Secretary of War Edwin M. Stanton grew apoplectic when he denounced Lincoln's interference in the management of military operations. Secretary of the Treasury Salmon P. Chase remarked that there was so little co-ordination between the departments that, when he wanted to find out what was going on in the government, he sent out a boy to get the latest copy of the New York *Herald*. Only Gideon Welles, the Secretary of the Navy, grasped the essential truth which escaped the notice of his efficient Cabinet colleagues. "[Lincoln] could have dispensed with anyone in his cabinet," said Wells, "and the administration would not have been impaired. But it would have been impossible to have selected anyone who could have filled the office of the First Magistrate as well as Mr. Lincoln." What Lincoln possessed and the others did not was an artistic sensitivity to what the tension levels of the nation could support and what it demanded of the President.

This faculty cannot be regulated. It cannot be taught. It is a kind of sublime madness, intersecting with the accidents of the medium in which it operates. It is largely unconcious of itself, only partly conscious of the means it uses; but it is totally aware of the objects it seeks out. It is a variable faculty, being half historian and half prophet in the way it operates. Its mission at times is to find and to state so that all can know the generating principle of that which *is*. At other times—and this is the Lincoln of the Gettysburg and the Second Inaugural addresses—its mission is to seek and state the generating principle of that which *shall be*. It is a sense of ensemble, based on a theory of arrangement in which a subject is shown as if for the first time in its true light. It is a talent which depends in great measure on the moral tone of the President's personality; less on his intellect—brilliant men can ruin a country—and more on the quality of his passions, his will and his imaginative faculties.

The faculty is shown in the President's capacity to foretell the course of events; in the problems he chooses to bring to the center of national attention, the time when he does it, the degree of gravity he attaches to the problem, the sense of lassitude or urgency he creates when he defines alternative solutions to it. It is shown in the degree to which he is a "great asker and patient hearer of the truth about those things" into which he ought to inquire. It is shown in the way he creates his own luck, or builds safety nets against misfortune. It is shown in how he stretches old forms to cover new functions, without exciting those of us who are suspicious of any change until we have had experience with it. But above all, the President shows his artistry by how he bridges the office of the President, which is defined and fixed by law, and the institution of the presidency, which, as it dwells on a plane of its own in direct view of the nation, is the hub of its reveries and boundless expectations.

This last, as I've said in a former connection, is perhaps the most difficult part of the unrelieved challenge to a President. He must move between the hard body of an office, *created* in a self-conscious way, and the mists of an institution, *deduced* from the temper of the nation and its sense of a mission in human history. More than one President has fallen into the gap between them. But those who have been most successful in meeting the challenge have uniformly held one position. They have spoken directly to the people, to gain from them the measure of support a President needs if he is to be effective in translating the national purpose to the Congress—just as he must receive from the Congress a continuing definition of the objects and situations the office of the presidency is to administer under law.

What all this means in a concrete case is best illustrated in the way Thomas Jefferson handled the purchase of the Louisiana Territory. The issue was a complicated one. First there was Jefferson's early doctrinal view that the states' delegations of power to the Federal government could not be enlarged by resorting to the implied powers of the Constitution. Upon this theory, the Executive and the Congress alike lacked any express authority to expand the boundaries of the United States by purchase and annexation. The second complication was Jefferson's early conception of the presidency. Though he was far from being an enemy of executive energy as such, at a time when the Federalists held the presidential office, and the Republicans were bidding for the rule of the House of Representatives, Jefferson argued that the Congress was the generating organ of the government and the special agent of the people. The President, therefore, could do nothing except what the Congress explicitly authorized. Upon this theory, Jefferson could not have sent James Monroe to Paris to negotiate the purchase of the "island" of New Orleans, and to open transit rights on the Mississippi River, closed when Spain transferred the territory to French rule. There was no explicit congressional sanction for the first half of this mission.

Nevertheless, the chain of events Jefferson set in motion without congressional authority brought the news from James Monroe in Paris that the whole of the Louisiana Territory could be purchased. Jefferson called the Congress back into special session to consider this prospect. He believed, for a while, that the Congress might have to appeal to the nation for an additional article to the Constitution, approving and confirming an act not previously authorized. But he also armed his congressional lieutenants with an argument to avoid the very act he felt might be necessary. "In seizing the fugitive occurrence which so much advances the good of their country," Jefferson wrote to John Breckinridge on August 12, 1803, "the executive have done an act beyond the Constitution. The legislature in casting behind them metaphysical subtleties, and risking themselves like faithful servants must ratify and pay for it, and throw themselves on their country for doing for them unauthorized what we know they would have done for themselves had they been in a situation to do it." Then, with the same aptitude Franklin D. Roosevelt showed in the use of pedestrian images to take the edge off radical acts, Jefferson fixed a homely image that might be employed to good purpose in the imminent debate. It was that of a guardian investing money for his ward until the latter came of age. He observed that the Congress could say to the nation: "I did this for your own good; I pretend to no right to bind you; you can disavow me, and I must get out of the scrape as I can: I thought it my duty to risk myself for you."

Several days after this letter was sent, however, Jefferson cast his own metaphysical subtleties aside. In a further message to Breckinridge, he stepped forward as a *party leader* and entrusted the ratification of the purchase treaty to a straight marshaling of party strength. He informed Breckinridge that since "word from France makes it undesirable to raise any constitutional questions about the purchase, it would be wise to have all friends of the treaty present on the first day of the session to insure its swift passage." The party whip was cracked. The friends were all present. And with the Federalists alone dissenting, the purchase was approved. Except for a shrill voice here and there, no one for very long challenged the constitutionality of what Jefferson had done, no more than they did in 1940 when Roosevelt announced the terms of the destroyer–naval base deal with England. No one for long lashed at Jefferson because he had ignored his own theories of limited government and a limited, though energetic Executive. What the people at large saw was a fulfillment by the presidential institution of their basic expectations. Jefferson had kept them at peace by dislodging France from its control over the port of New Orleans through which three eighths of American produce passed to its markets. He had enlarged to an incredible degree the sheer physical might of America, and he had opened up the highroad to material riches in a vast, fertile plain. But he did not stop here. He added a poetic dimension to the event. Louisiana, he explained, was not just a solution to a navigation problem. It meant the gain of an "empire of liberty"; a domain that would create and recreate new communities of free men should the old ones backslide on American ideals.

If Jefferson's handling of the Louisiana Purchase stands as an example of presidential artistry, Presidents lacking in the talent included John Adams, Madison, Van Buren, John Quincy Adams, William Henry Harrison (who held office for only one month), Tyler, Fillmore, Pierce, Buchanan, Grant, Johnson, Garfield, Arthur, Harding, Coolidge and Hoover. This is not to say they were bad men or were lacking in executive ability and intellect. But they shared one or more of five traits. Most of them failed as party leaders. Most of them compounded this failure by their inability to form a party *pro tem* that could cut across party lines and win the loyalty of millions of Americans. Most of them viewed the presidency as an office which worked with the Congress and the Court in a closed legal circuit. They all failed to project an image of a presidency with an organic responsibility of its own to help create what the people wanted. And most of them failed to grasp the potential of the presidency as an institution.

Of this group, two men are here considered.

1. *John Adams.* In the range of his political speculation, Adams was the equal of Thomas Jefferson and Alexander Hamilton and, in fact, held the middle place between their polar views. As a leader of the Revolution, and as the American minister to England, he made a vast contribution to the birth of the new nation. His conscience was of the highest order; his courage, equally so. Nevertheless, his presidential career was that of a flower whose roots grew toward the sky and not the earth.

He neither secured for himself a firm base of action, nor was capable of forming one. At first he went along with the Hamilton wing of the Federalist party and supported their financial and diplomatic measures. But having allowed himself to be identified with the non-agrarian interests—the "rich, the well born and the good"—he broke with the Hamiltonians rather than lead the country into a full-scale war with France. Yet he gained no profit from this in the agrarian pro-French quarters. The financial measures he had earlier supported had thrown the Southern planters and others into the arms of the Jefferson Republicans, while the sudden calling off of the impending war against France exposed Adams to the charge that he had needlessly taxed the nation to create an armament that was of no use. Not content to suffer an attack on one side by the embittered mercantile wing of the Federalist party, Adams invited a two-front war against himself by the notorious support he first gave to the Alien and Sedition Laws.

The "alien" portion of the laws was aimed at destroying "the foreign vote," principally of Scotch-Irish origin, which was gravitating in increasing numbers to Jefferson's party of the underdog, as it took possession of the Western wilderness. A Federalist on a trip among these long-limbed people, "with the long knife, the long gun and the long memory," had occasion to refer to them as "the most God-provoking Democrats on this side of Hell." And to curb the political provocations of these "foreign liars" and "savages,"—as the Federalists called them—the alien laws raised the period of residence for naturalization from five to fourteen years. During this interval, moreover, the President could deport any alien he judged to be "dangerous to the peace and safety of the United States." The sedition laws, on the other hand, were aimed at the native Jeffersonians. They were to be fined and imprisoned for subversive remarks or writings against the President of the United States.

The Federalist judiciary showed no reluctance to give vengeful force to these laws by every means, including a boomerang. On the eve of the 1800 elections, for example, Federalist agents reached deep into Republican-controlled upper New York to seize a Jedediah Peck, who had circulated a petition for the repeal of the Sedition Laws. The offender was thereupon carried through two hundred miles of Republican territory so that he could be brought to trial in New York. "A hundred missionaries, in the cause of democracy," wrote a contemporary New Yorker, "stationed between New York and Cooperstown, could not have done so much for the Republican cause as this journey of Jedediah

Peck from Otsego to the capital of the state." On each step
of the way, the frontiersmen, including those who had lately
been Federalist in their sympathies, had a visible proof of
what the Republicans had charged against the Federalists
in the Kentucky Resolutions of November 1798:

That if the acts before specified should stand, these conclusions
would flow from them; that the general government may place
any act they think proper on the list of crimes and punish it
themselves, whether enumerated by the Constitution as cognizable by them; that they may transfer its cognizance to the President or any other person, who may himself be the accuser,
counsel, judge, and jury, whose suspicions may be the evidence,
his order the sentence, his officer the executioner, and his breast
the sole record of the transaction; that a very numerous and
valuable description of the inhabitants of these states being by
this precedent reduced as outlaws to the absolute dominion of
one man, and the barrier of the Constitution thus swept away
from us all, no rampart now remains against the passions and the
power of a majority of Congress, to protect from a like exporta-
tion or other more grievous punishment the . . . peaceable inhabitants who may venture to reclaim their constitutional rights
and liberties of the state and people, or who for other causes,
good or bad, may be obnoxious to the views or marked by the
suspicions of the President, or be thought dangerous to his or
their elections or other interests, public or personal; that the
friendliness alien has indeed been selected as the safest subject of
the first experiment, but the citizen will soon follow, or rather has
already followed; for, already has a sedition act marked him as
its prey.

A few months later, Adams was overthrown. Two possible
alternatives had been open to him when he broke with the
Hamilton wing of the Federalist party. He might have
drawn to himself the sort of support that was rallying around

Jefferson. Or he might have tried to hold the loyalty of the Federalists who were part of the westward migration. But his earlier identification with Federalist economic orthodoxy made him suspect in Republican circles, though he had come closer to their economic views. On the other hand, his theoretical speculations on the nature of men and government made it impossible for him to accede to, much less lead the Republican demands on the head of civil liberties. And lastly, the Federalist machine he had helped to crank could not be halted before it wrecked its energy in the fatal execution of the Alien and Sedition Laws. Though Adams had jumped from the wheel, he was nevertheless blamed for what continued to move under its own momentum. The only positive good credited to him—the preservation of peace with France—was at the price of his self-immolation. This sort of act may provide a suitable theme for the elegiacs of historians as they retrace the death march. But it is not the sort of act which inspires a people with the sense of a united movement toward a great adventure.

2. *James Madison.* By any test of experience, James Madison was supremely qualified to hold the presidency. He had helped engineer the events that led to the call for a Constitutional Convention, left the imprint of his hand on the whole Constitution, and ably pamphleteered for its adoption. Through uncommon tact, he brought to his collaboration with Thomas Jefferson a practical sense of the possible and a softness of expression which won each end in view without compromising its heart. The rise and triumph of the Democratic-Republican party was his handiwork as much as it was Jefferson's. And on top of this, he had eight years of schooling in executive matters as Jefferson's

Secretary of State. Yet the sure touch he showed in lesser posts somehow palsied when the presidency was actually turned over to him.

The circumstances he faced were admittedly not easy. The Northern anchor of the Republican party, represented by the lower-income groups, had been uprooted by the embargo Jefferson imposed on commerce with warring European powers. Where these agrarian New Englanders had once been hostile to seaboard mercantile interests, they now began to edge over to their late enemies with whose prosperity their own suddenly appeared to be linked. The Southern anchor of the party was in no better shape. One of its prongs, represented by the planter interests, was well advanced on the road to economic decay; the radical Republicans, representing the second prong, announced that they would make no further compromises with the patronage-hungry Republicans in the Middle Atlantic states. As for these latter gentlemen, they too, had a bothersome announcement to make. It was that the support they had given in the past to Jefferson's agrarian policies had imperiled their political prospects in Middle Atlantic towns. They would have no more of this madness.

Only the backwoods part of the Republican alignment was unshaken in its devotion to the cause. This remaining center of strength, however, was fated to be the source of Madison's undoing. In one place, the Indians held lands coveted by cotton and grain growers. In another place, the Illinois prairies were thought to be sterile since they bore no trees, while the soil itself was too hard packed to be turned by pioneer plows. But as the population piled up behind this latter barrier to the westward march, attention was drawn

[77]

to a possible northward expansion into Canada. This meant a war of conquest; it also meant an end to the Jefferson-inspired Republican policy of temporizing with the English. Meanwhile, Tecumseh, and his brother, the Prophet, in pursuit of their own dream of a Great Lakes to the Gulf confederation of Indians, seemed to lend credence to the frontiersman's conviction that the English redcoats were behind every redskin outrage. As the lusts and fears of the farmer, trapper and fur trader all came to a focus in a nationalistic demand for war, the champion of the hour was not James Madison. It was Henry Clay, elected Speaker of the House of Representatives in late 1811. Clay saw the obvious truth that the President had no remaining natural source of strength except for the Westerners. Unless he came to an agreement with them, his chances for a second term would lessen. Madison was thereupon cast in the role of Adams, Clay in the role of Hamilton, and England in the role of France. But the outcome was different. Madison did not follow the Adams course of halting the drift to war at the price of a personal and party crack-up. With great reluctance, he recommended to the Congress that war should be declared against England. Not long afterward, the War Hawks kept their part of the bargain when a congressional caucus of Republicans in which they played a leading part endorsed Madison's candidacy and placed him on the road to re-election.

If no President could have resisted the pressure of the War Hawks, one might have expected that once a decision was made, Madison would rally the nation to prosecute the war. Instead, New England threatened to secede from the Union, as if to place itself out of range of the British fleet.

The raising and support of troops were undertaken in a slip-shod way. The men appointed as field commanders committed one blunder after another. William Henry Harrison, the only general to win a major land battle except for Andrew Jackson, was forced to resign from the army by the intrigues of Secretary of War John Armstrong, who wished to have the field command of all military operations. And it was only when Secretary of State James Monroe assumed the added duties of a Secretary of War that the dismayed nation was rallied to acts which won a semblance of honor from an otherwise shabby wartime performance.

It is not to be inferred that all the men who had the ability to guide public opinion were thereby made immune to the popular cry, "This will never do!" Ironically, those who were most successful in transforming public opinion into creative laws and programs were also among those who suffered the severest attacks. The abuse of "Mad Tom" Jefferson; of the "hangman," "adulterer" and "demagogue" Andrew Jackson; and of the "baboon," Abraham Lincoln, is legendary. And our memories are still fresh of what was said about "that man in the White House," Franklin D. Roosevelt, or that "haberdasher" Harry S. Truman. All these epithets seem to come with the presidency.

5

This will never do!

〓IIIIIIIIIII❑IIIIIIIIIII❑IIIIIIIIIII❑IIIIIIIIIII❑IIIIIIIIIII❑IIIIIIIIIII❑IIIIIIIIIII❑IIIIIIIIIII

Washington caught in a crossfire of the Federalists and Republicans –
His reaction to it – His critics press their attacks to the day of his
retirement – Similar attacks on other Presidents for great and small
reasons – Theodore Roosevelt and the issue of simplified spelling – The
distrust of leadership in a diseased state – American imitation of the
ancient style of Chinese warfare – Why the President does not take
legal action against his defamers – President as the source of compas-
sion – The presidential appeal to the ultimate verdict of history – The
historical sense in the presidency – Grant's plea to be forgiven –
Generous way in which the nation reacted to it.

It is said of George Washington that he was the first in
war and the first in peace. And so he was. But it was not
until some time after his death that he also became the first
in the hearts of his countrymen.

His presidency was a troubled one. In the most tranquil
of times, it would have taken no small talent to get a new
kind of government under way and to overcome the resist-
ance of those who preferred the system under the Articles
of Confederation. But Washington's difficulties were compounded by the influences the distant French Revolution

[80]

had set in motion. The garish light of that event colored and exaggereated the unsettled domestic and foreign problems before the United States. And as two parties, the Federalist and the Republican-Democratic, came into being to organize rival marches on those problems, Washington was caught at the center of the collision.

Earlier, Washington had confessed in his First Inaugural that he was "unpracticed in the duties of civil administration." Four years later, his political experiences led him to contemplate retiring at the end of his first term. He explained to James Madison that from the beginning he "found himself deficient in many of the essential qualifications, owing to his inexperience in the forms of public business, his unfitness to judge legal questions, and the questions arising out of the Constitution; that others more conversant in such matters would be better able to execute them." Not long afterward, at the height of the furor over the Jay Treaty, he had reason to regret consenting to a second term. "Every act of my administration," he said "[has been] attacked in such exaggerated and indecent terms as could scarcely be applied to a Nero—or even to a common pickpocket." Even Thomas Jefferson was writing of him at this time, "I wish that [Washington's] honesty and his political errors may not furnish a second occasion to exclaim, 'curse on his virtues, they have undone this country.'"

One might have supposed that as he approached his retirement, the national mood would have uniformly subscribed to Washington's self-portrait. "In every act of my administration," he wrote, "I have sought the happiness of my fellow-citizens. My system for the attainment of this object has uniformly been to overlook all personal, local and partial considerations: to contemplate the United States, as one great whole." But the endorsement was not universal. A majority of the Virginia House of Delegates voted down a proposed resolution that Washington's life has "been strongly marked by wisdom in the Cabinet, by valor in the field, and the purest patriotism in both." Young Andrew Jackson, blind to what the future held in store for him, had demanded that Washington be impeached at the time of the Jay Treaty "for the Daring infringements on our Constitutional rights." Failing here, Jackson became one of twelve Congressmen who voted against a cordial reply to the Farewell Address. And to the editors of the *Aurora* of Philadelphia, the leading Republican journal of the day, Washington's retirement from the presidency marked the end of a Babylonian captivity for the nation. "When a retrospect is taken for the Washington administration for eight years," they wrote on March 5, 1798, "this day ought to be a JUBILEE for the United States."

The only President who was spared Washington's experience was William Henry Harrison, who died one month after his inauguration. All the rest, gifted or pedestrian, wise or bumbling, have been attacked for acts involving the very continuity of the nation. They have also been attacked for acts as trivial as simplified spelling. When Theodore Roosevelt, an enthusiast, gave the public printer three hundred words to be used in simplified form in the Annual Message, he was to explain that he made no attempt "to do anything far reaching or sudden or violent, or indeed, anything very great at all." But, as often happens when the Congress is outfoxed by the Executive on an issue of major importance, it strikes back at an exposed bit of nonsense. In this case, it was simplified spelling—not because the Congress attached any importance to it, but simply to show a general displeasure with the executive. A sharp skirmish followed, and Roosevelt sued for peace.

I could not by fighting have kept the new spelling in [he explained to a friend] and it was infinitely worse to go into an undignified contest when I was beaten. Do you know—the one word as to which I think the new spelling was wrong—thru—was more responsible than anything else for our discomfort? But I am mighty glad I did the thing anyhow.

In the final pathological stages of the effort, attacks of this sort have led directly to the death of three Presidents and to countless attempts on the lives of others. If there is any pharisaical comfort to be drawn from these outrages, it is that America, unlike other nations, has never produced a doctrinaire justification for political murder. Here, John Wilkes Booth, hiding in a barn, his leg broken, found that he was not hailed as another Brutus or William Tell because he shot Abraham Lincoln. In a diary found on his body, Booth wrote: "After being hunted like a dog through swamps, woods, and last night being chased by gun boats till I was forced to return wet, cold, starving with every man's hand against me, I am here in despair . . . looked upon as a common cut-throat." The image was an accurate description not only of Booth, but of Charles J. Guiteau who shot Garfield and Leon Czolgosz who shot McKinley.

If another ground of pharisaical comfort is wanted, it is that among the people as a whole the distrust of leadership tends to limit itself to an American imitiation of the ancient style of Chinese warfare. To make the enemy lose face without a loss of blood, fearsome masks are worn by the combatants. Symbolic acts of mayhem are performed in ritual-

istic dances. Incense is burned and celestial bells are struck.
An elaborate jingle of verbal insults is aimed at the President
and those close to him. The broadest flourish of all comes at
the moment when the keynote speaker rises before the nominating convention of the party that is out of power. First he
whets his axe on the grindstone of several thousand fire-
spouting words. Then, while his audience shouts its ecstasy,
he chops off the head of the President. Surprisingly, except
for Theodore Roosevelt, no modern President while in office
or as a candidate has ever looked to the courts for relief.

There are many good reasons why they do not. The
primary one touches a leading element of the presidency. It
is that the President holds the ultimate power to pardon and
to grant reprieves. Though he is also our principal national
disciplinarian, it is demanded that his capacity to forgive
shall be the strongest of his impulses. The prosecuting attorney's mentality may do for a mayor or for a governor. But
it will not do for the head of a democratic nation; if nothing
else is shown by a President, compassion, at least, must be
shown. (It may be for this reason above all others that a
forgiving Abraham Lincoln serves us as our secular passion
play.) Again, no matter who the President is, whether a
Theodore Roosevelt or an Andrew Johnson, the nation feels
uneasy when the President singles out anyone for a special
attack. The attack may be fully deserved, as it was when
Johnson ripped into Thaddeus Stevens, who had made his
life miserable. Yet there is the feeling that no one is really
in a position to defend himself when the President holds him
up to the ridicule of the nation. Even the friends of the
President recoil when a man who is the ultimate source of
forgiveness prosecutes his private wrongs. On all sides it is

said that he is vindictive—that he is using the power of his place to crush defenseless private citizens—that he is demeaning the presidency by appearing as a party to a private fight—that he is trying to suppress free speech and free press—that the rewards of the place are so great that he should reconcile himself to its inconveniences.

This may also explain why our Presidents seek refuge in the hope that they will be "vindicated by history." Some of them, like Andrew Jackson, heard the verdict in their lifetime. As Jackson stepped down from the inaugural platform after his successor Martin Van Buren was sworn in, a shout leaped from the witnessing throng, wrote Thomas Hart Benton, such as "power never commanded, nor man in power received. It was affection, gratitude and admiration . . . the acclaim of posterity breaking from the bosoms of contemporaries." Others felt they would have to wait a while longer to get their full credit. As the aged Madison wrote to the aged Jefferson: "I indulge the confidence that a sufficient evidence will find its way to another generation, to ensure, after we are gone, whatever of justice may be withheld whilst we are here."

To help along the cause of delayed justice, many Presidents kept diaries, wrote autobiographies, or had their papers edited for study by the future. And of late, the presidential appeal to the ultimate verdict of history has assumed institutional form. This began when Franklin D. Roosevelt provided a central place where the records of his administration might be kept. Now that Harry S. Truman has made a similar arrangement, it is probable that all future Presidents will do the same.

One thing is certain. As they announce their plans, all will be assailed as egoists. It will be said of them what a Boston newspaper said of John Adams after he retired from the presidency: "Mr. Adams affects to believe that posterity will acquit him. It must be the posterity of a very distant age, so distant as to be wholly unacquainted with his conduct that shall pass a favorable judgment upon him." It is to be hoped, however, that the practice becomes firmly rooted, and not only because it would reduce the loss of presidential records containing a major part of our history. The human desire "to read well," and the knowledge that his secret thoughts would be exposed to future generations might act as a powerful spur to greatness, or a powerful deterrent to pettiness in those sensitive areas where the conscience of the President and not the law states the rule of what is right or wrong.

Where war and peace are involved, it is possible to pinpoint the connection between the President's sense of history and what he does. From the Civil War on through World War II, every President has done his best to hold his hand, so that the onus of starting the war would be recorded by history as falling on the enemy power. But his awareness that he will be judged by history shines through less dramatic events to which he is a party. Perhaps no one revealed this more clearly than President Grant, a man who otherwise won no celebrity for the delicacy of his feelings. In the Civil War years, he could seem unmoved when they called him a butcher. In the White House, he did not appear to be annoyed by the rank odors that rose from the corruptionists who flanked him on all sides. Yet toward the end, as if in a blinding revelation, Grant saw the whole of his presidential course to be one of neglect and failure. It brought from him a plea that he be spared the censure of posterity. In his last Annual Message to the Congress, he explained that it had been his "fortune or misfortune to be called to the office of Chief Executive without any previous political training." He went on to say that from the age of seventeen he had witnessed but two presidential campaigns, and in only one of them was he eligible to vote. Under the circumstances, therefore, it was reasonable to expect errors of judgment in his presidency. Then came these poignant words:

Mistakes have been made, as all can see and I admit, but, it seems to me, oftener in the selections made of the assistants appointed to aid in carrying out the various duties of administering the government, in nearly every case selected without a personal acquaintance with the appointee, but upon the recommendations of the representatives chosen directly by the people. It is impossible, where so many trusts are to be allotted, that the right parties should be chosen in every instance. History shows that no administration, from the time of Washington to the present, has been free from these mistakes. But I leave comparison to history, claiming only that I have acted in every instance from a conscientious desire to do what was right, Constitutional within the law, and for the very best interests of the whole people. Failures have been errors of judgment, not of intent.

The generous way in which the nation reacted to this manly statement recalls the common observation that only railroad wrecks make news, not the trains that arrive safely and on time. Perhaps the same thing is true of the President's standing with the people. It is the dramatic denunciation of his works, and not their quiet endorsement that fills the public ear and eye. Despite our many common scolds, this nation generally has a sober discriminating sense, and more than an ordinary capacity for human sympathy. Every

President has won some understanding for the fix he is in and the problems he faces. No one of them has lacked some friends, even among the people who strongly disagreed with his policies. Even Herbert Hoover received nearly 16,000,000 votes in 1932. And in any event, no President has been without means he can use to create a climate favorable to his purposes. What those means are, exclusive of actual policies, will be examined in the next chapter.

6

The President in his self-defense

IIIIIIIIIIIᴏIIIIIIIIIIᴏIIIIIIIIIIIᴏIIIIIIIIIIᴏIIIIIIIIIIᴏIIIIIIIIIIᴏIIIIIIIIIIᴏIIIIIIIIIIᴏII

The President's natural sources of strength – The deeply ingrained managerial sense of the country – The age of the place he holds – The fear of change – How this fear works to his advantage within his party – President also gains strength from the men around him – The difficulty he experiences, however, in the selection of his friends – Principles upon which American Cabinets are formed – Examples of Republic of Texas and the Southern Confederacy – Kitchen Cabinets as natural supplements to regular Cabinets – The ultimate source of President's strength is the reasonableness of what he says or does – Communications problems of English Prime Minister and American President contrasted – The means at the President's disposal to make himself heard above the tumult – Mark of affection shown for President – Reveals dualism of will to enlarge and will to diminish – What Charles Dickens had to say about the will to diminish – Where Dickens needs amendment – How the dualism serves the tone of our constitutional morality.

In parliamentary forms of government, the same men who as legislators plow the ground for coming events harvest and market the crops as ministers. In modern totalitarian states, too, the "agitators" and the "managers" tend to be the same people. But the American pattern is different. Here, though we often invite a fatal and false opposition between thought and action, we nevertheless distinguish between the "talkers" and the "doers"—between the legislative and executive functions. Patrick Henry and Samuel Adams, for example, were at liberty to agitate for a revolution. Yet its management was entrusted to George Washington, the engineer who held back at first. Again, Senator Robert A. Taft could be foremost among those who agitated for Republican policies in the Senate and across the nation. Yet it was General Dwight D. Eisenhower, the administrator, who was entrusted with the party nomination in 1952.

The special place we give to the manager shines through a primary term of speech. Almost the first question we ask when we have business to do in a new place is, "Who is in charge here?" We are pretuned to expect that somebody will be in charge—and that the somebody will be one man and not a committee. As long as the President, therefore, shows some capacity for "being in charge"; as long as he exercises a will to decide—even if his decisions are wrong—he has at his command a fund of support among a people who abhor a vacuum perhaps more than nature does.

Next to this cultural trait is the support the President draws from the age of the place he holds. In the last 165 years, people everywhere have experimented with various forms of an executive. But the American presidency, with its unbroken career, is now the most venerable of all executives among the major nations of the world. Its survival capacity alone gives distinction to the man who embodies it. Entering the succession of Presidents, he stands out as someone who is "bound to go down in history." And this fact can induce many people to bid for their own immortality by linking their story to the President's through service to him.

The President in his self-defense

A further resource at the President's disposal has been mentioned in another connection. It is the human fear of change. At election times in particular, our thoughts often bear the same notations ancient cartographers used to write in the margins of their maps. "Beyond this, lies nothing but sandy deserts full of wild beasts, unapproachable bogs, Scythian ice, or a frozen sea." In this mood, though we may find faults with a President, since the faults are charted, and sometimes predictable, we may prefer to put up with him rather than risk an adventure with someone else who might lead us from bad to worse. In the subtle activity of this will "to stay put" one can partially explain why fourteen Presidents who were elected or succeeded to the office were again nominated by their party and were elected for a second term. In Franklin D. Roosevelt's case, it was for four terms. Only six Presidents failed to win a second term after their renomination. Only four who wanted to be renominated— and they all came in the period before the 1880's—were turned down by their party. Even John Tyler was again offered his party's nomination, though the Whigs in Congress had announced earlier that their connection with him was at an end.

The advantages the President holds within his party are based on two main facts which touch on our disinclination to change. (1) Through the use of his patronage, he will have created a dependency that has a material stake in his survival. If he is overthrown, all who live on his bounty risk his fate. They have every reason of self-interest, therefore, to stick by him. They will desert only if the seditionists within the party show themselves strong enough to deny the President a further nomination; or only when the President announces that he has no interest in another term. In the latter event in particular, when the President's power to coerce and reward is lifted, small armies form around ducal figures who either promise to be a new source of rewards, or will reaffirm the existing pattern of rewards if they win the party's scepter and then the nation's throne.[1] (2) The second advantage the President holds is that the party cannot deny him a renomination without inviting the charge that it fooled the people four years before when it backed a man it now admits to be unqualified. To avoid any such self-condemnation, the party may be forced to conceal its errors by repeating them for a second time.

An added source of support for the President at all times is the sort of men with whom he surrounds himself. It is unfortunately the case, however, that while a President is free to pick his enemies, unlike a tyrant, he is not entirely free to pick his friends. To this extent, he is denied the benefit of Machiavelli's advice to the Prince. "The first impression that one gets from a ruler and of his brains," said Machiavelli, "is from seeing the men that he has about him. When they are competent and faithful one can always consider him wise, as he has been able to recognize their ability and keep them faithful. But when they are the reverse, one can always form

---

[1] Before the enactment of the Twenty-second Amendment, the chance that a President might run for a third term tended to hold his dependency together, and to this extent gave a semblance of order to his administration. Now that he cannot constitutionally succeed himself more than once, we can expect the end of every second term to take on the aspect of a Donnybrook Fair at the peak of its melee. The amendment may have an opposite effect, however, toward the close of a first term. As long as the question of re-eligibility was left open, a party that did not want to renominate its President could at least try to dump him. But constitutional permissions have a way of becoming categorical imperatives. Now that the law says explicitly that a President may have a second term, his party may be forced to renominate him as if in obedience to the Constitution.

an unfavorable opinion of him, because the first mistake that
he makes is in making this choice."

Where the President is concerned, his aides come to him
as a residue that has passed through four or five screens.
First, there is the geography of the country which must be
represented. Then there are functional groups, organized
on economic, ethnic or religious lines who must be represented. Next, there are the factions of the party which must
be appeased. After that, there is the Senate, whose consent must be won before any man can undertake the work of
a department or commission on a permanent basis. The only
active right that a President may have in the whole of this
process of natural selection is the right of veto.

So far, whenever Americans have set up any sort of government, these same principles for selecting and rejecting
executive aides have been in operation. In the Republic of
Texas, for example, Sam Houston, the first President, was
elected to the office for reasons apart from his military genius.
He had clearly expressed disinterest in the presidency,
thereby specifically qualifying for it on the moral grounds of
self-abnegation. He was not bound to any of the quarrelsome
political factions, and thus appeared to be the one man
around whom a new union could be built. But for their Vice
President, the Texans went on to choose Mirabeau Buonaparte Lamar, as intense a partisan as the men after whom he
was named; he had been foremost in the plots that brought
on the war with Mexico. This popular decision, which joined
a President of one temper to a Vice President of a distemper,
was duplicated in Houston's cabinet. To offset Lamar,
Houston chose as the first Secretary of State, Stephen F.
Austin, a one-time leader of the peace party and a candidate

[93]

against Houston for the presidency. So it went down the line. All the Cabinet posts were filled by a system of political and geographical checks and balances. Though the net effect often stalled instead of stirred the organs of decision, Houston could act in no other way. Despite its vaunts of independence as a nation, Texas, after all, was American.

So was the Southern Confederacy under Jefferson Davis. From the time Davis picked his first Cabinet, on through some thirteen changes in personnel or their assigned work, the men he appointed owed their place to politics brought in line with geography. A gift for social invention or executive ability was given credit only after a potential appointee passed the other pregnancy tests just mentioned.

The misfortune of the Confederacy—repeated in the Union—was that a public opinion, responsible for the arrangement, also damned the discordant result without recognizing that it damned its own handiwork. In midyear of 1861, a South Carolina congressman called the Cabinet a "farce." A Virginian writing in the Richmond *Whig* said simply that the Cabinet "is rotten and stinks." The embittered Senator Robert Barnwell Rhett in 1862 said that "inefficiency has characterized their doings from the beginning until the present moment." Midway in the war, a bill was introduced to limit Cabinet appointments to two years, coinciding with the life of the Congress. And at regular intervals during the war, various resolutions called for the removal of this or that person in the Cabinet, and finally, their removal as a body.

It is no wonder that the English-style innovation, by which the Confederate Constitution allowed Cabinet officers the right to sit on the floor of the Congress and to take part in its work, remained a dead letter. The point was debated a number of times in both chambers, but at no time was the right granted. Apart from a fixed contempt for Davis and his Cabinet, the ruling view seemed to be that if Cabinet officers sat in the Congress they would give the executive branch too much authority! There the case rested until General Grant put an end to the discussion—though it was picked up in the North and continues to the present day.

The manner in which the President of the United States secures his Cabinet can yield members who are hostile to each other. The textbook case is the enmity between Secretary of State Thomas Jefferson and Secretary of the Treasury Alexander Hamilton in Washington's administration. Or the members can be hostile to the President's program, as in the case of Jackson's first Cabinet. They can be contemptuous of the President as a human being. Witness the reactions of Lincoln's Cabinet. They may try to use their standing in the party to overthrow the policies of the President. The representative example is provided by Secretary of State William Jennings Bryan in Wilson's cabinet. Or they can try to use their standing with the Congress for that purpose, as Secretary of Commerce Jesse Jones did in Franklin D. Roosevelt's cabinet. The selection system can also yield members like Secretary of the Interior Albert B. Fall in Harding's Cabinet who use their place to enrich themselves through shady deals. It can lead to the appointment of men who feel they have no need to keep the President informed about what they are doing. And finally, it can yield Cabinet members about whom there is at least a reasonable doubt whether they are competent to direct their departments.

Nevertheless, the President is held responsible for their

presence in the Cabinet and for what they do. They often do very well. But when they don't, he cannot get rid of them without arousing a storm in the national group that has a passionate interest in keeping a particular Secretary next to the President.

The problem the President faces here is most acute at the start of his administration when he has not yet consolidated his position on a plane above the men to whom he owes his victory. When he goes outside the party leadership to pick his Cabinet, he invites a party storm. When he stays within the party, his first Cabinet frequently appears as the outward sign of what he—or his managers—had to agree to in order to win the party nominations and then the election. But as the President grows wiser in his choice of men outside the party or from within the party; as election debts are paid off, and the men to whom they were owed either wither or die off in one way or another, the President has more latitude in picking their successors.

They are screened for their place on the basis of the principles already mentioned. Yet in contrast to the first Cabinet, their names tend to originate with the President, rather than in forces beyond his effective control. As a rule, these "second Cabinets" lack the glamour of the first, though the men in them may be far more competent to do their specific jobs. What is cited in criticism of them is that they contain fewer party chieftains who have an independent mass base of support from which they can threaten the President. Moreover, since they owe their place to the President, and show signs of greater fidelity to him, they are suspected of being his puppets and his "yes men."

When all these adjustments are made to account for the

difference between the men around the President and those who flank a princely tyrant, the heart of Machiavelli's comment remains true. To create a good impression of his brains and the integrity of his purposes, the President need not limit himself to the company of the men who sit in his Cabinet. He is free to show the quality of his judgment in his choice of an informal body of advisors which passes under the name of a Kitchen Cabinet or the Palace Guard; occasionally, a Cabinet officer who is particularly intimate with the President may belong to it.

Taken as a group, these men owe their place by the President's side solely to his trust and to the talents they can lend to his cause—even if it is nothing more than a talent for amusement. They are there, moreover, as the inevitable by-product of the limitations inherent in regular Cabinets, which can rarely satisfy all a President needs. He must have supplementary advisors to whom he can turn for a candid discussion of problems, for new ideas, for a long view of where his administration is trending, and even for assistance in executing the day-to-day work of the presidency. Men of this sort are highly expendable. They can be sacked at any time without peril to the President's position; often, in fact, he can win popularity when he does just that.

In addition to the Kitchen Cabinet, there are numerous citizens of private standing who are respected for their virtue and talent. They may be national, regional, or local figures. But among their followers they can exert a far greater influence in conditioning a climate of opinion than can the elected representatives of the people. They are constantly invited to the White House "to consult with the President." Or they can be asked to serve on special commissions. When the President goes to their community, he may invite them to join his entourage for a day. And by the honor he pays in various ways to these natural, though unofficial leaders of the nation, he can draw to himself all the trusts and confidences gathered in them.

The ultimate source of support for the President—and this is also true of executives who lead other democratic nations— is the reasonableness of what he says he wants to do or actually does. All the arts of communication—reading, writing, speaking, listening and watching—are employed to this end, shared in by democratic leadership everywhere. Yet the nature of our presidency, mentioned in other connections, gives a special color to the way an American President can persuade the people that he is wise and reasonable. I repeat, first, that the President is placed outside the legislature. Second, he owes his place to a vote of the people and not to the legislature. Third, he holds that place for a fixed number of years. Fourth, the executive function—in one view of the Constitution—is enveloped in the unitary person of the President instead of a committee. And fifth, by an organic and direct grant through the Constitution, the President is invested with powers and duties which cannot be reduced by the Congress and which he cannot surrender to the Congress even if he wished to do so.

How all these traits lead to a method of presidential persuasion, markedly different from that used by other democratic executives, comes into sharp focus through a contrast with the English Prime Minister. The Prime Minister, to begin with, works from within the Parliament to whom he owes his place. When he is overthrown, the whole of the

Parliament is overthrown with him and all must go to the people and stand for re-election. (The instability of the French parliamentary system is due, among other things, to the fact that the Cabinet can be overthrown and the deputies remain in their seats.) The Prime Minister's party in England, therefore, has every reason to back him on any leading issue. Moreover, it is frequently joined by independents or fractional parties who have no treasury or nationwide organization to aid them in campaigns. These last would prefer to support the Prime Minister rather than hazard the burdensome costs and risks of standing for re-election time and again.

As long as the Prime Minister and his Cabinet survive, they have a constitutional mandate to lead the Parliament from above, while being directly responsible to it. In practical terms this means that the Cabinet holds the initiative in the work of legislation. Furthermore, by its procedural rules, the Parliament has imposed drastic limits to the amount of legislation that can be introduced from below through the so-called "private member bills." At the opening of Parliament, legislators who want to introduce bills of their own meet on an assigned day and draw lots for the privilege. The drawing stops automatically after fifty names and is not repeated again for the whole of that session. But even the lucky are assured of nothing more than a first reading of their bills. In an average sitting, only six of them will become law. Nor do these private member bills deal with leading public issues. With the astonishing exception of the measure that reformed English divorce proceedings, they are of the sort which clean up musty corners of the law. A 1951 example was the private member bill which expunged a web of statutes dating back to the thirteenth century by which the common informer who reported a breach of the law to the magistrate was rewarded through the fine paid by the accused.

Measures of this sort excepted, the legislation Parliament considers waits on what is sent to it by the Cabinet. This tends to eliminate from the center of parliamentary attention a great deal that is eccentric, local, special and contradictory in the operation of the American Congress. With all eyes focused on what issues from the Cabinet, and not on what is generated from below in the form of private inventions, the note struck by the administration comes through with a greater coherence of purpose and unity of direction.

A further result is that the Prime Minister can often arrange a sequence of debates at intervals most favorable to his own cause and least favorable to the opposition. Even when the opposition moves to the counterattack during the question period, the procedure of Parliament requires that the administration shall be informed in advance about the leading questions that will be asked.

The Prime Minister and his Cabinet are direct parties to the debate that follows. They present themselves in person to argue that what they did was right, or that what they want to do is wise. With an immediate vote in prospect, upon which their survival may depend, they are inclined to seek out the personal thrust that can discomfit the opposition. They will be derisive and satirical. They will wheedle and cajole. They will search for verbal inventions whose striking images may gloss over a doubtful point and conceal a flaw in the argument. Through all of this, as I said, they will have the backing of the party whose survival is bound up with the Cabinet's.[2]

The unique character of the communications problem an American President faces has these drawbacks. Since he stands outside the legislature, all executive representatives stand there with him. Since the Congress can overrule his policies without overthrowing itself at the same time, it can indulge its capriciousness at will. Since the work of social invention is designed under our system to rise from below, the Congress can state the terms of a national debate at a time most embarrassing to the business the Executive has in hand, and most helpful to the political fortunes of the congressional element hostile to the Executive. Since the American government is a federal one, the Congress in enacting its measures can give voice to a mass of local interests, though the result may contradict national aims previously agreed to. And from these and other sources of confusion, a tidal wave of sound crashes over the Executive.

Yet he has ample means to make himself heard above all other voices. On his Inauguration Day, it is his word alone which fills the land, as he sets the tone for his administration. What he says on that day he can restate four times throughout his term when he delivers the State of the Union Address, informing the nation of what he has done or what

[2] To the rank and file member of the Parliament, the skill he shows at forensics is really his only avenue to national fame. And while he will polish his oratory as a result, he suffers from the want of opportunities open to his American counterpart to show a talent for social invention. This basic difference between two legislative systems—and the kind of parliamentarians they produce—is highlighted by the fact that almost all English legislation bears the name of the minister who sponsored it, while all American legislation bears the name of the Congressmen who steered through its enactment.

he feels should be done. He repeats it again in his budget messages and, of late, in his economic reports. Filling in these broad brackets is the steady stream of messages, letters and documents he sends to the Congress as the law or political exigencies call for them. In his all-important veto messages, equal in power to two-thirds the combined strength of the Congress, he clearly states what should not be done, and he disassociates himself in advance from any sympathy for a law passed over his veto.

Though his place outside the Congress takes from his hand the direct power of command a Prime Minister enjoys in the Parliament, by addressing the people directly the President can ask them to whip the Congress into line with what he wants done. Though he is denied the benefits of a Cabinet which holds itself collectively responsible for any leading act of the administration, the President, unlike a Prime Minister, can repudiate any member or even the whole of his Cabinet and yet survive as an Executive. Though he does not directly participate in the congressional debate, the President is nevertheless represented there through his legislative friends, through his enemies (who, because of self-interest or conviction will support some of his acts), through Cabinet officers and principal aides who appear before Congressional committees, and through the heads of private organizations and citizens of national standing who share the President's views. The impact, as the President speaks through these people, may be less than if he stood before the Congress in person to share in a debate. Nevertheless, these speakers do serve as shock absorbers for the congressional and the national recoil, which might otherwise bowl over the President.

In addition, recent Presidents have been able to speak to

the nation directly through the new institution of the White House Press Conference. A harassed President, with a load of problems on his mind, may be pushed by sharp-witted reporters into offhand remarks which can have unpleasant national and world-wide echoes. He can be equally embarrassed by what comes out of press conferences held in places like the State Department, the Pentagon or by his party lieutenants in the Congress. But the balance of forces rising from this new institution generally works in the President's favor. If he chooses to act through the medium of the White House correspondent, the President can analyze and report himself as a news item. The most hostile editors know that unless they give him "coverage" they risk the loss of readers who will turn elsewhere to find out what is going on. The editors may fume against the President on the inside columns, but they cannot readily obscure the facts and the views the President states from his vantage point on the front-page pulpit.

Press conferences are not the only source of news which flows from the President. There are recurrent statements from that wraithlike figure, "the White House spokesman." There are the brief stories which highlight a bit of presidential comedy or humanity. There are proclamations calling for the observance of days and weeks set aside for worthy causes. There are letters released by the President addressed to private citizens, organizations and prominent political leaders. There are untold numbers of short addresses at White House award ceremonies where the President, on the receiving or giving end, weaves into the text of his remarks pointed references to current issues. There are the major addresses the President delivers in person before various national conventions, at the dedication of great public works, or in commemoration of great historical events. And, of course, there are the President's addresses direct to the nation at large, delivered over radio and television from his White House study. Through all these means the President can create a climate favorable to his cause while he states the rule of reason and urges its adoption by the nation.

One more thing should be said. If the people are quick to find fault with the President, they are also quick to show their affection for him. When they discover what his hobbies are, they deluge him with the means to enjoy them. Fossils were sent to Jefferson. Specimens of flora and fauna were sent to John Quincy Adams. Clay pipes were sent to Jackson. Whittling knives were sent to Calvin Coolidge. Stamps were sent to Franklin D. Roosevelt. Or the people learn what he likes to eat and drink and send him the biggest and the best, even if it is just a crate of lemons as in the days when "Lemonade Lucy" Hayes, a leader of the Woman's Christian Temperance Union, was the mistress of the White House. They give the President advice and encouragement when they feel he is in trouble. They appeal to him, confident that he will get them out of trouble. They outline his portrait with the "x" on a typewriter or reconstruct his profile out of bottle caps and matchsticks for a county fair exhibit. If they are fortunate enough to have a letter bearing his signature, they have it reproduced in the local press. They cut his picture out of the Sunday papers, frame it, and display it in a prominent place where it remains long after he has left the White House. If they have one of his autographed pictures, they place it next to the family photographs and to cherished scrolls. They name their children, business enterprises, cities and great public works after him. They visit his birthplace as though it were a shrine. In some cases, they draw on his life to instruct the young. They defend him against all who doubt his greatness.

They accept his choice of a successor, as when Jefferson blessed Madison, Jackson blessed Van Buren, and Theodore Roosevelt blessed Taft. Even when he retires from the presidency, they seek his views on public and personal matters. They either suspend or arrange to pay his debts, as in the case of Jefferson, Jackson and Grant. They help meet the financial needs of his widow, as in the case of Mrs. James Garfield. They give the President's widow a place of honor at all public events. For a while at least, they respond to the magic of the President's name through the political preferences they give to his sons.

Finally, there is the apotheosis. The face of the deceased President is stamped on a coin and postage series. Or his features are carved into the side of a mountain. Or the whole of his figure is cast in bronze and put in a colonnaded temple. Or it forms a mosaic in stained-glass church windows.

As this rings out in counterpoint to the sort of criticism a President encounters, we are drawn again to a dualism in the American political spirit. It is shaped by a constant clash between the will to diminish and the will to enlarge. Of the two, the will that would diminish, being more strident in tone, has always held the attention of foreign observers of our scene. It was all that Charles Dickens could hear when he visited America in the middle of the nineteenth century. As he sermonized on the spirit of jealousy and distrust which he felt ruled each transaction in our public life, he wrote for our benefit:

By repelling worthy men from your legislative assemblies, it has bred up a class of candidates for the suffrage who, in their every act, disgrace your institutions and your people's choice. It has rendered you so fickle, and so given to change, that your inconstancy has passed into a proverb; for you no sooner set up an idol firmly than you are sure to pull it down and dash it into fragments; and this because, directly you reward a benefactor, or a public servant, you distrust him, merely because he is rewarded; and immediately apply yourselves to find out, either that you have been too bountiful in your acknowledgements, or he remiss in his deserts. Any man who attains a high place among you, from the President downward, may date his downfall from that moment; for any printed lie that any notorious villain pens, although it militate directly against the character and conduct of public life, appeals at once to your distrust, and is believed. You will strain at a gnat in the way of truthfulness and confidence, however fairly won and well deserved; but you will swallow a whole caravan of camels, if they be laden with unworthy doubts and mean suspicions. Is this well, think you, or likely to elevate the character of the governor or the governed among you?

The shaft flies straight and true. But it grazes and does not hit the heart of the whole truth. Where the presidency is concerned, the people have raised both small and great men to that place. They have remained faithful to them, showered them with rewards, excused their shortcomings, have been content when they merely tried to do their best. Even when a President has visibly spurred the pace leading to a national calamity, the people have held back with patience and forbearance until a peaceful change could be made. Again, the advance knowledge of the abuse it might bring has rarely kept our principal public figures from aspiring to the presidency. The hope may lie deeply buried, but it is there. The simple fact is that those who meet the constitutional and political specifications of the post behave in a way that is visibly different from the behavior of those who do not qualify under our unwritten rules of "availability." The "available" ones are more inclined to take a national than a sectional point of view; on the other hand, they are more given to temporizing than to boldness.

We can also argue that former generations acted unwisely when they chose Buchanan over Frémont, Grant over Greeley, Harding over Cox, Coolidge over Davis. But we really don't know whether the losers would have turned in a better performance in the presidency, any more than we could have known in advance that those who stirred such great hopes would fail when the presidency was turned over to them. It is part of the glory and the terror of our political life that a man like Lincoln was unfit for everything except the presidency, while a man like James Madison was unfit for the presidency but magnificently fit for everything else. Yet we are not wholly at the mercy of fate because this is the case. Our politics and our cultural pattern, as will be shown in a moment, cast up the sort of men in the presidency who, if they can do the nation no enormous good, cannot readily do it enormous harm, even though they cannot be removed for four years. Besides this process of natural selection which is constantly at work among the people, there is the power of the Congress and the power of the Court, and the supreme power of the law, which act as safety valves when there is a human failure in the presidency.

Lastly, we can argue that a number of our Presidents were pilloried for shortcomings which were not their own, but those of the epoch in which they lived. But there is a far more important question than the measure of good or evil we do our Presidents or presidential candidates. It is the question of how we can maintain the tone of our constitutional morality as it affects us all, and not the leaders alone. For its bearing on this social need, the clash between a will to diminish and a will to enlarge, provided it is kept in constitutional bounds, is not a symptom of a national sickness. Rather, it creates the surface tension which keeps us taut and yet resilient, while we avoid the extremes either of calcification or flabbiness.

II

VIRTUE AND TALENT

7

A dialogue between ex-Presidents

John Adams and Thomas Jefferson in retirement – Resume old debate on meaning of aristocracy – Attempted distinctions between the natural and the artificial aristocrats – Application of the debate to the presidency – Doubts about the capacity of our political system to separate the natural from the artificial aristocrats – Related topics to be considered in this section.

Some years after they retired from public life, John Adams and Thomas Jefferson reached for each other by letter to renew a friendship that had been broken when they were active partisans. Beyond the healing of a personal breach between a "witch hunter" and a "Jacobin," the aim of their post-presidential correspondence, as Adams explained it and Jefferson agreed, was that "we ought not to die before we have explained ourselves to each other."

In the range of things they brought into friendly debate, the term "aristoi" or "aristocracy"—meaning "the best"—soon cropped up in their exchanges. It had first drawn their interest as far back as 1783 when Adams and Jefferson were our ministers to England and France respectively. Yet that early effort to reach some sort of agreement on the application of the term to America, and on the means by which the "aristoi" could be controlled, had been inconclusive. And in 1813, after a long interval when both men had been chosen as "the best" in the land, they again tried to settle a point on which they had differed thirty years before.

Adams began by asking: "Who are these 'aristoi'? Who shall judge? Who shall select these choice spirits from the rest of the Congregation? Themselves? We must first find out and determine who themselves are." The pillars of aristocracy, he continued, are beauty, wealth, birth, genius and virtue. "But anyone of the three first, can at any time, overbear anyone or both of the last two." The proof he offered was that even philosophers who hold that the "aristoi" are the "wise and the good," on marrying their children, "themselves prefer the rich, the handsome and the well descended to the wise and the good." This "natural aristocracy," Adams went on to say, may be based on foolish and pernicious things. But the willingness of people to be duped by it not only ought to be recognized; measures should also be taken to protect the government from its effects. He therefore proposed to siphon off the natural aristocrats and to give them representation in a separate legislative chamber. Here they could be kept from doing too great harm.

Jefferson admitted in reply that there was a natural aristocracy among men. But he insisted that the elements of wealth, beauty and birth merely defined the traits of a pseudo-aristocracy. The truly natural one, based on virtue and talent, he considered to be "the most precious gift of nature for the instruction, the trusts and the government of society." And he continued: "That form of government is the best which provides most effectively for a pure selection of the natural aristocrats into the office of the government." To give the pseudo-aristocrats representation in a separate chamber in order to keep them from doing mischief, as Adams proposed, would instead arm them for it and increase instead of remedy the evil they work. "The best remedy," Jefferson said, "is exactly that provided by our Constitution—to leave the citizens the free election and separation of the *aristoi* from the pseudo-aristoi, of the wheat from the chaff. In general they will elect the real good and wise. In some instance, wealth may corrupt and birth blind them, but not in sufficient degree to endanger the society." For in any event, "the recurrence of elections at short periods gives the people a chance to displace an unfaithful servant before the mischief he meditates be irremediable."

Adams' rejoinder to Jefferson narrowed the issue to a fine point. He said that the two were now agreed that there was a natural aristocracy among men, "the grounds of which are virtue and talent." But he was not sure whether they were agreed on the sense of the words they used. The word "talent," in particular, needed a more exact definition. He observed that education, wealth, strength, beauty, stature, birth, marriage, graceful attitudes and motions, gait, air, complexion and physiognomy, are talents, as well as genius, science and learning. Then he said:

Any one of these talents that in fact commands or influences two votes in society gives to the man who possesses it, the character of an aristocrat, in my sense of the word. Pick up the first hundred men you meet and make a republic. Every man will have an equal vote, but when deliberations and discussions are opened, it will be found that twenty-five, by their talents, virtues being equal, will be able to carry fifty votes. Every one of these twenty-five is an aristocrat in my sense of the word; whether he obtains his one vote in addition to his own, by his birth, fortune, figure, eloquence, science, learning, craft, cunning, or even his character for good fellowship, and a *bon vivant*.

Adams then veered off, almost as an aged Puritan's Freudian slip, to an examination of Lady Emma Hamilton. In swift words he sketched her career. It began with the time this "daughter of a green-grocer walked the streets in London daily, with a basket of cabbage, sprouts, dandelions, and spinach on her head." Then some painters saw that she had a "beautiful face, an elegant figure, a graceful step, and a debonair appearance." And finally, as the wife of the British diplomat, Sir William Hamilton, she not only caused the triumphs of the Nile, Copenhagen and Trafalgar, but separated Naples from France, and banished the king and queen from Sicily. "Such is the aristocracy of the natural talent of beauty," Adams observed, a bit winded after his account. And on this illustrative ground he rejected Jefferson's distinction of natural and artificial aristocracy. Aristocracy generally, he said, "is a subtle venom that diffuses itself unseen over oceans and continents and triumphs over time." He would, if he could, put it all into the Hole of Calcutta. This, however, was impossible since aristocracy, like the Phoenix, rises from its own ashes. How then should it be controlled? It should be chained in a "hole by itself" and a watchful sentinel placed on each side of it.

The two men continued to exchange thoughts on this topic for about six months, without ever explaining themselves to each other. Yet their debate is as relevant to our affairs today as to the affairs of 1783 or 1813. We can dismiss

out of hand any proposal to control an aristocracy by giving
it a separate legislative chamber. But the question of who
the aristocrats are, how they can be known, and how the
"natural" ones can be chosen for the trusts and the government of society is basic to any political inquiry, and in particular, to one about the presidency.

When choices are made for this post, does our political
system winnow the wheat from the chaff? Does it give our
supreme reward to the real good and the wise? Does it
prefer the seeming good and the seeming wise? What shall
be made of the men who were turned down for a range of
lesser posts before they won the presidency? When did they
become the natural aristocrats? And what shall be made of
the men who gained the presidency, only to be defeated
when they wanted to hold on to it? Did they once deceive
the people into thinking that they were the real good and the
wise? Or is what changes not the man but the wind that
strikes his fixed sails; does the wind determine who shall be
the real good and the wise; does *it* envelop unchanging men
to make of one a President, and to deny another the right to
continue as a President? But if the leader is carried forward
or back by the currents of a quixotic environment, how can
he be judged in moral and political terms when in any event
he is ruled by forces beyond his control?

The march of these questions can eventually encroach on
the enormous issue of fate and freedom, an area best cultivated by a theologian or by a poet. But within the borders
of political inquiry, I propose to pick up and advance the
thread of the Adams-Jefferson dialogue as follows: (1) To
trace the growth of the system by which our Presidents have
been chosen. (2) To examine various plans to reform that

system. (3) To abstract the kind of virtues and talents the system has commonly rewarded with the presidency. (4) To compare this abstract with the traits listed by John Adams as magnets for political loyalties. (5) To suggest how contemporary social trends, if they continue their present course, might modify the virtues and talents looked for in a President.

One concept will run through all this. It is that the search for a man who matches exactly what our society wants and trusts in the presidency necessarily narrows down the range of choice. Today, in a screening movement that curves upward from the most humble political offices, millions among us would qualify for the presidency on three or four counts of "virtue and talent." But we would fall by the wayside in increasing numbers as the tests continued. In the end, those who possessed the mystic combination of the "natural aristocracy" from which Presidents are chosen probably would not exceed more than one hundred men in a present population of 156,000,000.

8

Inventions in election machinery

IIIIIOIIIIIIIIIIIIOIIIIIIIIIIIIOIIIIIIIIIIIOIIIIIIIIIIIOIIIIIIIIIIOIIIIIIIIIIIOIIIIIIIIIIOIIIIII

The electoral system invented to screen presidential material – Electors chosen by state legislatures – Whole system collides with rise of political parties – Near disaster in 1800 as electors come under party discipline – Leads to Twelfth Amendment – Invention of Congressional caucuses to nominate party candidate – Breakdown in 1824 and its underlying causes – People acquire right of suffrage and right to vote directly for presidential electors – Jacksonian claim of a popular mandate re-examined – Changes in the wake of Jackson's defeat – Presidential nominations made by state legislatures in transitional period – Stages in the invention of the national nominating convention – The basic pattern is fixed in 1840.

The Constitution deals with a President's virtue and talent in deceptively simple and negative terms. It states that "No Person except a natural born Citizen, or a Citizen of the United States at the time of the Adoption of this Constitution, shall be eligible to the Office of President; neither shall any person be eligible to that Office who shall not have attained to the Age of thirty five Years, and been fourteen Years a Resident within the United States." It also states that "no religious Test shall ever be required as a Qualification to any Office or public Trust under the United States."

But does it follow that any boy who meets these facts of birth, age and residence can be the President?

The delegates to the Constitutional Convention did not think so. No task took more of their time or ingenuity than the invention of a device that would bar all boys from the presidency except the few thought suitable to the whole constitutional system they had in view. For the method of election, as they conceived of it, was not a detachable piece of machinery. They related its design (1) to the number of persons who would form the Executive, (2) the tenure of the Executive, (3) its powers and duties, (4) the means by which it could be controlled, and (5) the allocation of power among the states as sovereign bodies, and among the people according to their numerical strength.

When a basic decision was reached that one man alone would form the Executive, it was recognized that he could be chosen by a vote of the Congress, by the state governors, or by the people directly. Yet each alternative met with objections.

1. It was said that the congressional method, urged in a Virginia plan, would violate the agreed-upon separation of powers among the three branches of the government. It would continue the "tyranny of the legislature" by making the President dependent upon the will of Congress. And in any event, the mixed character of a Congress based on two different modes of representation would make a choice by this body an awkward affair.

2. The record of objections to an election by governors, as urged by Elbridge Gerry of Massachusetts, is sketchy. But apparently the delegates felt that it would violate the proposed division of Federal and state spheres of responsibility,

and would give the governors a whip hand over the national executive. This in turn would curb the energy that was wanted in the office, and thereby continue the evils associated with the Continental Congress.

3. Of the objections to a presidential election by direct popular vote, a distrust of the people's competence to decide a matter of this sort seems to have been only secondary. While a fear of "wild popular passions," evidenced in Shays' Rebellion, was never far from the Convention's thoughts, the strongest advocate of the direct method was Gouverneur Morris, New York's distinguished cynic, to whom self-government was a contradiction in terms. The one clear note of distrust was struck by Colonel George Mason of Virginia, an ardent democrat in different matters. It would be "as unnatural to refer the proper character for chief magistrate to the people," he said, "as it would be to refer a trial of colors to a blind man." The main cause of opposition to a direct choice appears to have been the fear of the smaller states that they would be placed at an enormous disadvantage by the voting strength of the big states.

At an early stage in the discussions, James Wilson of Pennsylvania, one of the leading architects of the presidency, proposed that "certain districts in each state . . . would appoint electors to elect outside of their own body." This germinal idea was to be cultivated and refined by men like Hugh Williamson of North Carolina, Gouverneur Morris and James Madison. But when it was first advanced it was rejected out of hand. The stated ground was that men competent to serve as electors would in all probability be occupied in other posts. The real objection, once again, was the fear that the method, involving as it did the principle of popular representation, would lead to the domination of the small states by the big ones. Indeed, the method did not triumph until the relationship between the states was compromised for the over-all needs of the constitutional system, and until the apportionment of electors was extended to embrace the states as well as the people.

Throughout the summer of 1787, the delegates blew hot and cold as they accepted, rejected and then brought the same plans up again for another round of debate. A report of an eleven-man committee, submitted on September 4, eventually joined together all the bits and pieces that had been fought over for more than three months. Yet the synthesis was unlike anything that had been previously endorsed. It provided that the people of each state, under methods prescribed by their state legislatures, would choose a number of persons as electors, equal to the total of senators and representatives of that state in the national government. The electors would then meet in their separate states and would vote for two persons who in their view were fit to be the President. After the votes were sent to the seat of the government and tabulated, the person who gained a majority would be the President; the one second highest on the list would be the Vice President. But if no one gained a majority, the Senate, with each state casting one vote, would select from among the five highest on the electoral list the man who in its opinion was best qualified for the presidency.

Four important amendments, approved on September 5, were embodied in what was to be the actual constitutional text. One amendment provided that "no person shall be appointed an elector who is a member of the legislature of the United States, or who holds any office of profit and trust under the United States." Its aim was to fortify the independence of the President, to curb any influence he might try to exert over an elector, and in general to remove the danger of election intrigues by men in the government. A second amendment provided that the president of the Senate would count the electoral vote in the presence of both chambers. This was to clear up an implication that the counting was to be done by the Senate alone. The third amendment, enacted on the motion of Roger Sherman, provided that the House and not the Senate would do the voting by states when no person won an electoral majority; moreover, it was to do this "immediately." The final amendment was addressed to the danger that the members of the three largest states could form a quorum and pick the President if the choice fell to the House of Representatives. On the motion of James Madison, it was agreed that when the House assembled for the purpose of electing a President, a quorum would consist of a member or members from two-thirds of the states, with a majority of all states necessary for a choice.

These and other details were then referred to the committee on style for a final polishing; the whole of the Constitution was resubmitted to the delegates for a discussion on September 12 and was approved five days later.

In the hard fight which followed immediately over the ratification of the Constitution, the electoral device which has since been excluded from the applause of history met with ready approval. Thus Alexander Hamilton remarked in the sixty-eighth number of *The Federalist* that "the mode of the appointment of the Chief Magistrate of the United States is almost the only part of the [constitutional] system of any consequences which has escaped without some censure, or which has received the slightest mark of approbation from its opponents." At the time, the four main benefits he claimed for the method seemed real enough. (1) It promised to make the Executive "independent for his continuance in the office on all but the people themselves," since the latter would presumably act through the Electoral College. (2) It would reduce the opportunity for tumult and disorder, since the multiple members of the Electoral College, and their convocation in separate places, would make it difficult for them to communicate their "heats and ferments" to the people. (3) The same "detached and divided situation" of the electors would raise an obstacle "to cabal, intrigue and corruption" since the College would come into being for the sole work of choosing a President and would pass out of existence when its work was done. (4) It would permit the choice of a President to be made by persons who were "most capable of analyzing the qualities adapted" to the station of the presidency, and who would be "most likely to possess the information and discernment requisite to such complicated investigations."

The process of election [Hamilton wrote in summary] affords a moral certainty, that the office of President will never fall to the lot of any man who is not in eminent degree endowed with the requisite modifications. Talents for low intrigue, and the little arts of popularity, may alone suffice to elevate a man to the first honors in a single State; but it will require other talents, and a different kind of merit to establish him in the esteem and confidence of the whole union, or of so considerable a portion of it as would be necessary to make him a successful candidate for the distinguished office of President of the United States.

Inventions in election machinery

The electoral system from the start veered past the purposes for which it had been formed. Though it was meant to be the means by which "the sense of the people" could operate on the choice of a President, it was not until the close of Monroe's tenure in 1824 that any appreciable part of the nation could make its electoral preferences felt in a direct way. Before then, the state legislatures, exercising a constitutional option, either kept to themselves the right of appointment, or generally curtailed the suffrage.

Fortunately, no difficulties arose in the crucial first two presidential elections. Washington twice won a unanimous vote. But the trouble ahead was foreshadowed when the electors, moving along complex factional lines, splintered their votes for what was known to be a vice presidential selection. By 1796, the factions had jelled into national political parties, the result being that John Adams won the presidency from Thomas Jefferson by only three electoral votes. In the 1800 election the electoral system crashed head-on with the presence of disciplined national parties and came off second best.

The constitutional authors had made no provision for political parties as an organic part of the government. But they were not blind to the prospect of their future rise. These men had seen the nation split into court and country factions during colonial days. They had seen it split again into Whig and Tory factions before the Revolution, during the war, and in the years before the Constitution was framed. Not being given to an angelic view of human nature, they foresaw that similar divisions would continue. In the words used by John Adams on a much later occasion, there would continue to be "the same running and riding, the same railing and reviling, the same lying and libeling, cursing and swearing . . . the same caucusing, assemblaging, and conventioning." A more stately expression of this outlook is contained in the tenth number of *The Federalist*. There James Madison observed:

A zeal for different opinions concerning religion, concerning government, and many other points, as well of speculation as of practice; an attachment to different leaders, ambitiously contending for preeminence and power; or to persons of other descriptions, whose fortunes have been interesting to the human passions, have, in turn, divided mankind into parties, inflamed them with mutual animosity, and rendered them much more disposed to vex and oppress each other, than to cooperate for their common good. So strong is this propensity of mankind to fall into mutual animosities, that where no substantial occasion presents itself, the most frivolous and fanciful distinctions have been sufficient to kindle their unfriendly passions, and excite their most violent conflicts. But the most common and durable source of factions has been the various and unequal distribution of property. Those who hold, and those who are without property have ever formed distinct interests in society. Those who are creditors, and those who are debtors, fall under a like discrimination. A landed interest, a manufacturing interest, a mercantile interest, a moneyed interest, with many lesser interests, grow up of necessity in civilized nations and divide them into different classes, actuated by different sentiments and views. The regulation of these various and interfering interests forms the principal task of modern legislation, and involves the spirit of party and faction in the necessary and ordinary operation of the government.

Madison also recognized that the cause and presence of these factions "in the necessary and ordinary operations of the government" could not be removed except by destroying the liberty which nourished them. But he hoped that the evils they produced could at least be held in check. Union, pure and simple, would be foremost among the means—as it still is. "The smaller the society," wrote Madison, "the fewer probably will be the distinct parties and interests composing it; the fewer the distinct parties and interests, the more frequently will a majority be found in the same party; and the smaller the number of individuals composing a majority, and the smaller the compass within which they are placed, the more easily will they concert and execute their plans of oppression." But if the sphere is extended, he continued prophetically, a greater variety of parties and interests are necessarily embraced, and this makes it "less probable that a majority of the whole will have a common motive to invade the rights of other citizens, or, if such a common motive exists, it will be more difficult for all who feel it to discover their own strength, and to act in unison with each other."

The prophet was among the first to provide the proof that what he said was true. In 1792, James Madison joined Thomas Jefferson on a celebrated "botany excursion" into the North. Besides the picking of a few flowers, the aim of the two men was to form an intersectional political entente, based on New York and Virginia, and drawing its main support from urban mechanics and small farmers. Called the Republican-Democratic party, it was at first little more than a loose federation of local units. But bit by bit, the roots were entwined, differences were arbitrated, and localisms were changed into the organized outlook of a national party. Thus, on the eve of the 1800 election, it was agreed in Republican-Democratic circles that a firm effort should be made, first, to win party majorities in state legislatures, and second, to have them appoint electors who would presumably vote for Thomas Jefferson as President, and Aaron Burr as Vice President.

Their efforts were so successful that the result was a near disaster. Since there was no way an elector could designate which of the two men he explicitly preferred for the first and the second office, the disciplined Republican-Democratic electors all voted for Jefferson and Burr as their presidential choice. The result was a tie, and the House was then called to elect the President as the Constitution provided.

In February, 1801, the House contained a number of lame-duck Federalists, members of the "class of 1798" who had first won their seats at the height of the anti-French, anti-Republican hysteria caused by the "X Y Z affair." Along with the other Federalists who survived the defeat of their party in 1800, these men saw two glittering prospects in the tie. They could prevent any decision from being reached; and in this way they could force a call for a new election. Or, as one of them expressed it, they could elect Aaron Burr "to cover the opposition with chagrin and to sow among them the seeds of morbid division."

The day was saved for Jefferson by the margin of strength Alexander Hamilton won for him among a handful of Federalists who had not gone mad.

Hamilton had not been beyond a temptation to subdue Jefferson by treachery almost a year earlier. In the opening months of 1800, he and Aaron Burr had engaged in a fierce election contest over the composition of the New York legislature. The larger issue was whether New York's electors would be controlled by Hamilton, or whether they would be placed in Burr's custody for use in Jefferson's interest at a later date. When the election went to the Burr forces, Hamilton proposed to Governor John Jay, a fellow Federalist, that an extra session of the lame-duck legislature should be called to deprive the incoming body of the power to choose electors. "In times like these," Hamilton informed the governor by letter, "it will not do to be over-scrupulous." There should be no objections to "taking of legal and constitutional steps to prevent an atheist in religion and a fanatic in politics from getting possession of the helm of state." Fortunately for Hamilton's reputation, Jay pigeon-holed the suggestion.

A year later, however, when faced by a straight choice between Jefferson and Burr for the presidency, Hamilton placed himself on the side of the angels. In the course of an exhaustive letter campaign, he urged the thought upon one Federalist that Jefferson was infinitely preferable, because he was "not so dangerous a man," and because he had "pretensions of character." Burr, on the other hand, was "the Catiline of America," "a bankrupt beyond redemption except by the plunder of his country." In another letter, Hamilton wrote: "For heaven's sake, let not the Federalist party be responsible for the elevation of this man [Burr]." And to another Federalist he wrote: "If there is a man in the world I ought to hate, it is Jefferson. With Burr I have always been personally well. But the public good must be paramount to every private consideration." Why not, he asked, seek an understanding with Jefferson?

The voting in the House began on February 11, with all but two members in attendance. Of the pair who were missing, one, however, was nearby. He was Joseph H. Nicholson, a Maryland Jeffersonian. Aflame with fever, he had been carried through a blinding snowstorm and then propped up in a bed prepared for him in a committee room next to the chamber. It was agreed that he could take part in the proceedings. On the first ballot, eight of the sixteen participating states, each with a single vote, went to Jefferson. This was one short of a majority of nine that was required to elect. The remaining states either went to Burr or were kept on dead center by their equal divisions between Jefferson and Burr supporters. Ballot after ballot showed the same line-up; the only change to be registered was in Mr. Nicholson's health. Instead of perishing, as most people feared he would, the strain and the excitement led to a great improvement in his condition.

By Sunday, February 15, after thirty-four ballots had been cast, some of the Federalists sensed that if they did not find a way out of the hole they had dug for themselves the people were in a mood to bury them in it without the benefit of any last words. At a party caucus that day, James A. Bayard, Delaware's sole representative, made the first break. Because the vote of his state could lead to the magic figure of nine, Bayard had been under intense pressure from Hamilton to support Jefferson. Yet he had his own game to play and would not abandon it so long as this hope flickered: that Burr would agree to manage the presidency in a Federalist way, in return for Federalist support in the House contest. No one knows whether it was honor or a wretched indecision which gagged Burr's lips. Whatever the cause, when he withheld the assurances that were wanted, Bayard at last announced to the Sunday meeting of Federalists that he meant to vote for Jefferson.

Most of the other men in the room were also agreed that something should be done to break the deadlock. But in a last flare of wishful thinking that a miracle might yet save the day, they pounced on Bayard and forced him to hold off. When the balloting in the House resumed on Monday, he still adhered to Burr. Another Federalist caucus was held on Monday night, and here a face-saving device gained the assent of everyone except a Connecticut member. It was agreed that the Federalists would vote blank the following day. In this way, the Republican minority in their state delegations could take the states into the Jefferson column, and the onus of ending the world would rest solely on their heads. But the Connecticut member, whose name is presumably lost to history, wanted no part of this moral equivocation. When he said that he would continue to vote for Burr, come what may, all the other New England delegations (except for Vermont which was split between Burr and Jefferson supporters) announced that they would do the same. In this hectic mood the Federalists approached the thirty-sixth and final ballot on Tuesday, February 17.

New Hampshire, Massachusetts, Rhode Island and Connecticut voted for Burr. Two states, Vermont and Maryland, were carried into the Jefferson column by the Republican members when the Federalist Congressmen from those states cast blank ballots. South Carolina's Federalists removed their state from the contest by also voting blank. Bayard, who had acted as the galvanic needle for the whole proceedings, similarly cast a blank vote for Delaware. These defections, together with the votes of the states who had been for Jefferson all along, gave him the victory by a count of ten states to six. Yet there appears to have been considerable truth in a wistful, post-mortem remark Bayard passed on to Hamilton. He observed that "the means existed of electing Burr, but this required his cooperation. By deceiving one man (a great blockhead) and tempting two (not incorruptible) he might have secured a majority of the states."

There was a delay of 132 years before one of the two legal causes for this bizarre experience was removed. With the enactment of the Twentieth Amendment in 1933, ending the phenomenon of a lame-duck Congress, men who have been defeated for election to the House no longer can help choose a President before the new Congress is sworn in. There was no delay, however, in dealing with the second cause. Immediately after the decision in Jefferson's favor, Hamilton drafted what was to become the Twelfth Amendment. Introduced at the first session of the new Congress and adopted four years later, it provided that electors were to state distinctly which of the two men they voted for was preferred as President, and which as Vice President. It also modified the House procedure if no person received a majority of the electoral vote.

With the rise of parties that could impose their will upon electors, some means had to be found by which each party could agree internally on its presidential nominee. The first solution, the congressional caucus, spanned the period between the fifth and tenth elections (1804–1824), and it paralleled a virtual monopoly of the political scene by the Republican-Democratic party. Since the man nominated in this way was certain of election, by indirection it was the Congress that picked the President, contrary to the express wishes of the Constitutional Convention.

The caucus system eventually stifled all political preferences except those of a self-perpetuating party oligarchy.

It also tended to place a President under obligation to the congressional leaders who had secured his elevation, with the incidental result that the Executive in this period began to show some of the traits of a prime ministership. Yet the caucus had its virtues as well. It introduced a greater degree of party responsibility for the actions of a President. It corrected the provincialism fostered by poor physical communications and by the rule which required electors to meet in their separate states when they chose a President. (The elector of the day had little contact with political leaders beyond those in a native or in a neighboring quarter; while the members of the Congress, who alone were in a position to know and judge the range of national talent, were barred by the Constitution from service as electors. To the degree that a caucus recommendation reflected intersectional agreements, the result when endorsed by local electors was anti-demagogic, antiparochial, and pronational.) Finally, the caucus was a logical place where like-minded men could consult and agree beforehand on the sort of individual who might win over a majority of the state electors. Had it not been for this pressure to concentrate votes on two or three main contenders, the House of Representatives might have been summoned quadrennially to pick a President.

The first major protest against the caucus was in 1808 when Thomas Jefferson wanted the Republicans to pick James Madison instead of James Monroe as his successor. A call for a party caucus was presently issued, the results to be binding on all who came. But Monroe's friends wanted no part of an arrangement geared to work against their interests. Thus a Congressman Gray of Virginia, a Monroe partisan, had this to say to his fellow Republicans: "I cannot consent,

either in an individual or representative capacity, to counte-
nance, by my presence, the midnight intrigues of any set of
men who may arrogate to themselves the right, which belongs only to the people, of selecting proper persons to fill
the important offices of President and Vice President. Nor
do I suppose that the honest people of the United States can
much longer suffer, in silence, so direct and palpable an
invasion upon the most important and sacred right belonging exclusively to them."

The excoriation of "midnight intrigues"—the phrase was a
forerunner of "smoke-filled rooms" at national nominating
conventions—was to no avail. The caucus was held, and as
expected it recommended James Madison to the attention of
the Republican electors. Madison won the presidency for a
first term without difficulty; the part played by a caucus in
securing him a second term has been detailed in another
place. But what is of special interest here is that, in the presidential succession of 1816, some of Monroe's supporters who
had been scandalized eight years before by the use of a
caucus raised no objections when the device now worked in
his interest. Indeed, with Monroe's triumph, the nation
lapsed into a period of political peace in excess of the constitutional authors' fondest hopes.

The rumblings of a new revolt against "King Caucus" took
on a distinct tone several years before the 1824 elections.
The Republicans where everywhere in the ascendancy,
though all was not well within their own ranks. Sixteen Republicans, later to be reduced to six, wanted the nomination
as Monroe's successor. When it became known in late 1822
that Monroe favored William H. Crawford, the Secretary of
the Treasury, past experience indicated that this support

would weigh heavily in Crawford's interest if a congressional caucus was held. Adherents to the other candidates—Henry Clay, Andrew Jackson, John Quincy Adams, John C. Calhoun, De Witt Clinton—lost no time in getting their favorites into the race by different means, primarily by nominations made in state legislatures. But the question debated on all sides was whether a Republican congressional caucus should be held at all.

The first outspoken support for it came early in 1823 from New York's legislature. The source is not surprising. Martin Van Buren, New York's up-and-coming United States Senator, was allied with the party faction—it included Thomas Jefferson—that backed Crawford's candidacy. The legislature of the state resolved:

> That although a nomination by the Republican members of Congress is not entirely free from objections, yet that, assembled as they are from the different quarters of the Union—coming from the various classes of community—elected during the pendency and discussion of the question and in a great degree with reference to it, they bring into one body as perfect representation as can be expected of the interests and wishes of all and of each; and that a nomination made by them in a manner which has heretofore been usual is the best attainable method of effecting the object in view which has yet been suggested.

A few months later, the Tennessee legislature, which favored Andrew Jackson's interests, joined the issue. It adopted a set of anticaucus resolutions and instructed the state's representatives in Congress to resist any call for a caucus meeting. These views were circulated among Republicans in other states, but party members in Maryland alone expressly adhered to them. Elsewhere, they were either scorned or tabled. An interesting rejection, fore-shadowing a future development, came from members in Lancaster County, Pennsylvania. They resolved that "the best and most exceptional method" for nominating a President would be a "convention of delegates from all the States of the Union." But they observed that this would be "entirely impracticable, from the immense extent of our country, and from the great expense necessarily incident to the attendance from the extreme parts of the United States." The best that was attainable under the circumstances, was "the old and tried mode" of nomination, namely, the congressional caucus. The physical facts behind the argument were incontestable. The Railroad Age did not dawn in America until 1831.

A call for the congressional caucus was eventually sent out. But the one held in the House chamber on the evening of February 14, 1824, advertised the imminent rupture of the party and the end of a system of presidential selection used for two decades. Though Republicans from sixteen states were present at the meeting, the heaviest concentrations came from New York, Virginia, North Carolina and Georgia. Eight states were not represented at all, while four states furnished but one member each. As was expected, a first ballot recommended the nomination of William H. Crawford as President; a further ballot recommended Albert Gallatin as Vice President. The proceedings had been frictionless. But the caucus was apprehensive over the national reaction to its work. "We will not conceal our anxiety," declared a committee which had been authorized to prepare an address to the country. "To our minds, the course of recent events points to the entire dismemberment of the party to which it is our pride to be attached." The prophecy proved morbidly accurate.

Back of the party skirmishing, and in a sense the cause of it, was a far more important human drama, nationwide in its scope. A disciplined political style, carried over by a handful of men from the days of English rule, no longer impressed the active memories of the living; almost two generations had been born as American citizens instead of British subjects. Old political alignments, old methods and old values could not contain the new juices.

In the South, the tobacco aristocracy of Virginia, whose four Presidents moved in the traditions of the English Whigs, approached economic exhaustion; at the same time their power of command also waned. Nor was the cotton aristocracy of the South much better off.

In the North, the industrial and commercial interests of the seaboard, spurred to increased activity by the needs of the War of 1812, had accumulated enough capital to accelerate their own efforts. The self-employed artisan could not compete with production thus concentrated in factories; as he lost his market, he was forced to turn himself into a wage worker who serviced the new machines. But as he brushed up against those who shared his fate, he came to see that through united action he could retain his self-respect and restore what he had lost in his social status.

Meanwhile, the Western hinterland formed a theater for events no less important in their political implications. With the end of serious harassments by the English, French, Spanish and Indians, empty regions filled up with a tide of immigrants turned grain growers. Land speculation was rife, while local capital for the creation of real wealth was always in short supply. Paper money and borrowing from Eastern quarters for local capital needs led to recurrent panics and to deep-seated enmities against those who alone seemed to benefit when others went bankrupt. And as a final turn of the screw, the existing tariff system appeared to favor Eastern commercial and industrial interests at the expense of the Westerner.

One result of the interaction of these many forces was a joint lunge by the frontiersman and the urban worker for the right of universal manhood suffrage, the frontiersman being the first to win it. But the older states along the Eastern seaboard of necessity moved in the same direction. To help check the loss of their population to the frontier, they gradually enlarged the base of politics by granting voting rights to those who had been denied them. As the suffrage movement picked up momentum (it ran parallel with mounting pressures for free and universal education) it was followed by a demand from the newly enfranchised for the right to vote directly for presidential electors. By 1824, this point, too, had been won in eighteen out of twenty-four states. Next in the line of change was the congressional caucus. The select circle of leaders who alone passed on the virtues and talents of a presidential aspirant would have to step aside for the opinions of the "average man," expressed directly in his franchise.

It was John Quincy Adams' misfortune that the "average man" actually thought himself to be abreast of the new power which lay just over the horizon. Thus, when Jackson failed to win a majority of the 1824 electoral vote, and the House elevated John Quincy Adams to the presidency, a leading factor in the furious Jacksonian reaction was the publication for the first time of the popular vote for electors. The results showed that Jackson received 152,899 votes; Adams, 105,321; Crawford, 47,265; Clay, 47,087. To Jackson's partisans, this was a popular mandate which the House wilfully chose to flaunt. Even at this late date it is easy enough to share their sense of outrage. Yet the inclination to do so probably is based in an admiration for Jackson's subsequent actions as a President. It cannot properly be based on the cold facts of 1824—any more than Jackson's presidential contributions to the growth of our democracy can be discounted as demagoguery simply because his pre-White House career showed little zeal for the cause of the plain people.

If the popular vote for his 1824 opponents is totalled, Jackson trailed behind by 47,000. Besides, in only five states were the four leading candidates represented on the popular ballot. In six others, only three were represented; in seven, only two. The remaining six states, where electors continued to be chosen by the legislatures, contained more than one fourth of the nation's population. And finally Virginia, Pennsylvania and Massachusetts, with a combined white population of 2,225,000, cast a total of only 97,000 votes for all candidates. How can one speak of a popular mandate when so many different sounding rods were in use, or when, as in the case of the three states just mentioned, only five per cent of the people were heard at all?

The notion that the people had been robbed of their victory nevertheless was drummed home for the next four years in parliamentary oratory, in invective, slogans and epithets. If the charge was undemonstrable, it did serve to clear the ground for new changes. The one-party government of the

Republican-Democrats was split down the middle into two distinct parties, each taking one half of the old name. With the simultaneous overthrow of "King Caucus," it was no longer possible for a presidential aspirant to entrust his chance for success to the impact of his personality on congressional circles alone. His stand on issues, formerly obscured by the inner disciplines of one-party government and the congressional caucus, once again weighed heavily.

Thus, almost imperceptibly, the forum and the object of "government by speaking" shifted from the members of the Congress to the nation at large. "Those who have wrought great changes in the world," wrote Martin Van Buren at this time, "never succeeded in gaining over chiefs; but always by exciting the multitude. The first is the resort of intrigue and produces only secondary results, the second is the resort of genius and transforms the face of the universe." The technical skills of oratory, he said, while important, were meaningless in the end without the "deep seated and habitual confidence" of a majority of the assembly and of the people in general. So much was this the case that he advised against any "overtures to leaders to gain over parties." The new leader, he said, should concentrate on winning over "the mass of the parties that he might be in a situation to displace the leaders."

In the interval between 1824 and 1828, four of the remaining six states changed from the legislative to the popular method for choosing electors. Delaware, a holdout, fell in step in 1832; South Carolina fought a rear-guard action for the legislative method until 1860. The net effect of these readjustments, all the work of local forces, was equal to an amendment to the Constitution. In particular was this true of one more development which remains to be mentioned. Before 1824, electors in a number of states were chosen individually on a district basis. By 1832, however, all states except Maryland and South Carolina had brought the electors together in a "general ticket" so that their vote went as a unit to the candidate who won a majority of the popular vote. Though this crushing assault on the constitutional independence of the elector signaled the absolute triumph of majority rule within each state, it also concealed an equal capacity to frustrate the will of the majority in the nation as a whole.

Upon the overthrow of the caucus system, presidential nominations revolved briefly around the action of state legislatures. Andrew Jackson in this way was put into the 1828 contest at the head of the Democratic party. The same was true of his rival, John Quincy Adams, the National Republican nominee. As the victor by 140,000 votes (the total cast in 1828 was 1,156,328, or more than three times the 1824 total) Jackson was the first President in almost a generation who won his post without obligation to the Congress as a collective body. Yet the nominations by state legislatures which set the stage for this triumph proved adequate only as a makeshift device for a transitional period. As the Jacksonians gradually consolidated their strength in victory, there were those who called for a new national medium through which party members could select their standard-bearers.

The method was found by one of the "third parties." In September, 1830, ninety-six delegates from ten states and the territory of Michigan met at Philadelphia for a national convention of the Anti-Mason party. Here they considered ways and means to serve the party cause across the nation. Arrangements presently were made for a second national convention to be held at Baltimore in September of the following year. Each state was allotted a number of delegates equal to its combined representation in both congressional chambers, to be chosen by people who were opposed to secret societies. The whole of this call to arms to fight secret societies was part of an elaborate political masquerade. Its true aim was to select a presidential candidate who could unite all elements in the nation who were opposed to a second term for Andrew Jackson.

The Anti-Masons originally settled on Supreme Court Justice John McLean of Ohio, but for a variety of reasons, in September, 1831, they were forced to turn to William Wirt. A former Attorney General in the Cabinets of Monroe and John Quincy Adams, Wirt was nominated for the presidency on a single ballot. The sequel was a high burlesque. A committee of Anti-Masons called on him—he was in Baltimore at the time—to inform him of his selection. When the amenities were disposed of, Wirt handed the committee a letter which he had evidently prepared some time before. It contained the startling news that the candidate-designate of the Anti-Mason convention once had been a Mason himself. Wirt observed that he had seen no harm in this affiliation until his political party was organized on the principle of opposition to secret societies. He concluded by saying that if the convention had nominated him under a misapprehension about his background, it should feel entirely free to substitute another name.

His letter was carried back and read to the delegates. These gentlemen, the progenitors of the national presidential nominating convention, proceeded to show a pragmatic agility of no common sort. On the one ballot which had led to Wirt's selection, 108 of the 111 votes were cast for him. In the face of the now open fact that he had been part of the very evil the Anti-Masons ostensibly were organized to fight, the delegates to a man voted to stand by him. Wirt and his running mate, Amos Ellmaker of Pennsylvania, eventually won seven electoral votes in the 1832 contest. In due course, the party itself passed into the historical limbo filled with wraithlike causes on the order of the Loco-Focos, the Know-Nothings, the Barnburners, the Hunkers, the Stalwarts and so on and on. Yet the Anti-Mason seed for a national presidential nominating convention was to take root, grow and eventually to flourish among the living.

Of the major parties, the National Republicans were the first to resort to it. In December, 1831, 167 delegates from seventeen states met at Baltimore to choose the party candidates for President and Vice President. The core of the meeting was the old congressional caucus, disguised by its convocation in a place conveniently near Washington, yet apart from it. Nevertheless, its annals seem to contain the genesis of practices which were later standardized in the nominating conventions of our day. The meeting had a credentials committee which passed on the legitimacy of each delegate's presence. There was a temporary chairman and a permanent chairman. Each delegate rose as his name was called and announced his vote for a candidate; in this case, it proved to be a unanimous chorus for Henry Clay. Each state also chose a member from its own delegation to serve on the committee which notified Clay by letter of his selection. There is the hint of a National Committee in this arrangement. A party platform was not adopted. Yet, allowing for the accidents of time and place, the address the convention issued to the country has a remarkably modern ring. It sharply criticized the Jackson administration "for its corruption, partisanship, and abuse of power; for the hostility it had manifested to internal improvements, for treachery on the tariff question, for the war on the Bank," etc.

Meanwhile, in Democratic quarters it was assumed that Jackson would be the candidate to succeed himself. Countless bodies had already placed him in nomination. But Jackson's wish to have Van Buren as a running mate met with fierce opposition. In casting about for ways and means to circumvent the objectors, the men around Jackson soon agreed that if the party leaders met in one place they would be more amenable to reason. Thus the New Hampshire Democrats, under White House prompting, came forward with the suggestion that a party convention be held. A prearranged echo was interpreted as the approving voice of the people, and an official call was issued. The convention was held in May, 1832, in the saloon of Baltimore's Athenaeum. And in this salubrious atmosphere, with every state represented except Missouri, the delegates endorsed Jackson's candidacy for a second term and picked Martin Van Buren as the vice presidential nominee.

It was this convention, incidentally, which adopted a rule that was fated to be a source of conflict inside the Democratic party for the next 104 years. It provided that "two thirds of the whole number of the votes in the convention shall be necessary to constitute a choice." Later, the rule enabled Southern Democrats to exert an indirect veto on any party candidate they felt was obnoxious to Southern interests. But the original motive appears to have been a desire to hamstring Van Buren's opposition. Since he was expected to run ahead from the outset of any balloting, those who opposed him would yield before the two-thirds barrier and join in making his triumph more striking.

The 1832 contest enabled the major political parties to gain first-hand experience with the device of a nominating convention. But the Democrats alone used it in the 1836 election; and then, only under a sharp nudge from Andrew Jackson. His determination to be succeeded in the presidency by Martin Van Buren once again ran into opposition; nowhere was it stronger than in Tennessee, where Democrats in the legislature nominated Senator Hugh L. White for the presidency. The Alabama legislature swung behind this action as did all but two members of Tennessee's congressional delegation. While Jackson's friends attacked Senator White directly as a "traitor," Jackson urged that a call be sent out for a national convention to be composed of delegates "fresh from the people." It developed, however, that a great number of the delegates who met in Baltimore in May, 1835, were fresh from the government jobs they held through the President's bounty. When they helped bring about a unanimous ballot for Van Buren, there was a cry that the old caucus system had been revived in a worse form than the original, in that timeservers had replaced legislators as the main actors. What gave special force to the charge was the free and easy way in which the delegates were selected and apportioned. Twenty-two states and two territories participated in the convention. But on the roll call of 626 names, Virginia, New Jersey, Maryland and Pennsylvania alone accounted for 422, or two-thirds of the total.[1] However, if some of the delegates were on the executive payroll as postmasters and the like, they were also the same men who were generally the leaders of the party's local rank and file. To this degree, the 1836 Democratic Convention more directly represented the people in party matters than did the tight little circle that formed the old congressional caucus.

Preceding these events in the Democratic camp, a large segment of the National Republicans a year before began to call itself the Whig Party. The name embraced no more than a hope in conservative quarters that Jackson could be prevented from securing the election of his hand-picked successor. All malcontents in reach were gathered together to form the barricade. Politically, the Whigs included Republicans who had supported John Adams and Henry Clay; states' rights Democrats who had turned away from Jackson when he threatened to use arms against South Carolina in the nullification threat of 1832; former Anti-Masons; former Jackson men, outraged by what they called his executive usurpations; and independents who had never taken part in politics but who were persuaded that the Jacksonian course led to "the imminent peril of our whole fabric of constitutional liberty and national prosperity."

[1] Equally significant was the conduct of a Tennessean named Rucker who happened to be in Baltimore at the time. When he learned that his native state had sent no delegates, Rucker made his own political sentiments known to the managers of the convention and was admitted to the floor. Without any authority from party leaders at home, he presently cast Tennessee's fifteen votes for Van Buren. The act passed over in the form of a verb "to ruckerize," meaning "steamroller" in modern political terminology.

Inventions in election machinery

The Whig leaders had enough contact with each other to know this much: that if they called a nominating convention, it would never agree on the one man to oppose Van Buren in the 1836 contest. So they decided to place five Whig leaders in the race, the theory being that if each of these men in his own sphere won enough electoral votes to deny Van Buren a clear-cut majority, the House of Representatives would then convene to pick the President. If this could be managed, a little luck with a few "great blockheads" and some not "uncorruptible" men might lead to the triumph of the Whig cause. William Henry Harrison, Hugh L. White, Daniel Webster, W. P. Mangum and John McLean eventually were selected to carry the banner of different Whig factions. But Van Buren won a clear electoral majority after a bitter battle.[2]

The climax to the long evolutionary line traced in these pages occurred in the next election. Following their 1836 defeat, the Whigs mulled over their tactical problem and decided that their chance for success in 1840 lay in a union of forces behind a single person. Accordingly, the call went out for a great "union and harmony" convention to meet at Harrisburg, Pennsylvania, on December 4, 1839.

At Harrisburg the contest narrowed down to a choice be-

---

[2] The 1836 election provided the only occasion in our history when the Senate was called upon to pick a Vice President. The Democratic nominee for this post was Colonel Richard M. Johnson of Kentucky, hailed as the man who had personally killed Tecumseh in the Battle of the Thames during the war of 1812. The main Whig contenders, who appeared in combination with several of the presidential candidates, were Francis Granger of New York and John Tyler of Virginia. But the electoral vote for Vice President was spread in such a way that no one received a majority. Since Johnson and Granger were the two highest on the list, the Senate, as the Constitution specified, chose between them. The balloting resulted in Johnson's election.

tween Henry Clay, the workaday party chieftain, and William Henry Harrison, the once forgotten military hero, who, to the surprise of many, had led the Whig field in the 1836 race against Van Buren. The decision between them was based on the straightforward principle of "availability," the first of its sort to rule a convention. Clay had made too many enemies to serve as the central peg around which the dissident Whigs could unite. On the national scene, moreover, he had been closely identified with so many "aristocratic" and unpopular causes that it was doubted whether he could attract to the Whigs any more strength than the conservative forces they already had nailed down. Harrison, on the other hand, suggested a kind of venerable neutralism that could serve as a point of union for all Whig factions. Besides, some of the more enlightened Whigs felt that the time had come to raid and displace the Jacksonians at their source of strength.

"Those may sneer who choose at appeals to popular sympathies," observed the Boston *Atlas*, the voice of a new breed of practical Whig politicians. ". . . But it is only by means like these, that masses of men, whether great or small, are ever brought to act together." Life in a democracy is such, the *Atlas* continued, that "in the long run those will always have the ascendancy in it, who take the most pains to secure the favor and good will, and to gain the ear of the people. Those who would have votes must descend into the forum and take the voters by the hand."

The political climate was favorable. Countless numbers of people, once loyal to the Democratic party, had grown restive when Van Buren failed to bring them the easy economic relief they wanted in hard times. If a Western Whig,

dressed as another Andrew Jackson and free of any doctrinaire loyalties to suspect Whig causes, was offered to them
as an alternative, he could draw to himself and the party the
victorious margin of strength only disaffected Democrats
could provide. Under the influence of this reasoning, the
Whig Convention extolled Clay in extravagant terms for his
services to the party. But it settled on Harrison as the presidential candidate.[3]

The delegates at Harrisburg had adjourned without writing a platform or a statement of principles. They had none to
offer on which the party could agree. But an indiscreet comment of a Democratic newspaper in Baltimore provided a
theme for songs, slogans, symbols, slander and buffoonery
which served them far better than any lofty professions of
party doctrine. The newspaper observed that Harrison would
be quite content on his backwoods farm if he were limited
to a pension, a log cabin and a barrel of hard cider. His need
of a pension was real. But the rest of the slur was miles wide
of the mark. Harrison, descended from Virginia aristocrats,
had been born in a mansion. His own home in Ohio was one
of the finest in the region; and his economic difficulties, far
from being those of a backwoods farmer, were due in part to
his expensive and ruinous speculations in land. Finally, in-

[3] The news came as a bitter blow to Henry Clay. He had remained
behind in Washington and had whiled away the hours of suspense in the
company of passing visitors and in intimate contact with the bottle. But
drunk or sober, his furious response to the work done at Harrisburg did not
die with him. Other political figures of the future who were to be barred
from a presidential nomination by the rules of availability were to re-echo
his feelings. "My friends," Clay stormed, "are not worth the powder and
shot it would take to kill them. . . . I am the most unfortunate man in the
history of parties: always run by my friends when sure to be defeated, and
now betrayed for a nomination when I, or anyone, would be sure of election."

[*147*]

stead of dipping into hard cider, his immersions were more often in the classics that lined the walls of his extensive private library. Nevertheless, the Whigs seized on the image of hard cider and a log cabin. They raised it as their standard and presently appeared on the political stage as the champions of all that was rustic and plebeian.

The democratic forces in the land, brought to a quickened sense of self-awareness by the Jacksonian revolution, were treated to a caricature of themselves. Yet they embraced it and were seduced by it in an exotic political performance unparalleled even by the Republicans in their 1952 success. Whigs everywhere slipped out of broadcloth and into homespun, out of silk hats and into coonskin caps, turned from august meetings and toward barbecues and clambakes. The virtues of the poor and the rights of the workingman were vigorously blared by a range of orators from fledglings on cracker barrels to Daniel Webster, who shouted: "The man that says I am an aristocrat is a liar!" It was the Whig log cabin against the Democratic "palace"; the Whig hard cider, available to all, against the champagne and the gold plates used by privileged Democrats. On lantern slides, on medallions, on lithographs and wood engravings, from watch chains and earrings, in pendants, on wheels, in windows, in town squares, in forest clearings, in rolling balls of tin or cowhide, in marching choruses, to the tune of fife and drums, in the sputtering glare of torchlight parades, in bonfire—by these and other means, the young, the middle-aged and the decrepit shouted their love for the hero of Tippecanoe—though the battle had been fought by a scrub team of nine hundred men some thirty years before against the blundering brother of Tecumseh.

Inventions in election machinery

"We have been sung down, drunk down, and lied down," one Democrat bitterly complained. "Are the Whigs contending for the privilege of living in log cabins?" another one asked. "Is there any despot in the land who prevents them from pulling down their mansions of bricks, of granite and of marble, and putting up log cabins in their place?" William Cullen Bryant, the Democratic editor and poet, tried his best to be reasonable. "The question," he said, "is not whether Harrison drinks hard cider. . . . The question is what he and his party will do if they obtain power." The Whigs saw no need to reply. Wrong men, standing for the right thing for the wrong reason, saw their tactic succeed as, one by one, the states went to the polls. The Whigs had embraced the people. "They have at least learned from defeat the very art of victory!" the *Democratic Review* protested. "We have taught them how to conquer us!"

With the simultaneous endorsement of the nominating convention by the two major parties, the device passed over as a durable feature of the presidency. In the years that followed, it produced "dark horse candidates" and "stampedes" and "bandwagons." It lent itself to the revival of the old congressional caucus in that the decisions of conventions were dictated from time to time by party leaders in the Senate, the House or both. It had its "big moments" when the ferments on the floor of the convention or in the gallery exploded in results no one could foresee. It underwent numerous changes in the system of accrediting and apportioning delegates. To foster the appearance of being a truly national assembly—and this has been a special problem of the post-Civil War Republican party—conventions tolerated unconscionable abuses in overweighting the voting

[149]

strength of various states. And finally, the convention system was flayed hip and thigh from the earliest days of its career. In 1859, Thomas Hart Benton described it as one of the two great "trials" taxing the American capacity for self-government, the other being slavery. Yet the essential features of the device have remained relatively unchanged since 1840. To date, it has given us twenty-six of our thirty-three Presidents.

9

Proposals for new inventions

IIIIIIIIIIOIIIIIIIIIIIIOIIIIIIIIIIIIOIIIIIIIIIIIIOIIIIIIIIIIIIOIIIIIIIIIIIIOIIIIIIIIIIIIOI

Persistent power of the electors in the choice of a President – Inequities of the system it fosters – Examination of proposed reforms – The abolition of electoral system in favor of presidential election by straight popular vote – The apportionment of electoral vote in each state according to per cent of popular vote – Proposals for reforming convention system – Direct national nominating primary contains explosive dangers – Preferential primary would preserve supreme benefits of the convention system and would reform method of selecting delegates – Proposals for reforming our political parties by realignments into distinct liberal and conservative groups – The liberal argument in support of this – The liberal argument in opposition – Conservatives not actively interested – Damaging effects on our politics and on the presidency if any such realignment could be realized – Note on contour plowing.

The names of electors now only infrequently appear on a ballot. Yet it would be incorrect to say that the nominating convention has wholly displaced the Electoral College as the instrument for choosing a President. First, the College has been a decisive factor in the victory of a candidate who failed to win a majority of the total popular vote. Second, in the absence of state laws to the contrary, electors still retain a latent constitutional right to vote their own preferences for a President. And as late as 1948, a Democratic elector in Tennessee did this when he voted for the State's Right candidate, as he had said he would.

To the direct power the College still wields one must add its enormous and unseen indirect power. In party contests for presidential nominations, the existence of the College tends to favor men who live in states with big electoral votes (and populations), and to bar from serious consideration the political talent found in the smaller states. In the period between 1900 and 1952, Ohio and New York alone have been represented in seventeen of the twenty-six combined Republican and Democratic nominations. Seven other states, Massachusetts, California, Kansas, Nebraska, New Jersey, Missouri and Illinois have accounted for the rest. On four occasions during this period, the Republicans and Democrats have pitted men against each other from the same big states, as in the 1904 nominations of New York's Alton B. Parker and Theodore Roosevelt; the 1920 nominations of Ohio's James M. Cox and Warren G. Harding; the 1940 nominations of New York's Wendell L. Willkie and Franklin D. Roosevelt, and the 1944 nominations of New York's Thomas F. Dewey and Franklin D. Roosevelt.

The general theory behind this, that in a presidential election people will vote their local pride in a home-grown figure, rests on shaky grounds. It is worth noting that of the varied array of defeated candidates since the start of the twentieth century, only William Jennings Bryan in 1908 and Thomas E. Dewey in 1948 carried their home base (and in 1948, Dewey's victory in New York was 450,000 votes less than the combined strength of the Democratic and Progressive candidates). In no other case did a candidate, defeated across the nation, salvage the electoral vote of his own state. Nor have the defeated vice presidential candidates, nominated in part with express reference to the character of their states, been much more successful in securing them for their parties. Yet the theory of local pride persists as a rule for the motives and acts of nominating conventions.

If the College intrudes on contests for party leadership to the disadvantages of men who come from small states, it overcompensates for this in a general election. The College permits the small states to exert a voting strength wholly out of proportion to their population. Thus, Nevada, with a present population of 160,000, gets three electoral votes, assigned on the basis of its two Senators and one Representative. The ratio here is one elector for every 53,000 people. New York, with a present population of 14,830,000 gets forty-five electoral votes, assigned on the basis of its two Senators and forty-three Representatives. The ratio is one elector for every 329,000 people. As between the two states, each electoral vote in Nevada has six times the effective representation of a New York vote. Though this is the extreme case, the same sort of disproportion works on a regional basis in favor of the South, the Rocky Mountain region, and part of New England. As regions, they are over-represented in the College at the expense of the great population centers of the Middle Atlantic States, the Midwest and the Pacific Coast.

In addition, the existence of the College is a powerful deterrent to the emergence of "third parties." Since the electoral vote of each state generally goes as a bloc to the candidate who wins a majority of the popular vote, third parties face enormous difficulties in registering their strength in effective electoral terms. For example, in 1924 the Progressive Party of Robert M. La Follette polled a national vote of 4,822,856. This was more than one-half the size of the Democratic vote, and almost one-third the size of the Republican. Yet the distribution of La Follette's popular ballots in the forty-eight states produced a Progressive electoral vote only one-tenth the size of the Democratic, and one-thirtieth the size of the Republican vote. A barrier of this sort tends to discourage insurgent elements and to crowd them back into orthodox party channels. Incidentally, the same circumstance handicapped the Republican party in the South until 1952. Not until then did the sizable popular vote it amassed below the Mason and Dixon line in the previous decade register itself in a single electoral vote.

Of the amendments advanced over the years as solutions to the situations just described, two deserve brief notice.

1. It is proposed that the whole of the electoral system should be abolished in favor of a presidential election by a straight popular vote. The method, so it is claimed, would do justice to the weight of third-party opinion. It would lead to an across-the-board registry of national sentiment for a candidate, as contrasted with a present registry based on the outcome of forty-eight self-contained elections in the states. It would end the constant danger that an accidental spread of several thousand popular votes could give an electoral majority to a candidate who trailed behind in popular preferences. In short, it is claimed that the amendment would eliminate all chance for tyranny by a minority of the people, and would advance instead what Thomas Jefferson in his First Inaugural called "the vital principle of Repub-

lics"—namely, "absolute acquiescence in the decisions of the majority."

Adoption of the proposal, however, would not be an unmixed good. Run-off elections might be necessary in order for a candidate to secure a majority of the popular vote. On the other hand (as will be shown presently) if a straight plurality elected, and three strong candidates were in the field, the victory could go to the one who polled only a shade over one third of the popular vote. Even if the scheme were so worked out as to end the tyranny of the minority, it could undercut an existing constitutional safeguard against the tyranny of the majority. Specifically, it would deny to the less populous states the extra padding of the two electoral votes representing their United States Senators. If this automatic adjustment between the weight of population and the weight of functional interests was removed, the presidential preferences of the smaller states would be perpetually subordinated to the preferences of the great population centers.

One need not agree with the use to which John C. Calhoun put his close analysis of constitutional government—it was to justify the right of states to nullify the acts of the Federal government—yet his remarks have an intimate bearing on the subject being considered here and throughout this chapter. I quote:

There are two different modes in which the sense of the community may be taken; one, simply, by the right of suffrage, unaided; the other, by the right through a proper organism. Each collects the sense of the majority. But one regards numbers only and considers the whole community as a unit, having but one common interest throughout, and collects the sense of the greater number of the whole as that of the community. The other, on the

[*155*]

contrary, regards interest as well as number—considering the community as made up of different and conflicting interests, as far as the action of the government is concerned—and takes the sense of each, through its majority or appropriate organ, and the united sense of all as the sense of the entire community. The former of these I shall call the numerical, or absolute majority; and the latter, the concurrent or constitutional majority. . . . As there can be no constitution without the negative power and no negative power without the concurrent majority, it follows, necessarily, that where the numerical majority has the sole control of the government, there can be no constitution; as constitution implies limitation or restriction—and, of course, is inconsistent with the idea of sole or exclusive power. And hence, the numerical, unmixed with the concurrent majority, necessarily forms, in all cases, absolute government.

2. A different electoral reform was urged by the late Senator George Norris. Under its provisions, the College would be abolished, but not the electoral system. Each state would remain an electoral unit with the same relative strength as at present. The distribution of the electoral votes within each state, however, would be divided among the candidates in proportion to the popular vote cast for them in each state. A plurality of electoral votes would elect, in contrast to the present requirement of a majority. The merit claimed for the plan is that it would elevate a President by an electoral vote which would more closely mirror the national popular vote. At the same time, it would not violate the existing safeguards for small states. In the allotment of electoral votes to these states, they would retain the protection of two votes, represented by their United States Senators.

The main objection to this plan, parodixically, is concealed in a merit it shares with election by a straight popular vote. The merit is that it would eliminate the role the House now plays when no candidate wins a majority of the electors. True, the presence of strong parties has made frequent intervention by the House unnecessary. Except for the unique 1800 and 1824 contests, one of the dominant political parties has always managed to gather in an electoral majority. Yet it does not follow that what has been will always be. The rise of a strong third party, and its survival as a durable feature of our politics, could lead to chronic electoral divisions where no one would win a majority. And the House would be called again and again to choose the President in an atmosphere that invites tumult and intrigue. There is, then, a strong case to be made for an election by a plurality, with the incidental result that the House would be denied any role in a presidential contest.

Yet the existing arrangement should not be cast aside without a careful weighing of what would also be lost. At present, when no one among three or more strong contenders wins an electoral majority, the lesser interests have at least a faint if imperfect chance to register a "second-best choice" by means of the balloting in the House. Guided by an affinity of their interests, they can combine with each other to form a victorious majority, or they can form it by adhering to the interests which may hold a plurality. But if the election was by a straight popular vote or by a straight electoral plurality, with the House ruled out as a factor, the parties who in combination formed the real majority but failed separately to win a plurality would have no way of registering their second-best choice.

Unless run-off contests were held, the end result in a

three-way race might be the opposite of that intended by the proposed reform. It might obscure instead of express the true preferences of the electorate. In a three-way race, as I have already implied, there would be a mathematical possibility that a candidate who polled only thirty-four per cent of the popular or electoral vote would nevertheless win the presidency on the basis of a plurality over the two candidates who polled thirty-three per cent each for a total of sixty-six per cent. Could any such victor be secure in his authority? We have had minority Presidents, but none so markedly in a minority. The forces who mustered almost twice his strength but had no second chance to readjust and seal their preferences in a winning combination would certainly assault each of his acts as those of a usurper.

If a choice must be made between the disorder that would be generated in this way and the disorder invited by the intervention of the House, the latter seems the lesser of two admitted evils. It at least has the virtue of being contained within a concrete political organism, and of resulting in a specific yes or no decision on the right of one man to act as President.

In summary, if the general principle of the amendment proposed by the late Senator Norris is acceptable on other grounds, it probably would be wise to reinstate the rules (1) that a majority of electors instead of a plurality would be required to elect and (2) that the House would exercise its present rights in the event no candidate won a majority.

The question of merit aside, the adoption of any organic change in the present electoral system seems remote at the time of this writing. A political hurricane, of course, could force a profound reorientation of outlook. Short of one, it is unlikely that the Republican and Democratic parties will voluntarily open the road to the emergence of strong third parties. Nor is it likely that the Southern states, those of the Rocky Mountain region and part of New England will voluntarily surrender the political benefits they draw in a general election, if not in party matters, from the existing inequalities in the Electoral College. And without their support, any amendment would fail to be ratified.

Could the electoral system be partly altered by state action alone? Legally, yes. The Constitution vests the method of appointing electors exclusively in the states. It does not compel the electors to vote as a unit for the candidate who wins a total of the popular vote in any state. Mention has already been made of an early practice whereby electors in some states were chosen on a district basis, and cast individual votes. Even during the twentieth century, split electoral votes were cast in Maryland in 1904 and 1908; California, in 1912; West Virginia in 1916, and Tennessee in 1948. If the states then were to enact laws apportioning the electoral to the popular vote—there being no legal bar against it—the results when registered in the Electoral College would approach the aim of the Norris proposal. But again, it is unlikely that a political party in habitual control of a state would selflessly back a change that might increase the effective representation of an opposition party in the College.

If nominating conventions do their work well, by the range of good alternatives they present to the people they tend to reduce the imperfections in the electoral system. In its impersonal registry of victorious support for good men the system itself seems personally good. Yet a feeling also persists that the conventions either do bad work, or that they do not represent the true wishes of the people. Insofar as this is true, they compound the mischief which rises from the electoral system. We are therefore obliged to ask: Is there a better way of nominating a President? Two proposals will be examined.

1. There are those who urge that the nomination of a President should be taken out of the hands of party leaders and entrusted to the people directly. Thus the proposal for a constitutional amendment providing for a direct, national party nominating primary. Over the years, support for this course has come from some of our foremost political scientists. Their names alone—they include Woodrow Wilson—raise a strong presumption in its favor. Yet one oddity should be noticed. Most advocates of the amendment revive it on the eve of a nominating convention that threatens to work against their political preference. The same men lose interest in reform when the convention ratifies their particular bias.

But suppose the amendment was viewed on its own terms, divorced from the ebb and flow of partisan enthusiasms. Would it gain the end for which it is framed?

The answer is no. Two items alone in a campaign agenda loom up as stumbling blocks. The first is the need for a party platform. If it is assumed that candidates should be chosen with a platform in mind, when, in what place, and by whom would the platform be written? The second item involves the relation between a presidential and vice presidential candidate. If it is assumed that these two should be chosen with reference to the political forces they bring into balance, when, in what place and by whom would they be paired off as a team? So long as the assumptions underlying these details express political values the community wants to pre-

serve, the physical incapacity of a direct primary to provide
for them would inevitably lead to this paradox: a convention
of some sort would necessarily be convoked to overcome the
impotence in a device that was to replace the convention
system.

As another disadvantage, in a national primary, a candidate would either have to build a personal machine in forty-
eight states, or come to terms with the existing local leadership. In the nature of the case, an incumbent President who
wanted to be renominated for a second term would by his
control of patronage hold an organizational advantage his
party rivals could not readily overcome. This detail aside,
the party's collective responsibility for the choice of the
nominee would be diffused. The convention system at least
has the virtue of centralizing responsibility and attention. It
not only places the party as a whole on record in support of
its candidate; it identifies the particular group of men who
engineered his selection and the means they used in the
process.

Each added facet of a direct primary involves new difficulties, though they vary in importance. If numerous candidates entered the field, rarely would any one of them win by
a straight majority. So unless run-off primaries were held,
the best to be hoped for would be a victory based on a plurality. And it could happen that this plurality would be only
a fraction of the total vote that was cast. There would be no
opportunity, as there is in a convention, for those who in
combination formed the real majority to reshuffle themselves
again and again until there was a consensus in support of
one man. Thus an amendment designed to locate and
amplify the voice of the real majority might instead gag it.

The amendment, if adopted, would also strike at the independent voter—as distinguished from the indolent one. The active independent voter performs two crucial functions. First, he often serves as a kind of better conscience for both major parties when he raises the standard of the paramount community interest. Second, to the extent that his support is necessary for the success of a political project, he acts as an invisible rein on party extremists with their chronic cry that the argument is exhausted and all must stand to arms. These two sobering functions, however, would come to an end with the advent of a direct primary. Since the independent would not be registered as a party member, he could not participate in the nominating primaries unless most state laws were changed. On the other hand, it is highly unlikely that rank and file party members in a polling booth, each faced by a pragmatic decision of the moment, would come within hailing distance of the respect nominating conventions give to independent opinion when they weight the appeal of a prospective nominee in a general election.

Then, too, the mechanics of a primary race—the exactions of time and machinery—would tend to rule out the "last minute" selection of an "independent" candidate. And some of these have been among the best in our political history. It is also to be remembered that despite its riotous aspects, the convention system enables public figures to observe the proprieties of our constitutional morality without personal or party loss. Thus, a Republican Convention in 1916 could draft Charles Evan Hughes, though he could not properly seek a nomination in person because of his position as a Supreme Court Justice. Again, a convention can tactfully seize and exploit political values which suddenly bubble to the surface. In doing this, it can relieve a public figure from an embarrassing prior commitment, or from an embarrassing dependence on anything except the united will of the party. Thus the Democratic Convention in 1952 could draft Governor Adlai Stevenson, though he could not properly seek a nomination in person when he was already pledged to run for re-election as Governor of Illinois; nor would he accept the nomination if it was presented as a gift of the outgoing Democratic President. And again, for all the charges that they are boss-ridden, conventions have shown a prudent capacity to brush past the first rank of party leaders to select candidates whose party affiliations are sketchy, but whose qualifications for the presidency promise a victory which the established chieftains could not win. Thus the Republican Conventions of 1940 and 1952, respectively, preferred Wendell Willkie and General Eisenhower to the tried and true leaders of the party.

Conditions being equal, General Eisenhower alone among this group could have been nominated in a direct primary. The others, pinned down by their special situations, could not have made an effective primary race. They needed the independent leverage of a convention to elevate them to the role of party nominee. A value judgment is admittedly concealed in what has just been said. It is that men like Hughes, Stevenson and Willkie were more suited for the presidency than their rivals who came to the conventions with substantial support. The reader who agrees—without demanding specific proof—may nevertheless raise three major objections, phrased as questions. (1) Cannot the same internal independence of a convention lead it to reject men of superior talents while it elevates those with lesser ones? The answer is yes. This has happened a number of times. (2) Even if a convention makes a good choice, is it not anti-democratic when it is made contrary to known and fairly clear expressions of the popular will? In a strict construction of democratic theory, the answer again is yes. The wisdom of a particular decision does not by itself purify the non-democratic means by which it is reached. (3) In the abstract, is a bad political device which sometimes produces a good result to be preferred to a good device which sometimes produces a bad result? The answer here must be no. In politics, as in art, form has a way of creating its own substance. If the form is good, it will contain the internal means to correct any imperfect material thing it produces. But if the form is bad, it will lack the internal means of repeating the material good it produces accidentally.

Yet none of these questions and answers turns the argument against the nominating convention and in favor of the direct primary. For the convention upholds in an extralegal way the constitutional concept on which our government is based: that majorities and minorities alike shall have a limited initiative and a limited veto. Each, that is, shall give a little and take a little in reaching an agreement of the moment; and each shall keep open the avenue for a continuous re-examination of what was agreed upon, until dissent from the majority decree is dissipated and a natural consensus is realized. Could a direct primary do this in the particular choice of a presidential candidate? Could it gather together and bring to bear on that choice the concurrent voices of a people infinitely varied in temperament and material needs? Could it act as a kind of subgovernment refining the discords between the weight of sheer numbers and the "concurrent majority" of interests, before all alike move to a higher plane of battle in the actual lawmaking process? It could do none of these things on a national scale. The nominating convention alone appears to be structurally adequate for this work.

If it were abolished, the conversations it makes possible between transcontinental interests, the common language it gives to them, the common means of self-protection with which it arms them, the compromises it imposes on them, would also come to an end. A Babel would rise on the debris. As each direct primary showed the presence of a hard-core vote which could win its way every time, the lesser interests would inevitably secede to form a new party where they, too, could win perpetual victories. Thus, as interest drew apart from interest, eventually each would stand alone. Instead of the coalitions our parties now seek before they bid for the management of the government, we would have the ideological and fractional parties which lead to coalition governments after elections are held.

Yet this would be the least of the evils. Since reducing the size of political parties would also reduce the number of those whose agreement was required for a party stand, we would invite the rise of a deadly elite, which has thus far had little success in breaking through the concentrated restraints of a national nominating convention. I have in particular mind the bellowing demagogue skilled in vituperation and obscurantism; the plausible liar who calls for a general slitting of throats in the name of a transcendent political or religious good; the doctrinaire who would relieve mankind from the burden of thinking any more; the class hero who would have you believe that his property—or lack of it—is a sufficient warrant for the rule of the land; the ruralist to whom the pastoral idiocies of the farm and forest provide an automatic refuge from the harsh realities of human existence. All these, now held in check by the Republican and Democratic conventions on pragmatic grounds, if not on the grounds of justice, would be liberated to seize what they could.

Elsewhere, the impulses of negation and self-destruction have formed the flowers and music along the route of these types as they marched to the seats of supreme authority. Are we immune from those same impulses? The constitutional authors did not think so. In their non-angelic but Christian view of human nature, they concluded that Americans, being of the stock of Old Adam, could also hail a serpent as a hero, though he inspired patent and indisputable villainies. It was with this in mind that they provided three sentinels in the form of the three branches of the government. Each was to serve the people in a special way; and each was to keep a watch over the other in the course of that service.

Nothing has happened since 1787 to void the need for sentinels. We have not been transfigured into pure spirits, like angels. What has happened since 1787 is that a sensitive part of our affairs has been entrusted to the care of subgovernments like political parties. And Old Adam is there, too, as the main actor. If this is agreed to, it follows that our political parties must contain the same constitutional safeguards that protect the government proper against madness. I have tried to suggest that the convention system, by its internal mechanics, does offer that safeguard when a party chooses its presidential candidate.

2. The second of the two proposed reforms for presiden-

tial nominations would preserve the convention system, but it would alter the method by which delegates are chosen. The approach is best expressed in a draft bill now being considered by the legislature in the state of Washington.

The bill rejects the unit rule common to the handful of states which hold preferential primaries before the national convention. In these latter states, the candidate who wins the most primary votes also wins all the delegates. Under the Washington plan, the delegates would be divided in proportion to the total primary vote cast for each candidate. Moreover, the delegates would be bound to vote at the convention in accord with the primary results, until they were released by their candidate or he received less than ten per cent of the total convention vote.

The Washington plan also provides that candidates can be entered in the primary on being certified by the national committee of the party, by the state central committee or by a petition signed by at least one thousand registered voters in a state. The consent of the candidates would not be required. Nor would they have the power to withdraw their names. Also, the primary would be an open one; registered voters, regardless of their previous party preferences, could vote in either the Republican or Democratic primary, but not in both. Finally, a late date for the primary—the third Tuesday in May—is proposed so that all the presidential aspirants will have emerged and will have had a chance to do some campaigning.

(This formula can now be extended to bring about a simultaneous national *preferential* primary. The means are present in a proposed bill before the Congress, sponsored by Senator Paul H. Douglas of Illinois and Representative Charles E.

Bennett of Florida. In essence, the Douglas-Bennett bill would authorize the Attorney General to negotiate agreements by which the Federal government would share with the respective states the costs of the Washington-style primaries. Each state could make its own detailed primary rules, as long as the preferential balloting was held concurrently with the other states.)

A national application of the Washington plan invites some of the secondary objections listed in connection with a direct nominating primary. It might force candidates to build personal machines in forty-eight states, at a high cost of money and energy. And it would create psychological conditions unfavorable to the last-minute selection of "independent" candidates. But on balance, the plan provides a workable answer to the major objections that can be raised against both the direct nominating primary and the convention system as it is now constituted.

Most delegates who come to the national conventions are now chosen not by preferential primaries, but by state committees or by state conventions. The Washington plan would not remove the grounds for "boss" influence inherent in this latter arrangement. But it would substantially reduce its scope. To repeat, the means lie in the right of one thousand or more registered voters to enter a slate of delegates in the primary by means of a petition; in the apportionment of delegates to candidates according to the total popular vote they received; and in the fact that the primary would be open to all voters, regardless of their previous party preference.

In its provision that the consent of a candidate would not be required before his name was placed on a ballot, the

Washington plan also contains an indirect means for relieving the embarrassment of men who could not properly make an open personal bid for the nomination. A genuine "draft" would be possible. Moreover, by binding delegates to their candidates, the plan would introduce in the convention a note of greater responsibility to party members at home. At the same time, the provisions for the release of delegates under stated conditions would ensure for the convention the flexibility it needs if it is to do its work well. And in this respect, above all others, the Washington plan deserves support.

There remains still a third area of reform which could have a direct, and in a sense a transcendent influence on the choice of candidates and the election of Presidents.

It is said that there are wings inside both the Republican and Democratic parties that have more in common with each other than with their parent bodies. According to this school of thought, these wings should be detached, and with like joined to like two new parties should be formed: one, to include all "liberals," and the other, all "conservatives."

The benefits claimed for the proposed realignment are these. (1) The two new parties would not suffer from a tyranny of minority elements as the old ones now do. Each could press its course on a straight line, unencumbered by dissenters who want to move in an opposite direction, or at a slant, or to stand still. (2) Party platforms would present voters with clear-cut alternatives instead of, as at present, with choices that are often as vague as a line drawn in a gas cloud. (3) On being presented with definite choices, voters would come to the polls in far greater numbers than they do now. (4) A victorious President would not only enter the

[*169*]

White House with a specific mandate; but—since what he could be expected to do would appear very clearly in a party platform—the nation could hold him to a strict account.

For the most part, the initiative for this general proposal has come from liberal circles. Over the years, liberals have argued that the pattern of the nominating conventions necessarily drives the parties into conservative paths. They observe that the professionals who run the conventions want a candidate who can make the most friends and be the smallest target for enemies. This means that he will necessarily be all things to all men, even though the times may demand a bold stand on vexatious issues. This sort of choice is bad enough in itself, but it is not even made in the open. It is made in a conspiratorial air of secret pledges, second-choice ballots, horse trades, blandishments and alliances between two factions based on a common hatred for a third faction they want to head off. Yet it is from the interaction of these amoral forces that a Lilliputian becomes a Gulliver simply because men of principle and courage made too many enemies in their career of creative partisanship.

To win any hearing at all from the major parties, the argument continues, liberals are forced to narrow down their demands. Even so, their modest requests presently take on an illicit tinge because they are entrusted to the "politicians." On the other hand, when the major parties bait their platforms with warm sentiments to attract liberals in the general elections, they rarely pay off in the event of victory. Nor are the rewards any greater when the two major parties in a case of *extremis* are compelled to nominate an advertised liberal for the presidency. When he wins, he frequently shows an irresistible inclination to go respectable. He fawns on his late enemies within and outside the party and makes them his counselors. At the same time, he drifts away from the liberal elements whose hard work in the campaign should have won for them the right to stand by his side.

The liberal cause can suffer more from a President of this sort than it suffers from any dedicated enemies. Those who elected him become disenchanted. Those who fought him and later seduced him become contemptuous. Yet his failures, originating in the loss of a mass base of action, are charged to liberals because they were conspicuously identified with his campaign triumph. Still worse, by helping him in his first bid for the presidency, they place him in a strategic position where he can force his nomination for a second term. From these cumulative causes of frustration, the will of the liberal in time goes flaccid. In the end, he is so far a victim of this mood that he stays indoors, does nothing, and laughs in knowledgeable cynicism at enthusiasts who ride out to tilt with windmills.

Since all this is the case, the argument concludes, liberals can best serve their cause by withdrawing from both the Republican and Democratic parties. If they built a party of their own, the going would be hard at first. The timid would balk and stay home. The sensual midway would cry for the known fleshpots left behind. Among the mass, however, the call to end their captive state within the old parties would arouse energies equal to any obstacles that might be met. No longer would liberals and the great mass of independents appear as mendicants, begging a concession they could readily get if their numerical strength were organized in a house where they alone were master. The mere institutional form of a separate party would make it possible for liberals to assume tasks not originally foreseen perhaps, but which harmonized with the progressive spirit that brought the party into being. In due course, its monumental achievements would lead to a remaking of America after the imprint of the liberal imagination.

If the will to realign our parties has generally found its strongest expression in liberal circles, the strongest objectors to the proposal have also been liberals. These people call attention first to the prospective groups who might be expected to join the new party. If they were like the ancient Persians who first considered a public issue while drunk, reconsidered it while sober, and then acted if their views coincided in both conditions, there would be some hope for them. But the prospective recruits change their mood from moment to moment. What they feel while drunk is never what they feel when they are sober. In a flush of anger at the President and his party, they want to smash the tables of all political laws and go it alone. On second thought, they grow cautious. They want specific benefits from the President, from his party, or even from the rival party. And they fear that a loss of bargaining power would follow a political secession. They also fear that the loss of their vote for a man who can't possibly be elected by an infant party—or even be registered in any impressive electoral strength—would ensure victory for the worst candidate of the old-line parties.

Nor do the difficulties stop here. Who would lead this new party? First-class men outside the established leadership of the old-line parties either are not widely known, or they lack the broad appeal requisite for national leadership. A vast distance separates Maine from Texas, and the Florida Keys from the state of Washington. To be seen above the intervening barriers, a personality that would lead a nation must be of a special sort. However dimly he appears on the horizon, millions of men and women must be able to recognize themselves in his image. Synthetic means, of course, can sharpen the image. Rutherford B. Hayes described the process when he undertook the build-up of his presidential successor, James Abram Garfield.

We must neglect no element of success [said Hayes]. There is a great deal of strength in Garfield's life and struggles as a self-made man. Let it be thoroughly presented—in facts and incidents, in poetry and tales, in pictures, on banners, in representations, in processions, in watchwords and nicknames. How from poverty and obscurity, by labor at all avocations, he became a great scholar, a major-general, a Senator, a Presidential candidate. Give the amplest detail—a school teacher—a laborer on the canal—the name of his boat.

Yet all this takes money and organization and intricate lines of communication. The problem would be simplified if a first-rank leader from one of the old parties undertook the role of candidate for the insurgent venture. These men, however, are not easily come by; and when they are, they are generally on the national downgrade. In any event, most men of this sort nurse secret ambitions of gaining the presidency with the help of an old-line party. Unless they lose all hope for success, they will not readily abandon the efforts of a lifetime to lead a cause that has no organization, no funds, no press, no jobs, and in all probability, couldn't get on the ballot except in a handful of states.

For reasons of this sort, the search for liberal goals must be pressed from within our present political parties. This in no way means that their faults should be glossed over. For low reasons, they often cry fire in a crowded theater, and just as often ignore a real fire when it singes their feet. Yet in their time, the two major parties have led bloodless revolutions which produced spectacular gains. Whether by accident, design, an afterthought, or from the pressure of forces of which they were only vaguely aware, they have led a steady march toward economic equality and broader civil rights.

Again, though the two old-line parties have nominated and elected Presidents whose supposed liberalism turned sour, they have been offset in their number by a happy paradox. Conservatives who won party nominations have just as often turned out to be bold advocates of liberal causes. Andrew Jackson and Harry S. Truman are two massive cases in point. Indeed, a conservative tarnish gives a protective luster to a liberal cause. Observing the tarnish, the talkative and the wise nod their heads in understanding. They know that the liberal cause was embraced simply to win and to hold power, and they applaud this as a "smart" or "fast" maneuver. But let the same cause be openly professed on its merits by a known liberal; let its adoption be urged on the sole ground that it is just, and the man and the cause will swiftly be anathematized as enemies of all that makes for stability in the community.

So runs the general tone of the liberal opposition to a realignment of our parties.

Save for Southern secession, the 1948 Dixiecrats, and the spasmodic agitation in Republican circles on the eve of their 1952 convention, a debate of this sort has not actively engaged conservative thinking. Conservatives generally have been content to seek control of the two major parties, without inquiring whether they should form a new one of their own. Thus, in the pre-Civil War years, before the cocked pistol of slavery blew out everyone's brains, the Southern slaveholders undertook to capture the Democratic party, while the Northern mercantile interests made a similar effort in the case of the hydra-headed Whig party. But, at the same time, each went to some pains to draw liberal support to its side.

The Southern slaveholder, for example, claimed that he upheld the true version of liberty proclaimed in the American Revolution. Similarly, he identified himself as the shield of constitutional government, protecting minorities from the tyranny of the majority. When the occasion warranted, he wept from the pulpit and in print over the mistreatment of Northern workers. This general appeal to opinion outside the slavocracy was climaxed by the phenomenon of the "dough-face" Democratic presidential candidates. It was hoped that these Northern (or border) state men with Southern (or expansionist) principles would draw support from otherwise hostile farm and labor groups in the North and along the Middle Border. Their vice presidential running mates, more-over, were chosen to check any incidental losses in the North or the South because of the presidential selection. Thus James K. Polk of Tennessee was paired with George M. Dallas of Pennsylvania; Franklin Pierce of New Hampshire with William R. King of Alabama; and James Buchanan of Pennsylvania with John C. Breckenridge of Kentucky.

The Northern mercantile forces used the same tactic. Working from within the Whig party, they found it useful to placate two sources of opposition. To join otherwise hostile grain growers of the West and laborers of the East with the financial and commercial interests of New England and the

Middle Atlantic states, they embraced Henry Clay's concept of an "American System" where everyone got a piece of the national pie. When this proved inadequate as a bait, as I have already stated, they brought William Henry Harrison out of retirement. On another occasion, in a bid for the support of southern planters, they found it useful to nominate a reverse doughface in the person of Zachary Taylor of Louisiana. Here was a man of Southern birth and residence who nevertheless had safe Northern or at least nationalist principles.

The pattern of conservatism and its concessions to liberal sentiment carried over into post-Civil War politics. Of the many examples on this head, the team of President William McKinley and Senator Marcus A. Hanna is the most compelling. In our day, these Republican leaders have become the comic cartoons for standpat politicians. Yet they were nothing of the sort. At a time when the Republican party seemed to be little more than the antechamber of our biggest corporations, the pair bore themselves in such a way that large segments of the labor and farm population hailed them as champions. This took some doing; it was Joe Cannon who said of McKinley that he kept his ears so close to the ground they got full of grasshoppers. Yet McKinley and Hanna managed to catch the national sound and to give the appearance of guiding themselves by it. They twice captured the sources of political strength William Jennings Bryan had earmarked for himself.

Viewing the history of our political parties in a single glance, one is reminded of those giant-dwarf images at a carnival featuring concave and convex mirrors. The liberal standing before the one sees the need to shrink his claims in a bid to win or at least neutralize the conservative opposition in and out of his party. The conservative standing before the other sees the need to enlarge his political appeal in ways that might win over or at least neutralize the liberal opposition. The optical distortion can be a passing thing, or it can remake a party in its own image. Yet all poles of political opinion are forced to exaggerate themselves—whether by elongations or contractions—to foster a sense that they offer hospitality to aims other than their own. And this is because no group in the nation is big enough to form a majority of fifty per cent plus one per cent all by itself. Indeed, on the single occasion when men neither could nor would reach out for sources of political strength other than what they themselves represented, all parties died, the government collapsed, and we had our Civil War.

The idea of a "pure" conservative party and a "pure" liberal party in America, then, has the same air of unreality as a plan to have a mountain range without valleys or a river without banks. Of themselves, mountains imply valleys as rivers imply banks. And the same is true of our party life. So long as we don't want a welter of one-interest or ideological parties, by the very nature of our diversity each party will and must have a mixed character. In particular must this be true under our Federal arrangement where the legislative impulse is designed to come from below, and not from above as in England.

A party figure, and especially one who sits in the Congress, may be called on to support the abstract his party makes for its national purposes, especially during a presidential campaign. But he is also expected to voice the sentiments of local quarters that might have lost out when that abstract was made. There are times when he can ignore the local source of his power, and can vote his best conscience, even though the result offends regional interests. But in some cases, inevitably, he will have to buck the party and its existing presidential leadership. This means that majorities and minorities, and liberal and conservative divisions will necessarily be present in each party. It also means that the price of a "pure" liberal or a "pure" conservative party would be an endless series of purges of all those who in a passing parade of issues failed to keep step with what some drum major said was high orthodoxy, whether of a liberal or conservative beat.

Suppose, nevertheless, that it was possible to form a "pure" liberal and a "pure" conservative party. Would it result in a better or worse politics than we have known? And how would it affect the character of the presidency? The probabilities seem to be these:

1. It would expose each party to the peril of annihilation any time it committed its united strength on a crucial public issue, and the commitment was based on a very wrong guess. With the destruction of the party that guessed wrong, there would be no force to hold the remaining party in check. From a two-party government we could become a one-party government, and by the logic of monopolies the one in time could become the state.

2. As each party dropped all dissenters who want to check the majority, each, now free of all internal restraints, might fly to an extreme position, carrying millions of Americans with them. With the parties in this polarized condition, the leading traits of party government in a democracy would be imperiled. Coercion might replace consent, if points of

difference appeared impossible to reconcile. From the same cause, a party might refuse to surrender the government to a rival through fear of what it might do. Even if the exchange of power took place peacefully, the alterations in existing relations and proportions in the community could be drastic. For there would be brought to the seat of government a body of people, interests and opinion never before represented and totally out of sympathy with what they had displaced. Upon gaining control of the apparatus of government, and by pile-driving their majority opinion through it, they could wrench a whole social order out of its socket.

The peaceful and orderly transfer of power between the Labour and Conservative parties in England cannot be cited in refutation of this. Though they seem to be divided along sharp ideological lines, the Labourites and Conservatives have an underlying affinity based on the fact that (1) each at bottom is a coalition of interests; (2) each has wings which overlap those of the rival party; (3) the presence of internal divisions within each party forces them into compromises which place the two parties within hailing distance of each other; (4) a deeply entrenched civil service invisibly imposes its own authority on both parties and acts as a source of continuity in the government; (5) and the same sort of authority and continuity is imposed by the Crown and the facts of empire to which both parties are deeply attached.

3. The effect on the presidency of the proposed realignment could do one of two things. Either it would turn a President into a prime minister, or, if he insisted on being a President of the United States, it would enlarge his grounds of conflict with the party that put him in office. For the uniformity of party opinion as expressed through the Con-

gress would act as a fixed hoop, and the President could do nothing unless he jumped through it. In the nature of things this would subordinate the Executive to the Legislature. On the other hand, if the President refused to jump, he would invite the charge that he ignored the explicit mandate on which he and his party had been elected.

Now if it had been the intention of the delegates to the Constitutional Convention to create a Prime Minister, they would have had the Congress choose the President. But they did nothing of the sort. They explicitly located the root source of a President's mandate in the people, acting through their electors. And here we come to the heart of the matter.

With the rise of national parties after the Constitutional Convention and with the emergence of the President as a party leader in Jefferson's day, a natural conflict arose between the first historical expectancy that a President would speak for all the people, and the subsequent partisan expectancy that he would speak only for some of them. Almost all our Presidents have been caught in this opposition. Almost all of them gave their own party members ample cause for complaint. The weak ones succumbed entirely and took the party view; the titans, the national view. Despite their skill at working from within parties, Jefferson, Jackson, Lincoln, Wilson and the two Roosevelts, for example, still found it necessary at times to cut loose from their party base and to argue the case of the people as a whole. And in so doing, each in his own way and in his own person became the party *pro tem* for millions of Americans who could find no place that suited them in any existing major political body.

Proposals for new inventions

Woodrow Wilson, lecturing on this theme at Columbia University in 1907, put the case this way:

It is the extraordinary isolation imposed upon the President by our system that makes the character and opportunity of his office so extraordinary. In him are centered both opinion and party. He may stand, if he will, a little outside the party and insist as it were upon the general opinion. It is with the instinctive feeling that the country wants [such a man] that nominating conventions will often nominate men who are not their acknowledged leaders, but only such men as the country would like to see lead both its parties. The President may also, if he will, stand within the party counsels and use the advantage of his power and personal force to control its actual programs. He may be both the leader of his party and the leader of the nation, or he may be one or the other. If he lead the nation, his party can hardly resist him.

In any clear-cut realignment of our parties along liberal and conservative lines, could the President then stand a little outside the party and insist on the general opinion? Could he lead the nation as well as the party? Could he be the rallying point for many millions who would still belong to neither party? The probabilities are that he could not. All the inducements would be present to crowd him into the straight and narrow path of a party leader, while the broad vistas of national leadership would be barred to him.

A final comment seems applicable to most of the reforms considered in this chapter. Some years ago in the American Midlands, it was felt that the mark of a good farmer was the straight furrows he plowed up and over hills and then down on the plain again. The one who plowed in swirling lines according to the contours of the earth was thought to be addlepated or profligate. Yet it turned out that every time the rains fell, the straight furrows became troughs for water

[*181*]

that cut a little deeper and a little broader until in the end the top soil was eroded and the dust gagged all life. The Midlands farmer learned at last that the man who respected what lay beneath his feet, who had the sense to treat each plot differently, who plowed not on a straight line but in turns that matched those of the earth, brought the farming art to the aid of nature. He built, in passing, a series of tiny dikes that held the water and made it walk instead of run off the soil, with the result that it refreshed but did not devour the earth.

Long before this lesson was learned in the world of American agriculture, our political institutions either developed or were formed originally as a social counterpart of contour plowing. But the current mood is one of impatience with what we have inherited from the past. Some alterations in the legacy may, of course, be needed. If they are undertaken, however, it is to be hoped that we do not abandon sound constitutional principles and embrace fatal ones in the name of reform. Above all, it is to be hoped that we do not succumb to the alien belief that we can best show our political virtue by drawing razor-sharp lines up hills and down the other side and onto the plains. For if this should be our decision in any political area, including the one that covers the choice of a President, then as surely as it is true in the natural world, we shall erode our rich political life and choke on the dust.

10

The laws of natural selection

IOIIIIIIIIIIIIOIIIIIIIIIIIIIOIIIIIIIIIIIIIOIIIIIIIIIIIIIOIIIIIIIIIIIIIOIIIIIIIIIIIIIOIIIIIIIIIIIIIOIIIIIIIIII

*The natural aristocracy from which Presidents are chosen – Physical
beauty unimportant – Physical stamina while important cannot be
gauged – The women in the life of candidates important only as symbols of a felicitous family relationship – The rules of exclusion from
the natural aristocracy – The Northern talent – The English talent –
The Protestant talent – Importance of the martial talent uncertain –
Commanding role of the small-town talent – The family origins
talent – The legal talent – The political talent – Summary of all the
rules of selection – Remarks of John Winthrop on the perilous relationship between the leaders and the led in a free society.*

At the opening of this section I said that the search for a
man who can be an exact transcript of what a whole society
wants and trusts in the presidency necessarily narrows down
the range of choice. Many millions among us would easily
pass a number of tests for presidential virtue and talent. But
in a present population of 156,000,000, probably not more
than 100 men now possess the combination of traits that
qualify them for the "natural aristocracy" from which Presidents are chosen. The evidence is admittedly inexact. Yet if
all the men who have held the presidency were placed
around a single table, their points of similarity would suggest

[*183*]

distinct laws of natural selection which drastically limit those who might hope to join their company.

1. *Beauty.* Few among us would agree on the character of beauty. But if the physical characteristics of our past presidents is the rule for judgment, then it is apparent that this talent, to which John Adams attached such great importance, is the easiest of all tests before a White House hopeful. Our Presidents have been long, short, lean and fat in body; erect, stooped and squat in posture; red, black, blond and bald in hair; straight-toothed, buck-toothed and false-toothed.

Thomas Jefferson, over six feet, first won fame as the homeliest scholar at William and Mary College. And after his death, his friend, James Madison, still felt the need to write defensively to a biographer that Jefferson's hair had not been "*red,* but between *yellow* and *red.*" Moreover, said Madison, Jefferson's nose had been "rather under, certainly not above, common size." Martin Van Buren, a diminutive President, was a bright blond who dressed accordingly. Jackson, well over six feet and cadaverous, was described by a celebrated English actress as a "good specimen of a fine, old well-battered soldier." Theodore Roosevelt, on the other hand, was medium in height, near-sighted, with a high voice and a keyboard display of dentistry. Some vendors, changing the musical image, palmed off small whistles as replicas of "Teddy's teeth." John Quincy Adams was completely bald. And it was said of him that when he got excited, it "was manifest in the flaming redness of his bald head, which acted as a chronometer to his audience."

Abraham Lincoln was likened by General McClellan to a "baboon"; though now it's high praise to say of a political figure that he appears "Lincolnesque." William Howard Taft was of such great girth that he once got stuck in a standard-sized White House bathtub—so it is claimed—and a special-sized one had to be installed for his use. General Zachary Taylor, as seen by a soldier, was "a plain old farmer looking man with a keen eye and a large nose." He was short and very heavy; and, said the soldier, on horseback he "looked like a toad." General Ulysses S. Grant, the least imposing of military heroes, was of a similar mold. He was "short, stooped—lumpish in body." William McKinley, with deep rings under his eyes, recalled a benign and well-fed under-taker. Those who observed Calvin Coolidge said his face was grammatically incorrect in that he should have grown an apostrophe above his lips to indicate a deletion of life. And Herbert Hoover, said the sculptor Gutzon Borglum, looked as though "a rose would wilt if you put it in his hand."

As disparate a trio as Woodrow Wilson, Warren G. Harding and Franklin D. Roosevelt would probably be among the few to match our inner image of how a President should look in his physical form. As for the others, however, it is probable that if we met any of them for the first time without knowledge of who they were, we might feel we stood before men with great inner force. But not until one of them was on his way to the White House would his physical traits seem appropriate in a President. Alfred Landon, a successful oil man, is a fairly recent case in point. He came to look like a President at the moment when he was nominated by the Republicans in 1936; and the image deepened each time the *Literary Digest* poll published further results pointing to his victory. Then, suddenly, when the count of ballots on election day showed a landslide for Franklin D. Roosevelt, there was a swift face changing. Landon's lines returned to those of a successful oil man. If he had won, either he would have developed the full "face of a President," or we would have developed it for him in our minds.

An item of dress, however, can excite warm emotions as a symbol of a political position or a personal style. It can be a brown derby, a crushed fedora, a coonskin cap, a shoestring tie, a flowing cravat, a pair of red suspenders or simply no socks. All these can make the crowd roar, though the specific cause for the roar is governed by the manners and morals of the day. The best example is the checkered career of beards and mustaches as a sign of manliness. At present, we would accept the décor of a beard on a Supreme Court Justice; there it suggests the quality of Michelangelo's Moses. But if a presidential hopeful wore one, he would be suspected of a Bohemian bias, or perhaps of an impetigo rash on his face. The presidency, having gone through the beard phase from the end of the Civil War to the time of Grover Cleveland, and then the businessman's mustache from Cleveland to Woodrow Wilson, has gone back to the smooth-faced phase of the period from Washington to Lincoln.

It remains to be seen whether television will lead to a natural physical selection among men who aspire to the presidency. We know that the camera lens can bring the secrets of a man into a pitiless light. And it can also play cruel tricks on gifted individuals who are afflicted with distracting facial mannerisms. Yet it seems unlikely that television will cast up a physical prototype of honesty and verve, like a face stamped on a coin, which a candidate must match at the risk of being dismissed as a counterfeit. Nor is it possible as yet to pinpoint the extent to which the fate of two presidential candidates in a campaign is influenced by their television performances.

2. *Physical stamina.* A capacity to endure great physical exertions should be a major requirement in the presidency. Yet the public has no way of judging this point despite the prognosis various doctors volunteer. Nor is there any hard and fast connection between acute mental strains and longevity. It is true that the first eight Presidents lived to an average of almost eighty-one years, while the Presidents from Theodore Roosevelt to Franklin D. Roosevelt lived to an average of sixty-five. Yet it is impossible to accept this difference of sixteen years as an absolute measure of what the modern presidency exacts from the men who fill the station. Aside from those whose lives were ended by assassination, there were five Presidents in the more tranquil nineteenth century whose age at the time of their death was below the contemporary average. On the other hand, in the twentieth century, Presidents Harding and Coolidge, who raised no sweat while in office, died at the ages of fifty-seven and sixty respectively. And in addition, Harry S. Truman and Herbert Hoover promise, happily, to increase the contemporary average of longevity by a good many years.

One can say that the presidential hopeful, at least, is under a moral bond to disclose to the nation the true state of his health. But does he really know what it is? Andrew Jackson always seemed to have one foot in the grave, but he lived to a ripe old age. Grover Cleveland underwent a secret operation for cancer of the mouth, yet he, too, lived into his seventies. William Henry Harrison, though advanced in years, was in excellent health. But one month after his inauguration, he walked in a rain to get away from a plague of office seekers, caught cold and died. Zachary Taylor, inured to hardships by his life in the field, sat in a blazing July sun at the dedication of the Washington Monument. Thereafter, he returned to the White House, wolfed some cherries, gulped down some cold milk, and was dead a few days later of a fever. Who could foretell the survival of the first pair and the sudden death of the second?

Besides, the will to believe in personal survival is among the strongest of human impulses. It can gloss over all the aches and pains of the present and interpret them as passing spasms. Indeed, the difficulty of fixing the true state of an individual's health has produced an extended and inconclusive constitutional discussion. The issue arose when President James Garfield lingered on his deathbed for days after he was shot, and when President Woodrow Wilson lay paralyzed for many weeks. Neither one could physically perform his duties. But who was to make a constitutional finding of fact about the President's "disability" so that the Vice President could act in his place, without risking punishment as a usurper? Was the finding to be made by the Vice President? By the Cabinet? By the Supreme Court? By the Congress? No such finding was made in either case. The family and personal staff of both disabled Presidents continued to improvise ways of discharging the official powers and duties of the office. In any realistic sense, it was they who favorably determined the question of disability in obvious defiance of the facts.

In appraising a candidate's power of endurance, the one rule of thumb the public seems to follow is the actual age of the presidential aspirant. The general assumption is that a man in his seventies is not equal to the strains of the White

House. But apart from this maximum age limit, the public seems to share the candidate's own view that he will somehow be immune to death from natural or violent causes. This is best shown in our attitude toward the selection of a Vice President. Though the latter topic, taken by itself, does not fall logically under a discussion of presidential stamina, a digression on some aspects of the subject is warranted because of what the death of a President can lead to.

One need not agree with Mark Hanna's estimate of Theodore Roosevelt when he learned that Tom Platt and Matthew Quay of New York meant to get rid of "Teddy" by kicking him out of the state and upstairs to the vice presidency. Yet Hanna's protest on other grounds is correctly addressed to a chronic oversight when Vice Presidents are selected. He exclaimed: "Don't any of you realize that there is only one life between that mad man Roosevelt and the Presidency? Platt and Quay are no better than idiots! What harm can Roosevelt do as Governor of New York compared to the damage he will do as President if McKinley should die?"

To the time of this writing, seven Presidents, or one fourth of the total, have died in office. They completed only five of the twenty-eight years to which in the aggregate they had been elected. The other twenty-three years were filled by men who had been elected not to the presidency but to the vice presidency. This does not mean that all of the "seven by chance" were unfit for the higher station. Three of the seven—Theodore Roosevelt, Calvin Coolidge and Harry Truman—went ahead to win the office in their own right. As individuals, most of them at least equaled the performance turned in by some of the men who were elected specifically

[*189*]

for the job. Yet even the most competent of these men suffered in the presidency from a psychological hangover, dating back to the mood in which they were chosen for the vice presidency. It was John Quincy Adams who best stated it. He had earmarked himself for the presidency in 1824, and hoped at the same time that Andrew Jackson would consent to be his running mate. Though Jackson was the older of the two by only a half year, Adams reasoned that the vice presidency would "afford an easy and dignified retirement for [Jackson's] old age." Then, as an afterthought, he added: "The Vice Presidency . . . [is] a station in which the General could hang no one."

Similarly, we feel that in the Vice President we are simply choosing a presiding officer for the Senate. Or that we are giving a consolation prize to a man who wanted a chance at the presidency, but failed to win it. Or that we are humoring a wing of the party that came off second best in the convention. Or that we are merely building up sectional strength for a winning party formula. Or that the presidential candidate "should have the right to pick his running mate"—even if this eventually means that one man alone picks the presidential successor.

The habit of joining the presidential and vice presidential candidates as Siamese twins on a ballot adds special force to the psychological hangover. The arrangement violates the spirit of the Twelfth Amendment, which states that the electors shall cast "distinct ballots" and shall compile "distinct lists" for presidenial and vice presidential nominees. At present, of course, electors do nothing of the sort. They simply register the results of an indivisible ballot cast by the voters. It is also true that if the two officers were divided and voted on separately, a President and a Vice President of different parties might result. Yet the voter who likes one of his party's candidates and loathes the other, and cannot register this distinction, has every reason to feel that one half of his right of suffrage has been taken away. Since that half is most frequently his freedom to choose the Vice President, this officer can appear to be an interloper from the moment of his victory.

When there is a death in the White House, and the Vice President is suddenly called on to uphold, defend and protect the Constitution to the best of his abilities as a President, a good part of the nation shudders in apprehension over what this strange successor will do. The "deals" in the Convention which put his name in nomination as a Vice President, the blessing given to the nomination by the lately deceased President, the exhausted delegates who shouted their approval in half-empty halls—these memories are now exhumed and acquire a sharp poignancy.

Party leaders who had a chance to be the Vice President but turned it down at the convention soothe the bite of a missed opportunity by damning the man who accepted what was offered. Those who tried to block him in the convention but failed feel doubly robbed. Among the people at large, those who wanted to vote against him in the election but could not do so because his name was linked with a presidential candidate of whom they approved feel themselves doubly coerced. Cabinet officers and other key figures in the entourage of the deceased President begin to fear that the resignations they submit to the successor as a matter of form will be accepted. So they tell themselves, their friends, and, in their general air, they also tell the new President that he

[*191*]

is a porch climber—which may, unfortunately, be an all too accurate description; that what he wants done was never done that way before. And by means of this sort, they can force what they fear the most. The new President may accept their resignations. He may even ask for them.

But as these men depart one by one from the center of the national stage each vacancy and each replacement swells the current of national uneasiness. What issues from the White House seems to be based not on law, but on accident and caprice. And this feeling lingers on, even when the President by chance later wins the White House in a direct election. Even those who vote for him still feel that what he does was not meant to be. This psychological disarray was acute even in a former day when the nation was preoccupied with its internal affairs. But now, when we must make hard and costly decisions in our external affairs, and when these must be backed by careful deliberation and choice, the appearance of a happenchance President can have a divisive power, deadly in its effects. There will be those who will want to believe that the need to bear the costs and to make the decisions are all due to an accident in the presidency. From the pressures generated by this mood, leadership of any sort tends to be suspect as an illegitimate intrusion, sent from a foreign quarter to bedevil men and women who would certainly live as angels if they were left to themselves.

This uneasiness might be lessened if political parties nominated their Vice Presidents, and the nation voted for them, with all the concentrated seriousness given to the choice of a President. But this sort of reorientation seems unlikely, unless the nation suffers a stupendous calamity at the hands of a Vice President who succeeds to the presidency

by chance. Short of this method of progressing through disaster, serious consideration ought to be given to an old proposal, revived by Senators William Fulbright and George
Smathers after the 1952 election. They would divide the
four-year tenure of a president into its two phases, corre-
sponding to the congressional elections. If the President died
within the first phase, the Vice President would complete
only what remained of the two years. An election of a new
President for a four-year term could then be held coincident
with the election of a new Congress. If the President died
within the second phase, the Vice President as now would
complete what remained of his term. In this method, the
nation would have a direct and early voice in the choice of a
presidential replacement.

The Constitution imposes only two restrictions on the
enactment of this legislation by the Congress. First, the
presidential election must be held throughout the nation on
the same day, and second, the term must run for four years.
The Fulbright-Smathers proposal would respect these
limitations; it would also respect an implied constitutional
assumption that the terms of a new President, the whole of
a new House and one third of the Senate would have a
starting date in common. Moreover, it would restore what
probably was the original intention of the constitutional
authors—that the Vice President was to be a caretaker of the
executive functions until a President was regularly qualified to fill that post. The one serious drawback to the proposal is that a President's death in the course of the first
two-year phase might fall so near to a congressional election
that our political parties would have little time either to
choose a new standard-bearer or to present his merits to the

[193]

nation. And the mischances of any such work done in haste would have to endure for a full four years. But if there is a quieting answer to this challenge, then the proposal of Senators Fulbright and Smathers seems unassailable on any other ground. It appears to be the best answer to the profoundly unsettling sequence of events which follow a miscalculation about the physical survival of the President.

3. *The women in their life.* Up to this point, the rule of exclusion from the presidency is not too strict. Almost anyone can pass the "beauty test." And almost anyone between the ages of thirty-five and his late sixties who gives the appearance of good health can pass the stamina test. The rule of exclusion begins to tighten when the aspirant is judged by how he matches an idealized version of all that is felicitous in home and family life. In this respect, the man who wants to be President is held to a rule of performance far more straight-laced than the one most European democracies impose on their political leaders. Not infrequently the European leader, without the loss of reputation, has kept his mistress in public view. Though the woman may be denounced for giving her lover bad advice, the fact of the liaison itself tends to be accepted as normal. It can excite gossip, envy and even admiration when the leader is getting along in years. But only rarely does it lead to political exile.

A presidential aspirant is denied any such latitude; and a divorce in his background is a handicap which he and his friends weigh at length for its political effects. This is true even when the divorce bears not the faintest hint of anything that is dishonorable. Our performance here, incidentally, is in marked contrast to Catholic France, which did not deny Clemenceau the prime ministry because he and his wife had parted company. Nor, in the current speculation of Anglican England, is the divorce and remarriage of Anthony Eden regarded as a serious bar to his future assumption of the prime ministry. The difference can be explained in two ways. Since the French and English Prime Ministers are chosen by the parliament, the mores of the people at large do not exercise a direct impact on the selection process. But more important, in neither country does the work of upholding the virtues of home and family fall to the political executive. It falls to the titular head of state, who is the President in France and the Crown in England. In America, however, because the President has a dual and indivisible character as the head of state and chief executive, the duties of the Crown as they involve home and family fall to him.

With the 1952 nomination of Governor Stevenson by the Democratic party, a first step was taken to modify the harsh law which excluded divorced men even from consideration for the presidency. Not until a case actually arises can we know if the rule of exclusion would apply to a remarriage after a divorce. Presumably, party leaders would take into account the inevitable objections from religious circles to whom these remarriages are immoral or in defiance of "God's law." Nevertheless, it is to be hoped that political parties in the future will show a discriminating respect for the facts of each particular case, and will not lay down an automatic bar against a presidential aspirant who has suffered a domestic misfortune, often many years before he rose to public prominence.

One aside is in point here. It is conceivable that a Lady Emma Hamilton, to whom John Adams assigned such a deadly influence, has crossed a presidential path from time to time. But if the loving dalliance was transferred to the White House, it was carried off with such great discretion as to leave few traces for a night-prowling historian to detect. In general, women who carried weight at the White House were elderly and rich widows who filled their loneliness by bringing men together with men, not men with themselves. Or they had newspapers at their command, to advocate and to scold. Or they were matrons who arranged salons where personal ambitions and factional interests were advanced. Or they were women of great intelligence and drive who won attention by the merits of the causes they embraced. But evidently no woman with the cut of a courtesan has sat in a bubble bath, deciding public policy, while a President perfumed the water for her.

Nor is it possible to image a President's wife as the central figure in that kind of tableau. In taverns and smoking rooms across the land, rank jokes are often told about presidential wives. Broad hints of something illicit also titillate many ears. But they do not pass over into a supportable public accusation. The facts have been too obviously against the story-tellers. Presidents' wives receive delegations of Girl Scouts, visit mine shafts, encourage American industry by writing thank you notes for grass hats sent them, talk over old times with members of the home-town bridge club, or just keep out of sight. As a group, the history of their career in the White House has the limited scope of a magazine like *Better Homes and Gardens*. It is a repetitive account of who sat where on what occasion; eating what; how much it cost; what was said about it afterward; whether the succeeding President's wife changed the color of the room—all climaxed by congressional protests about the expense of maintaining the nation's "chief servant in a palace as splendid as that of the Caesars and as richly adorned as the proudest Asiatic mansions."

If it could be learned that even one White House mistress smiled invitingly to someone on the outside, the history of the inside would be considerably enlivened. But the very name Abigail Adams, the first of the presidential wives to live in the place, makes even a thought of this sort seem obscene. A woman of extraordinary parts, it was she who laid down the *Better Homes and Gardens* format for the female side of the White House story. "I will use the unfinished barn-like room on the East side of the house for a laundry," she wrote. And ever since then, a good part of the story dealing with presidential wives turns around the alterations they may have made to that one celebrated room.

From the days of Abigail Adams' sharp mind, tongue and pen, to Elizabeth Virginia Truman's modesty and reserve, the White House knew a charming and bustling housewife in Dolly Madison; an elaborate social ritualist in Eliza Monroe; a snob in Louisa Johnson Adams; a religious fanatic in Sarah Childress Polk; a shy frontier woman in Margaret Smith Taylor, who was more at home in a tent than in the White House and who stayed out of sight with her sewing basket and her corncob pipe; a former schoolteacher of Cayuga County, New York, in Abigail Powers Fillmore, who bought the first books for the mansion's bare shelves; a heroine of the W.C.T.U. in Lucy Webb Hayes; a number of invalids like Ida Saxton McKinley; a just-in-from-a-ride-in-the-country woman in Edith Kermit Roosevelt; a discursive woman in Helen Herron Taft; a charitable woman in Lou Henry Hoover; a woman of energetic compassion in Anna

Eleanor Roosevelt, and several nags like Mary Todd Lincoln and the shrill Florence Kling Harding.

This gallery is not only a disappointment to those in search for irregularities in the behavior of Caesar's wife. It is also a disappointment to writers of women's fables in which the wife makes the husband great. Except for a few cases, like Abigail Adams and Eleanor Roosevelt, the wife was either one more hurdle the husband had to surmount before he attained the presidency; or she influenced his rise neither for good nor evil, usually maintaining the same neutralism after he gained the presidency. Or she poured vinegar down his throat when he was spread-eagled on a cross. In short, in their effect on their husband's career, first ladies of the land are supremely like wives of husbands in private stations across the nation.

4. *The Northern talent.* I referred, in a former connection, to the way presidential nominating conventions discriminate in favor of men who come from big states and against those who come from small ones. An obvious refinement—and its consequence—remains to be stated here. Ever since the Civil War, the sense of *place* has worked in favor of the men who come from the big states in the North, while it has acted as a rule of exclusion against the Southerner, no matter how big his state. In part this is due to the pervasive hangover of Civil War animosities. In part it is due to specific anti-Southern prejudices among the Negroes of the North; neither party wishes to alienate their vote by presenting them with Southern candidates. And until recently, the absence of effective two-party competition in the South was also a factor. In the politics of net gain, Northern Republicans saw no point in bidding for the South by offering them a

Southern candidate, when victory in the region seemed hopeless in any event. The Democrats, on the other hand, saw no point in offering the South a Southern Democratic presidential candidate, when the region as a whole was felt to be safely Democratic.

But the greater part of this rule of exclusion is based on two facts, so obvious that they are commonly ignored. First, the North, taken as an entity, holds a decisive majority in the count of population. And with respect to the value of *place*, it imposes its own preferences on the Southern minority in the exact manner of a majority formed around any other principle of selection. Second, though the industrialization of the South has been greatly accelerated in recent decades, and in particular since 1940, it has not yet reached a stage where its politics offers an industrial-commercial-agricultural composite. The Southern image remains primarily an agricultural one, and thus it seems alien to the first two elements in the composite forming the Northern majority.

In the decades ahead, further industrialization may create a different pattern, and from this a different base for Southern political action. Indeed, we shall never be truly reunited as a people until the Southern genius for politics, which was once in the vanguard of a progressive democracy, is again restored and allowed full play on the national scene. But as long as the presidency lies beyond the reach of the Southerner, he will apply his talents to two extremes. On the one hand, he will turn toward local affairs. On the other, his great imaginative faculties will reach out and grapple with politics on a global scale. The national area which lies in between the local and the global will suffer the loss of his attention. And this loss has a way of compounding itself.

Elsewhere the hope of winning the presidency exerts a subtle pressure on a leader to change from a provincial to a national outlook. Though a Northerner, he must, in a sense, also be a Southerner. But the Southern leader has no such inducement to think like a Northerner and to embrace a national view in matters which go against the local grain.

The Southerner asks himself: Why risk an overthrow by local forces when the promise of an offsetting victory in the national arena is so ephemeral? When he bids for the presidency, he does so either half-heartedly, belatedly, or purely as a defense measure to veto some Northern candidate. Except where there is a clear coincidence of Southern needs and those of the urban North, the concessions he makes to the national point of view are interpreted as a device to get past the barrier of the nominating convention, and not as evidence of long-standing convictions. Many watch the sudden alteration in astonishment; but few take it seriously. So the sense of *place,* unmentioned by John Adams in his description of the natural aristocrat, works against the men from the South.

5. *The English talent.* If the presidential hopeful passes all the tests up to this point, he now encounters a rule of exclusion represented by the "English vote." The "vigorous seedlings from the old world nurseries," to quote Vernon Parrington, take root and flourish here only when they are of the kind that can be grafted on and sustained by the dominant English trunk. For though we are a nation of many overhead branches, America *is* English in its speech and literature, in its concepts of limited and responsible government, in its common law, in its Bible, and in the mere count of its population. Some 80,000,000 Americans trace

their descent to the British Isles, to form the largest single "interest" in the nation. It is not spoken of as the "English vote." Nor does it act as a solid bloc. But it forms the cultural frame within which all other "interests" and "blocs" must make their adjustments.

Though John Adams does not mention it in his description of the natural aristocrat, nowhere does its pervasive authority in social and political matters appear more strongly than in the identity of our Presidents. Of the thirty-three men who have held the presidency up to now, twenty-eight traced their descent back to Great Britain (exclusive of what is now the Republic of Eire). In a more detailed breakdown, eighteen had forbears who came from England proper; two came from Scotland; one came from Wales; six were of Scot-Irish origin, and one a mixture of English-Scot-Irish. Of the remaining five Presidents, three were of Dutch and one was of Swiss origin, representing ethnic strains that seem to be first cousins to the English in the images they offer of reserve, rationalism and devotion to personal freedom. General Eisenhower, who rounds out this group of five, can be classed either as Swiss Mennonite or Germanic in origin.

How the authority of the English vote is exercised is shown most clearly by an example drawn from neighborhood behavior when a new family moves in. From behind drawn blinds, the old inhabitants watch the goings and comings of the intruders to see if their advent will disturb what has been safe and predictable. Suspicion and conflict charge the air. Bit by bit, however, as the new family mows its lawn, trims its flower bed, sprays the trees, neatly wraps its garbage and deposits it in fly-proof cans, it is generally concluded that the strangers belong to the human race after all.

In time, the new family is enveloped by its neighbors and subtly acquires the characteristics of the street. No longer do its children have rocks thrown at them. They join in throwing rocks at still more recent invaders who must run the gauntlet of assimilation.

Something like this process of accommodation has occurred in the presidency of the twentieth century. Thus far, the English vote with its Dutch and Swiss allies has chosen all our Presidents in the century—exclusive of General Eisenhower, if he is considered to be of Germanic origin. But we have also had three major contenders who fall outside the English alliance. The first was Robert M. La Follette, of French Huguenot origin, though in his 1924 bid he spoke more for the German and Scandinavian immigrant who formed his mass base than for the scattered French. In 1928, the bid was made by Al Smith, of South Irish origin, and in 1940 by Wendell Willkie, of Germanic origin. These instances seem to reflect a continuing process by which immigrant waves are digested by the English majority, infused with its characteristics, and then reissued for public currency as Englishmen by adoption, much as the Roman Emperors adopted promising men and made them their heirs.

As the assimilation cycle does its work, the individual seems to acquire his status from that of his group. He may be a first-generation American, or his forebears may have been in America for several centuries. But he appears to be acceptable to the English alliance some three or four generations after the group with which he is identified—sometimes erroneously—appears in bulk on the American scene and gains acceptance. In this special sense, Al Smith's candidacy can be said to have climaxed the assimilation of the South Irish immigration in the 1830's, though Smith was the first of his family to be born in America. As a third-generation American, Wendell Willkie's candidacy climaxed the assimilation of the 1848 German immigration. General Eisenhower's forebears had been in America for over two hundred years, though as a candidate he seems to have been dissociated from the Swiss-German Mennonite immigration of the 1700's and erroneously linked in the popular mind with the 1848 German immigration.

If the foregoing generalizations have any more validity than a flying guess, they can be extended to say that the Scandinavian-American, representing the 1870–80 immigrant strain, may be the next in line to win acceptance from the English alliance. And after the Scandinavians may come the Italian-Americans, representing a 1900 immigrant influx.

6. *The Protestant talent.* The Constitution explicitly states that no religious test shall ever be required as a qualification for any office or public trust in the United States. In this, America differs from England, where priests are barred by law from holding any elective office, and where the Crown is limited by law to Protestants. Yet it labors the obvious to say that we have raised an extra-constitutional test of religious qualification for the presidency. It has not only made the post a Protestant possession; except for the 1928 candidacy of Al Smith, all major candidates for the post have also been Protestants. Here, then, is another "talent," unmentioned by John Adams in his description of the natural aristocrat.

The prejudices that have blocked Catholics and Jews from access to the office have been real, deep and, in some of their manifestations, ugly. But a sweeping indictment of intolerance cannot be sustained on this count. Catholics and Jews exercise a veto in the choice of presidential candidates. They are placed high in party councils; the Democratic party now customarily selects a Catholic as the national chairman. And both religions are generally represented in the personal entourage of the President.

While the decisive Protestant majority votes its religious preference, as if the government by law was organized as a Protestant state, the existence of a supra-Protestantism is worth noting. If present figures on Protestant sects can be used as a very rough gauge to the proportions that might have prevailed in the past, the results show no connection between the size of a sect and the number of Presidents it produced. To illustrate, the Baptists, with a present church membership of over 16,000,000, claimed but two Presidents; the Methodists, with a membership of over 10,000,000, four. In contrast, the Unitarian Church, with a membership of 75,000, has claimed four Presidents; the Reformed Dutch, with 134,000, two; the Congregational Christian Church, with 1,204,000, one; the Disciples of Christ, with 1,738,000, one; the Protestant Episcopal Church, with 2,378,000, ten; Presbyterian bodies, with 3,508,000, five. Of the three Presidents who are not represented in this grouping, Jefferson expressed a preference for the Unitarian faith; Hayes sometimes attended the Methodist Church but never joined, while Lincoln expressed a preference for no church.

The failure of Baptists and Methodists to produce Presidents in proportion to their numerical strength can be explained in several ways. In both cases, that strength represents millions of Negroes who have yet to attain any of the major offices from which Presidents are chosen. Next, the numerical strength also represents many millions of Southern whites who have been kept from the presidency by the rule that excludes Southerners as a whole. And finally, the doctrinal views and religious practices to which the Baptists and the Methodists subscribe have made them the "folk sects" of American Protestantism. Both seem to appeal to people of uncertain economic or social status; when any of these people rise to commanding places in the life of their communities they usually go over to the more fashionable or "intellectual" sects. Since we pick our Presidents from men who generally have been "successful" in some sort of endeavor, the choice tends to center on a person who would not normally be drawn or held by Protestant evangelism.

Three large Protestant sects have yet to produce a President. They are the American Lutheran Conference, with 2,024,000 members; the Lutheran Synod Conference of North America with 4,100,000; and the Latter-day Saints, (Mormons) with 1,113,000. (Figures are not available for Christian Scientists.) In the first two cases, the failure is largely due to an overlap between religious and ethnic factors. Lutherans in the main are represented by German and Scandinavian strains spread through the North Central states. Since they are among more recent immigrant groups, they come under the rule of exclusion mentioned in a former connection. The Mormons present a different case. Though they have won wide and well-earned respect for themselves as individuals, the nineteenth-century suspicion of the sect as a whole regrettably lingers on. Moreover, Mormon concentration in the intermountain region places them outside the areas from which we tend to choose our Presidents.

If we are to make a balanced appraisal of the part re-

ligious intolerance has played in the choice of Presidents, it
would be well to remember that this evil has worked a two-
way street. In the 1884 presidential campaign, it led to the
defeat of James G. Blaine at Catholic hands. There were
good reasons why Blaine should not have been elected President on the Republican or any other ticket in that or in any
other year. But anti-Catholicism was not one of them. On the
contrary, he had been sharply accused of "coddling the
Catholic vote"—until he was visited toward the close of the
campaign by a group of clergymen, assembled to give him a
clean bill of health on other grounds. As Blaine came down
the staircase of the Fifth Avenue Hotel in New York, the
chairman of the group drew near. This gentleman, later
described by the *New York Sun* as "an early Paleozoic
bigot," felt it within himself to say: "We expect to vote for
you next Tuesday. We are Republicans and don't propose to
leave our party and identify ourselves with the party whose
antecedents have been rum, Romanism and rebellion."

In all probability, Blaine did not hear what was being
said, or he was too tired to understand that a bomb with a
sputtering fuse had been tossed at him. In any case, he did
not repudiate at once the opinion expressed in his presence.
But a quick-witted reporter who was on the scene seized
the remark and ran with it to Democratic headquarters. The
next Sunday morning, every Catholic churchgoer in America
knew about it either from the pulpit or from handbills distributed before church doors. Blaine's later disavowal of the
bigot's views never had a chance to catch up with the allega-
tions that shook the Catholic community. In an enraged reaction to the slur on their religion, Catholics everywhere turned
on Blaine as if he personally had been the author of the

canard. In New York, the Irish administered the *coup de grâce*. It had been expected beforehand that their vote would give Blaine the state. Instead he lost New York by eleven hundred votes, and with it, the election.

In the 1928 elections, the current of bigotry was reversed, as if to even the historical score. This time, Protestants were primarily at fault. Al Smith came under vicious and disgraceful attacks, despite Herbert Hoover's efforts to halt the work of the hatchet men. Nevertheless, the 6,376,504 votes by which Hoover defeated Smith is not conclusive proof that religious invective, though massive in volume, was decisive in influence. The gap between the victor and the vanquished was a million votes fewer than in the 1924 election when Coolidge defeated Davis, and three quarters of a million fewer than in 1932 when Roosevelt defeated Hoover. It is true that a million Southerners broke with tradition and voted Republican, while unknown numbers boycotted the election. But their reasons are not clear. The traditionally Democratic states of North Carolina, Texas, Florida and Virginia, for example, are not the great strongholds of Protestant fundamentalism. Yet they swung over to the Republican column, while the fundamentalist strongholds, which should have been most deeply swayed by the charge that Smith would build a tunnel connecting the White House with the Vatican, gave him their majorities. On the other hand, six of the fourteen states that political map-makers classify as Catholic voted against Smith—including his own state of New York. The Democratic party, however, did register substantial gains in the great urban centers.

A compound of factors, of which religious bigotry was but one, seems to have tipped the scales against Smith. He was a sharply delineated big-city figure. This made him suspect in rural areas. He had been identified with Tammany Hall. This raised the bugaboo of machine politics. He had urged the outright repeal of prohibition, while Hoover called it "an experiment noble in purpose." On the basis of this difference, Hoover apparently drew a majority of the women's vote, including that of the dry Catholics. But above all, the America of September and October, 1928, probably saw no real need to change the Republican administration. On the surface, things were in excellent shape. As Machiavelli observed, before there can be a Moses, there must first be a people of Israel who want to get out of Egypt where they are held in bondage. Though Al Smith could talk of progressivism and reform and mean it, in 1928 the children of Israel found Egypt to their liking.

There is also the fact that not since the days of Charles Evan Hughes had the Republican party nominated a man with a better public record. Hoover matched each of Smith's strong points, and in some respects outpointed him. Like Smith, he was a man of rock-ribbed honesty. In a theater larger than Smith had ever worked in, Hoover had skillfully directed vast humanitarian projects involving Americans and foreigners alike. He had been a Secretary of Commerce in two cabinets at a time when the prestige of the business community was at its zenith. In his post as Secretary, he had sponsored measures that aided business, simplified the operations of his department, and given sensitive direction to the growth of radio and airplane manufacturing, two infant industries then in the forefront of public interest. For a society seemingly without acute social problems, for one whose bounties simply had to be administered competently, a Great Engineer in the presidency was not an unwise choice. What is really astonishing is that Smith actually polled 15,000,000 votes.

No one can predict the future prospects of a Catholic who aspires to the presidency. Our present preoccupation with the anti-Communist fight might work in his interest. Though Catholic Europe has crumbled or is in danger of crumbling before the Communist onslaught—at a time when Protestant Europe has stood firm under attack—there are those who believe that Catholic generalship is better equipped to fight the battle of the century. If this view wins wide currency in America, a Catholic aspirant might gain a political bonus from the mood of the era. However, though he wins a party nomination, he may have a hard time on the national scene in reviving the enthusiasm liberal Protestants showed for Al Smith.

A sizeable number of liberal Protestants who once dismissed the trumped-up charge of a "Catholic conspiracy" in America have unfortunately come to view Catholicism as a monolithic whole, preoccupied with enlisting a religious tradition in the defense of the economic and political status quo. There is a grave error here. It can be laid in part to the exaggerated displays some of the metropolitan papers, in pursuit of their own aims, have given to the attacks of Catholic priests on various Protestant-backed social measures. What this part of the press has wilfully failed to report are the eloquent dissents from these attacks voiced by other Catholics, priests and laymen alike. A Christmastime mention may be given to the Pope's strictures against the excesses of both capitalism and communism. But the year-long efforts of Catholic priests, journalists, professors, labor and lay leaders to defend the rights of persons against economic or political oppression get scant notice. As an example: for all the treatment part of the press gave it, the stirring declaration by fifty Catholic bishops against the evils of McCarthyism might just as well have remained unuttered.

Since he has been presented with only one side of Catholic activity, the liberal Protestant has come to suspect the whole of it, and is now among the first to strike the warning note against any apparent concessions to Catholic influence. To the extent, then, that a Catholic aspirant for the presidency would now be judged not on his own merits, but as "the tool of a priestly plot," he would lack the liberal Protestant support essential to his success.

8. *The martial talent.* The other talents considered to this point have lent themselves to fairly distinct judgments. But the military talent is difficult to assess, except in its specific application. The military mind may be damned in one case for its rigidity; in another, it may be hailed for its reasonableness and objectivity. The power to command may appear to some people as a power to oppress; to others, as a power to liberate. One general may be loved, and another one hated. Because of this ambivalence, it is virtually impossible to say that the military talent, by its inherent nature, works for or against an aspirant to the presidency. About all that can be offered under this head are a few rough generalizations.

In the period from 1789 to the eve of the 1952 elections, nine Presidents—Washington, Jackson, William Henry Harrison, Taylor, Pierce, Grant, Hayes, Garfield and Benjamin Harrison—once held active field commands as generals. In addition, Johnson held the rank of general as military governor of Tennessee during the Civil War, and Arthur was quartermaster general of the New York state militia. Nine other Presidents—Jefferson, Madison, Monroe, Tyler, Buchanan, Lincoln, McKinley, Theodore Roosevelt and Truman—also performed military services of various kinds in ranks from private to colonel. (In a comparable period, the Duke of Wellington was the only general to attain the English prime ministership.)

However, a direct grant of the presidency as a reward for conspicuous wartime leadership was limited to Washington, Taylor and Grant. In no other case was military talent by itself a decisive factor in the selection of a candidate or in his election-day victory. Five men who won fame in the field—Generals Lewis Cass, Winfield Scott, John C. Frémont, George McClellan and Winfield Scott Hancock—were defeated as the presidential candidates of major parties. Other military figures of equal prominence failed to win even a party nomination. Admiral George Dewey, the hero of the Spanish-American War, coveted the Republican nomination but killed himself off by remarking: "It's easy enough to be President; all you have to do . . . is to take orders from Congress." General Leonard D. Wood, who won fame in World War I, mustered impressive big-business backing in his bid for the Republican nomination in 1920, but his hopes were shattered when Senator William E. Borah denounced the Wood candidacy as being "too diamond studded." And in 1944 and 1948, General Douglas MacArthur's glory brought him only scattered support from the delegates to the Republican National Convention.

Even the generals who eventually won the presidency had no easy victories. Jackson was turned down by a vote of the House of Representatives in 1824. William Henry Harrison was rejected by the voters in 1836 when he made his first bid. At the Democratic Convention in 1852, Pierce emerged as the dark-horse choice on the 49th ballot. In 1876, Hayes lost the popular vote and gained the presidency only through a rigged procedure which gave him a margin of one vote in the Electoral College. In the 1880 Republican convention, Garfield, who had managed John Sherman's bid for the party nomination, became the dark-horse choice on the thirty-sixth ballot, to break the deadlock between Sherman, Grant and Blaine. In the election contest of 1888, Benjamin Harrison lagged behind Grover Cleveland in the popular vote and won the presidency only on the basis of his electoral majority. And finally, General Eisenhower had to wage a vigorous campaign first to win the Republican nomination in 1952, and thereafter to hold his party together in the election canvass.

More important than all this, from the time of the first President to the eve of the 1952 elections, the phenomenon of the general in the White House coincided with the age of the amateur soldier. Before that age came to an end with the introduction of the General Staff in 1903, the Revolutinary War produced one general-President; the War of 1812, two; the Mexican War, two; the Civil War, four. Of the lot, General Grant was the only one who had been trained at West Point, while Taylor was the only one who pursued an unbroken career in the army. Again, except for Washington and Grant, not one of these general-Presidents ever held a field command whose force exceeded one half the size of a modern infantry division. The scope of warfare throughout this period, the relatively simple weapons, the size of the

The laws of natural selection

armies and the location of the enemy were all made to order for the amateur.[1] An ambitious lawyer with the right political friends could raise a force of some size in his local community and become its chief officer. Hayes did this and so did Benjamin Harrison. An ambitious politician with the right connections in a state capital or in the White House could suddenly appear in the uniform of a general at the head of troops. Pierce did this. Even a teacher, with some knowledge of German and French, could translate a pamphlet by Frederick the Great or Napoleon and be thought competent to direct a battle. This was true of Garfield. Or a militiaman on the frontier who mixed fighting with other pursuits—as did most male adults there—could be elected by his partisans or appointed to the rank of major general. This happened to Andrew Jackson and William Henry Harrison.

It is also relevant that, except for Tyler and Grant, every general-President in the age of the amateur soldier had broad experience in civil offices before he attained the presidency.[2] Jackson, for example, devoted but six years of his pre-presidential career to matters that were exclusively military. He had been a highly successful lawyer, a prosecuting

[1] The age of the amateur was vividly described by General Grant, who remarked to his staff after the Battle of the Wilderness: "I could not keep from thinking of the first fight I ever saw—the Battle of Palo Alto [during the Mexican War]. As I looked at the long line of battle, consisting of three thousand men, I felt that General Taylor had such a fearful responsibility resting upon him that I wondered how he ever had the nerve to assume it; and when after the fight the casualties were reported and the losses ascertained to be nearly sixty in killed, wounded, and missing, the engagement assumed a magnitude in my eyes which was positively startling. When the news of the victory reached the States the windows of every household were illuminated and it was largely instrumental in making General Taylor President of the United States."

[2] Even Grant served for a brief period as Secretary of War in the Johnson Cabinet.

attorney, a Congressman, twice a Senator, a judge, a planter and a breeder of race horses. He was in his early forties when he took the field for the first time at the head of troops; forty-six when he won the Battle of New Orleans, and forty-seven when his fighting days were over. It was not until he was sixty-one that he won the presidency. His military glory made his name known throughout the land; but without his further identity as the leader of frontier political forces, it seems highly unlikely that he could have been elected to the White House.

Much the same story can be told of William Henry Harrison. Before his victory at Tippecanoe Creek, where he commanded about nine hundred men, he had been Secretary of the Northwest Territory, and later its governor. At the age of forty-one, while the War of 1812 was still on, Harrison resigned from the army, following the Battle of the Thames, in which Tecumseh was killed. Twenty-six years elapsed before he attained the presidency at the age of sixty-seven. In the interval he twice represented Ohio in the Congress; served in the state legislature; returned to Washington as a Senator; was sent to Columbia as the United States Minister; was recalled by President Andrew Jackson, and sank back into obscurity until he was brought out of a humiliating retirement by the Whig politicians in 1836.

The general-Presidents of a former age, whatever might be said for or against them, provide no basis for prophecy about the possible performance of General Eisenhower in the presidency. Here, for the first time, is a professional soldier, trained and reared to command by the General Staff. This is something new under our political sun. If in the future a martial talent of any sort is explicitly looked for in the presidential candidate, it is probable that it will be the talent of a professional. A lawyer, a businessman or a schoolteacher may still rise through the National Guard to command a division. But the identity and achievements of such a man are now altogether engulfed by the enormous size of the new military establishment and by the global scope of modern warfare. All the nation can single out among the milling mass are the achievements of those who command armies numbering in the millions. And these men are not amateurs.

Though they lack experience in partisan political matters— enjoyed to the hilt by most generals in the age of the amateur—the handful of top professionals may have offsetting virtues. The least important one is their administrative experience in directing huge enterprises. For the family resemblance between civil and military administration goes no further than a structural similarity in the chain of command. What goes on within that chain is fundamentally different. The twin duties of the President as a civil administrator are first, to win the right to administer certain policies, and second, to win support for those policies even as they are being administered. In all of this, he must work within the frame of laws established by Congress and interpreted by the Courts, while he is answerable to public opinion. The military administrator, on the other hand, is spared the need to win universal consent for his policies. That is the duty of civilian leadership. Again, the top military administrator does not have to win the voluntary co-operation of his subordinates in the execution of a policy. He can coerce them into co-operating for he holds in his hands the powerful sanctions of a court-martial, leading in certain circumstances to a loss of civil rights or to the death of anyone who breaches discipline. Finally, the art of the military administrator, best shown in time of war, has a broad streak of improvisation, exercised against the capabilities of an enemy. It is not exercised within a framework of detailed laws enacted and interpreted by the legislative and judicial branches of the government.

What can be cited to the credit of the top professional soldiers is the kind of experience they now acquire in dealing with national and international matters. Total wars of this century have also totalized the preoccupations of those who direct wars. How, where, when and in what quantity they employ a force of armed men may be determined by diplomatic questions; the size of the labor force, the rate of its production, the allocation of materials, race relations, religious matters, the administration of occupied areas and so on, all concern them. This may help prepare them for the presidency, though it is by no means a complete preparation which guarantees in advance a successful tenure in the White House.

Though the professional soldier frequently shows a marked bias in favor of the industrial captains with whom he has had close contact in the production of war materials, he is not alone in this feeling. Countless civilian political leaders share the same bias. Again, the professional soldier who is actually elected to the presidency offers no more threat of Caesarism than does a civilian in the post. (As a matter of fact, the one trait common to most generals in the White House has been their weakness. They placed a halter around their necks and a bit in their mouths, while they turned the reins over to congressional leaders. They would do far better if they viewed themselves not as a chief of staff but as a commander in chief.) To continue: The professional might offer it as his opinion that certain military projects should be undertaken to achieve such and such diplomatic and political objectives. On the basis of trust previously won, the nation might ratify the proposal and suffer acutely in the sequel. But disasters of a similar character can be initiated by a civilian in the White House. Nor is there any clear proof that a professional soldier in the White House would by nature be more autocratic than a civilian. From ancient to modern times, despotisms have been directed as often by civilians as by warriors.[3]

What should give us concern is not a professional soldier in the nation's chief office. Mussolini, Hitler and Stalin were not the products of military academies. But as civilians they could not have attained or maintained their dictatorships without the support of the military. And it is this fact—the use of indiscriminate and unjust force of any kind—that should alert our watchfulness. Whether the chief executive is drawn from civilian or military ranks, other talents being equal, is unimportant.

9. *The small-town talent.* As the perfectors of a mass production system which other peoples try to imitate—even at the point of a bayonet—Americans might be expected to assign to workers and to urban life generally a place of central importance. The statistics seem favorable. The 1950

---

[3] Sparta, the prototype of a garrison state based on a military brotherhood, was ruled for more than four centuries by a handful of civilians called the Ephors. Elected annually from the body of citizens, and served by a secret police, they could put anyone to death, including kings and regents. The Council of Ten in Venice, one of the more spectacular tyrannies of the Renaissance, was composed of merchant princes who made and broke generals and admirals.

census showed an urban labor force of 40,485,000 as against a combined rural farm and non-farm labor force of 19,000,-000. Also, the same census showed that only fifteen per cent of our population now live on farms, while eighty-five per cent live in towns and cities; and of these last, more than 80,000,000 live in metropolitan districts of 130,000 or more people. Yet here is one area where nostalgias are infinitely more powerful than the rule of majorities based on statistics.

There is a feeling that cities—and big ones in particular— are somehow un-American; that what goes on in them imperils all that is sacred to the American spirit. The roots of this prejudice lie deep in the early statements of Jeffersonian democracy. It was kept alive by the native-born's reaction to the influx of immigrants who, when free lands were no longer available, tended to cling to the big cities where they could find work in factories. Distrust of the alien, moreover, was compounded by his efforts to better his lot by joint action. Somehow, that appeared to imperil the existing order.

The identity between the rural and the respectable shows up in many ways. The urban dweller is often among the first to say that big cities are un-American. And indeed, the great ambition of first-generation Americans bent on assimilation is to move to the suburbs, and there join a vacuous mummery which is the next-door neighbor to farm life. Equally revealing of the union between the rural and the respectable is the use of rural images in our language. Log cabins are virtually meaningless to most Americans. Yet we still use this rustic image when we speak of the broad prospects open to a young man of ambition and talent. A tenement building, the urban counterpart of a log cabin, has far greater meaning in our life experience. Yet popular speech does not say

that "any boy born in a tenement can be a President." Tene-
ments smack too much of alien and "foreign ideas."

Even the happier aspects of urban life get scant mention in
political talk. In recent years, for example, a charming book
was written on *Country Life in America as Lived by Ten
Presidents of the United States.* But no one has written on
Big-city Life in America as Lived by Ten Presidents. In fact,
it was not until Chester Arthur succeeded to the presidency
that we had a big-city man in the White House (he was
born in Fairfield, Vermont). As the New York *Tribune* com-
mented:

> In Arthur we have a new type of man in the White House.
> There have been Presidents of all kinds. We have had stately
> Virginia gentlemen of the old school, and self-made men from
> the West. We have had soldiers of several varieties—the rough
> and honest and despotic soldier, the simple and docile soldier.
> We have had rural statesmen who were born to country seats
> and died upon them, after bestowing solemn political auto-
> biographies upon . . . the country. We have had one or two
> Presidents who grew up amid the healthful poverty of the fron-
> tier . . . and who in all their upward progress through the
> world never wore off their simplicity. But the "city man," the
> metropolitan gentleman, the member of clubs—the type that is
> represented by the well-bred and well-dressed New Yorker—the
> quiet man who wears a scarf and a pin and prefers a sack coat to
> the long-tailed frock coat that pervades politics, and a derby hat
> to the slouch hat that seemed to be regarded in various parts of
> this union as something no statesman should be without—this is
> a novel species of President.

It is still a novel species. In the first half of the twentieth
century, we've had no President except for William Howard
Taft who was conspicuously identified with big-city life.

Though they have come from states with a broad industrial and commercial base, as well as an agricultural one, all have been personally identified with the small town or the rural countryside. The place names were Oyster Bay and Hyde Park, New York, for the two Roosevelts; Staunton, Virginia, and Princeton, New Jersey, for Wilson; Corsica and Marion, Ohio, for Harding; Plymouth, Vermont, and Northampton, Massachusetts, for Coolidge; West Branch, Iowa, and Indian Territory for Herbert Hoover; Independence, Missouri, for Truman; and now, Abilene, Kansas, for Eisenhower. Even defeated candidates who have spent most of their adult life in great metropolitan centers have gone to some pains to re-establish their connections with the small towns where they spent their youth, whether in Rushville, Indiana; Otsego, Michigan; or Bloomington, Illinois, in the respective cases of Willkie, Dewey and Stevenson.

Identity with the small town and the rural district, then, is another talent looked for in a President—though John Adams failed to mention it in his description of the natural aristocrat. The bias in its favor serves in its own way as a constitutional check on the tyranny of the big city. Unfortunately, it is also used to justify the obstructive work of a tyrannical rural minority. These men and women are dependent on the products of mass-production industry. They have introduced the factory system into their own midst, and indeed would perish without it. Yet they advance the bombastic contention that city life is based wholly on a worship of "materialism," while rural life is rooted firmly in the virtues of the human spirit. As this preposterous view serves the further claim that those who live close to the soil are "better Americans," it has provided a moral armament for a strategically placed rural minority to block measures the urban majority needs for its survival; needs that in no way threaten the legitimate interests of the minority who live in the countryside.

10. *The family origins talent.* Here is one trait that coincides with John Adams' description of the natural aristocrat. While four presidents were of log cabin birth, four American families alone produced eight presidents, or one fourth of our total. These were John Adams and his son John Quincy; James Madison and Zachary Taylor, who had grandparents in common; William Henry Harrison and his grandson Benjamin; and the two Roosevelts. Six additional Presidents were born into families of wealth and influence. George Washington was one of these. So was Thomas Jefferson, who not only inherited a large estate from his father, but on his mother's side was related to the Randolphs, the bluest of Virginia's blue bloods. James Monroe was another President born to the manner. John Tyler, who came from a long line of Virginia leaders, had a state governor for his father. So did Franklin Pierce, whose father had been governor of New Hampshire. The father of William Howard Taft was a Secretary of War and Attorney General in the Grant Cabinet; in the Arthur administration, he served as American minister to Austria and Russia.

In addition to these fourteen Presidents, born into what might be considered "upper-class families," thirteen came from middle-class groups. One of these was Andrew Jackson, who though born after his father's death was by no means penniless. His early years were spent in the home of his uncle, James Crawford, a man of means by frontier standards. Moreover, through his mother, Elizabeth Hutchinson, he was related to leading families in North Carolina, clustered around four other Hutchinson girls who had left North Ireland with the frank aim of finding husbands in America. Rutherford B. Hayes, also born after his father's death, was reared in relative comfort by his uncle Sardis Birchard who sent his nephew to the best institutions of higher learning in America.

Herbert Hoover, after the death of his father, a blacksmith, was also reared by an uncle. A parsonage was the cradle of Chester Arthur, son of an Episcopalian minister, as it was for Grover Cleveland and Woodrow Wilson, both sons of Presbyterian ministers. Martin Van Buren's father was no howling success as a farmer or tavern owner, but neither was he a primitive frontiersman. James K. Polk's father was a farmer and surveyor, the latter profession carrying with it considerable prestige in a land-conscious community. Ulysses S. Grant's father did not make the county ring with his name, but in his dual work as a farmer and tanner he was still a cut above the unwashed masses. William McKinley's father was an ironmonger; Warren G. Harding's, a country doctor; Calvin Coolidge's a storekeeper; Harry Truman's a farmer, livestock dealer, trader, speculator and enthusiast who was ready to fight in defense of any principle, whether it was his own good name, that of his children or of Democrats generally. Though General Eisenhower's father did a varied assortment of work to feed his family, he probably belongs with this group.

Presidents who came from the lowest strata were Millard Fillmore, James Buchanan, Abraham Lincoln, James Garfield and Andrew Johnson. The first four were actually born in log cabins; Johnson is our only President born of a "proletarian." His father was a porter at an inn and sometimes served as a church sexton.

This handful, compared to the number of middle- and upper-class Presidents strongly suggests that our choice is weighted in favor of men who had early advantages based on parental wealth, education, social or political influence. Though all were subjected to exacting tests before they reached the summit, they apparently owed much to the extra push they gained from the accident of their origins. Obviously, the question of where the ruler comes from, while important, is secondary to the question of whether he is fit to rule, in whose name he rules, and how he rules. If our aim is the justice of a whole society, it makes no more sense to give a man the presidency (or any lesser office) simply because he was born either in humble or comfortable circumstances, than it is to deny him the post on those grounds.

A contrary view would necessarily assume that men born in the same social strata turn in the same sort of political performance. Yet the history of the presidency shows no such pattern. As an "economic man," Millard Fillmore should have been another Lincoln. His youth was marred by hardship and suffering which equaled if they did not exceed those Lincoln knew. Yet Fillmore emerged as an elegant gentleman, given to perfumed baths, a sybarite in all his tastes, Janus-like in his political views, and a hard infighter for the patronage with which he hoped to crush the antislavery wing of the Whig Party in New York. Fillmore often spoke of the time he wanted to aim an axe at the head of the swindling clothmaker to whom he was apprenticed as a boy. He would say that his youthful struggles made him

[223]

"feel for the weak and unprotected, and hate the insolent tyrant in every station in life." But two of the tyrants he singled out for special attention were Andrew Jackson and Abraham Lincoln.

In contrast, Presidents like Jefferson and the two Roosevelts—each the American counterpart of a European aristocrat—were "traitors" to their class. Each spoke for those who lived on the ragged edge. Each tried to strengthen republican institutions by making them work in the interest of all classes. In this, they were one with Lincoln, born at the other end of the social scale. Indeed, if there is any recurrent political pattern, it is that the troubled conscience of men who inherit wealth often makes them far more generous and resilient in their social attitudes than the self-made man with his purse-proud "good conscience."

11. *The legal talent.* Along the route of their formative years, almost all our Presidents acquired what we would now regard as a classical education. Twenty-four acquired it at colleges and universities. The others acquired it through programs of self-instruction. This kind of education does not by itself guarantee virtue. Still, a knowledge of what humanity has said, experienced and argued about for five thousand years does exert a sobering influence on the mind. It may not tell a man what he ought to do in a specific case. But the sense of the past at least drops a strong hint about what he should *not* do.

Related to this is another talent unmentioned by John Adams. Twenty-three of our Presidents at some stage of their career came under the intellectual discipline of the common law, with its strong accents on precedent and on formal order within which change takes place. Eight of the remaining ten Presidents were trained in a branch of science. It was mathematics and surveying for Washington; theology for Madison; medicine and military tactics for William Henry Harrison; military tactics for Taylor, Grant and Eisenhower; education and theology for Garfield; and engineering for Hoover. Harding received university training in the liberal arts, and thereafter went into the newspaper profession. Johnson alone was trained in a trade and moved directly from it into politics.

Among the Presidents who made their living from the law, not one limited his briefs to a special clientele. The clients were as varied as the community itself. Lawyer-candidates who violated this canon have suffered a loss of political support. In the 1924 campaign, John W. Davis, the Democratic candidate, was heavily attacked because he was an attorney for J. P. Morgan and Company, the New York Telephone Company and the New York Rubber Exchange. His previous record as a labor lawyer for coal miners and glass workers, as a co-author of the Clayton Anti-Trust Act, as a United States Solicitor-General, and as our Ambassador to England, was lost to sight. Similarly, as the Republican candidate in 1940, Wendell Willkie could not overcome the handicaps of his law practice. He was called by the uncharitable "a simple barefoot Wall Street lawyer." The more charitable called him, "the Abe Lincoln of Wall Street." When he answered that his office was not on Wall Street, but on Pine Street one block away, some felt that the streets were still too close for comfort. As later events proved, this estimate of Willkie was unfair. But in 1940 as in 1924, it was feared that any man who appeared as a special pleader for a special interest would continue to do that in the presidency.

[225]

12. *The political talent.* If we are completely dominated
by the values of the business community, as many people
have charged, somewhere along the line we should have
produced a businessman President, or at least one whose
main training had been in business. Nothing of the sort has
yet occurred. Despite the recurrent cry for "business in government" and against "government in business," our Presidents have always been chosen from among men who
showed some talent for "government in government." Nine
had previously served as Vice President; five as Secretary of
State; three as Secretary of War; one as Secretary of Commerce; two as Assistant Secretary of the Navy. In addition,
their number includes twelve generals; ten Senators, fourteen governors; twelve who had served in the House of
Representatives; seven ambassadors, twelve state legislators,
and eight who had served in municipal administrations.
Except for Wendell Willkie, who never held a public post,
all our major defeated candidates have represented an
equally wide range of political experience.

The absence of a businessman President can be explained
in several ways. By the nature of his work and his concern
with immediate economic rewards, the businessman tends to
exclude himself from direct participation in political contests. More often he chooses to act indirectly from behind
the scenes, or to seek appointive jobs where the people as a
whole do not pass on his fitness. If he eventually decides to
seek office in an election, he is frequently pitted against
rivals long schooled in the ways of political agitation. Thus
he is generally killed off before he reaches the way station in
which his qualifications for the presidency can be judged.
Often the businessman kills himself off by his tendency to

view the problems of government solely in terms of administrative efficiency. He talks at length about getting one hundred cents' worth for every dollar spent. But he says little about who is to provide the one hundred cents, on what social policy it is to be spent, who is to spend it and when it is to be spent. If he wins an election, his silence on these questions can soon prove his undoing. The mass puts him down as a "blue-nose reformer," preferring in his place someone who may blink at administrative irregularities but who also shows some disposition to meet all kinds of human needs.

The rules and mores he mastered in his private enterprise, moreover, are virtually useless in the top reaches of the government. Whether he was elected or appointed to office he is not free to buy and sell, or to hire and fire. What he does is ruled by the Congress. It is interpreted by the Courts. It is guided by the President in the light of political exigencies. Meanwhile, he is thrown in with a group of men who, for the most part, are strangers to him. He may hire a few people and discharge a few others. But he can neither engage nor "lay off" the many thousands in a department or agency. They are there by the permission of Congress, and they are protected by the Civil Service Commission. Nor does the businessman in government deal solely in measurable impersonal things. He deals in human beings, in their constantly changing values and aspirations, registered in votes. He has no profit index to judge his competence by. Whether he is competent or incompetent, he can be expelled in the first case and extolled in the second, depending on the tone of political forces in collision. He can draw flawless blueprints of how things should work. But he has none of the coercive instruments he used to make the same sort of plans work in his business. To survive in government, the businessman must also be an artist. A money-making gift is no more a substitute for the art of political combination based on consent than politics is a substitute for religion, or religion for politics. Each has a different method and a different object of action.

It is too early to predict the course of General Eisenhower's businesslike administration. Though his Cabinet was formed according to the laws of selection discussed in a former place, by his appointments of conspicuous businessmen the whole of big business now stands protected only by an eggshell defense. Its fate is in the hands of its top representatives in the Eisenhower entourage. This is a risky situation, particularly since it comes after a persistent twenty-year demand to restore the authority of business in public affairs to its pre-depression status. No other element in the economic community during the twentieth century has ever placed or been able to place itself in so exposed a position. Consciously or not, labor and agriculture have always managed to shape up some sort of defense in depth so that if its representatives, identified with one political faction, failed in their communal work, the interest as a whole could still gain a hearing through representatives identified with an alternative faction. Business, however, has currently deployed its full strength on a single distinct line in a curious disregard for the subtle checks and balances that make for political survival.

If its representatives manage to help maintain our prosperity, to end the Korean War with honor, and to lift the danger of a general war, then the prestige of business as a whole may rise to new heights. If they fail, business as a whole may suffer a bankruptcy of public trust, a reaction unwarranted by nature of the enormously complex problems we face, but invited by the indiscreet boasts of omniscience voiced in leading business circles.

It is still possible that a businessman President may emerge at a future date. As the prestige that goes with political authority tends to increase, more businessmen may enter public life at an earlier age, to compete for the intermediate posts from which Presidents are chosen. Moreover, a continuing preoccupation with national defense in the last thirteen years has drawn into government a flow of businessmen to help direct many aspects of our military and foreign policy. Great numbers of them flounder in the unfamiliar surroundings and are spared disaster only by the timely intervention of bright young lawyers or old file clerks. But the best of them who survive the "in-training program" gain a broad view of what government is all about. They also gain an aptitude for making political sense of the sort that can catch the national ear. These men, in fact, may be the salvation of the Eisenhower administration.

It will probably be more difficult for a labor leader to win the presidency. While labor has made great advances in the past two decades, the word "labor" still means "crisis" to many millions of Americans. In its organized state, it has not yet been fully accepted as a permanent and natural part of everyday life. In actual size, labor is the largest single economic group in the land. Yet labor by itself could not elect a President even if its present divided strength were united. It can achieve its objectives only in fraternal alliance with farmers and with our so-called middle-class groups. This

[229]

was true even in England, whose Labour Party represents a broad cross-section of the population. It is doubly true in America, where labor suffers the added handicap of being regarded in some quarters as a suspicious by-product of organized foreigners in big cities.

Still, our labor unions—which represent only a minority of the total labor force—have a way of acquiring the outer signs of respectability. The time span needed to achieve this appears to be a little over a generation. In the latter decades of the nineteenth century, the element most feared in our society was the railroad worker. He was commonly identified with the events of the Paris Commune of 1871; in some places, railroad workers were arrested for sedition on the ground that they sang the "Marseillaise." But now our Railroad Brotherhoods seem like mild, elderly, highly respectable gentlemen whose support is eagerly sought by political leaders of all persuasions. The American Federation of Labor underwent the same experiences. The Congress of Industrial Organization, as the most recent arrival on the scene, naturally invited a repetition of the old pattern. But in the past fifteen years, the violent outcry that the CIO was a nest of Communists has gradually subsided, and it has made considerable progress toward being accepted as an American institution.

As our labor organizations mature, they often produce a top leadership identical with the management of some of our great corporations. The leadership is often bureaucratic, undemocratic, rigid in its attitudes, and a practitioner of nepotism on a broad scale. In some cases, it degenerates into power based on brute force. But maturity has produced another type of labor leader who is the counterpart of the type of enlightened businessman now represented in the Committee for Economic Development.

It was sufficient in the old days if the leader of a union showed courage in "fighting the bosses"; if he could stand a few beatings now and then; if he beat up a few other people now and then; and if he showed a talent for social agitation. But the labor leader of today has to have opinions about the state of the nation, not merely the state of his union. He is called before the Congress to testify on a wide range of public issues which have no direct connection with higher wages and shorter hours. He has to be an inventor in the realm of public policy, just as he has to run a union whose business activities cover a range of things undreamed of a few decades ago. He surrounds himself with a staff of assistants drawn not from the working ranks, but from the universities and professions. Some of these recruits are put in positions from which they can in time succeed to the presidency of the unions without an apprenticeship at the work bench.

It is unlikely, however, that the new-style labor leader could gain the American presidency in an epoch of full employment. Labor itself would see no urgent need to change a political leadership that presides over the current output of bounties. But if the economy goes into a sharp decline, then, with the sympathetic assistance of hard-pressed farmers and segments of our middle class, labor might produce its first President.

To summarize the whole of the foregoing: The natural aristocracy from which our Presidents are chosen is the residue of what is left when we subtract (1) all females from the total population, (2) all males who do not fall into the age group of 35 to 67 years, (3) all who were not born as American citizens, (4) all whose ethnic strain is not compatible with that of the English alliance, (5) all men who are ill, (6) all who have experienced spectacular marital difficulties, (7) all colored peoples, (8) all non-Protestants (9) all Southerners, (10) all who come from small states, (11) all who have been conspicuously identified with big-city life, (12) all whose family origins cause unease to our middle and upper classes, (13) all lawyers conspicuously identified with a specialized clientele, (14) all individuals conspicuously identified with a special segment of the economic community, (15) all without some experience in major offices of government, whether at the international, national, or state and local level. If these rules of exclusion are applied to the entire population—with millions lopped off at each turn—the minority that can pass all these tests at any one time is probably in the neighborhood of one hundred men.

Taken as a whole, the results of our selection system seem to fall somewhere between the opposite views of John Adams and Thomas Jefferson. None of the auxiliary grounds of distinction—birth, wealth, beauty, strength, marriage, graceful attitudes and motions, eloquence, gait, air, complexion or good fellowship—have by themselves brought the presidency to any man. But neither has the selection system pushed past the barriers of added "talents," cast up by our majorities, to give a pure reward of the presidency to men conspicuous for their learning and genius. In this special sense, there are inherent limitations on the election of great men to that office. Yet the broad implications of the latter view can be challenged on grounds examined in a different connection.

The laws of natural selection

First, even if the selection system brushed aside all artificial talents and elevated the "real good and the wise," there is no proof that men of this sort would make superior presidents. Second, the greatness of the great Presidents we have known does not lie in what they could have done if they were philosopher kings with unlimited power. It lies in the way they used both their will and their imaginative faculties within the framework of limited government to secure approval for social projects. And there is no system on earth that can determine in advance whether the intellectually good and the wise will prove equal to this essentially artistic sort of performance. The proof comes only when the materials of the presidency are placed in a man's hands.

This perilous relationship between the leader and the led in a free society was forcefully stated in America as far back as 1624. In that year, John Winthrop, the deputy governor of the Massachusetts Bay Colony, joined his fellow magistrates in interfering in the local election of a militia officer. When a war of words threatening the peace of the settlement presently broke out, the magistrates bound over some of the objectors to the next court and summoned still others to appear before it. But the dissidents refused to be cowed. The magistrates found themselves accused of exceeding their authority; and as the chief among them, Winthrop was impeached. When he was eventually acquitted after three months of wrangling, he proceeded to draw this moral for the courthouse crowd:

I entreat you to consider that, when you choose magistrates, you take them from among yourselves, men subject to like passions as you are. Therefore, when you see infirmities in us, you should reflect upon your own, and that would make you bear the

[233]

more with us, and not be severe censurers of the failings of your magistrates, when you have continual experience of the like infirmities in yourselves and others. We count him a good servant who breaks not his covenant. The covenant between you and us is the oath you have taken of us, which is to this purpose: that we shall govern you and judge your causes by the rules of God's laws and your own, according to our best skill. When you agree with a workman to build you a ship or house, etc., he undertakes as well for his skill as for his faithfulness, for it is his profession, and you pay him for both. But when you call one to be a magistrate, he doth not profess nor undertake to have sufficient skill for office, nor can you furnish him with gifts, etc., therefore you must run the hazard of his skill and ability. But if he fail in faithfulness, which by his oath he is bound unto, that he must answer for. If it fall out that the case be clear to common apprehension, and the rule clear also, if he transgress here, the error is not in the skill, but in the evil of the will: it must be required of him. But if the case be doubtful, or the rule doubtful, to men of such understanding and parts as your magistrates are, if your magistrates should err here, yourselves must bear it.

The same moral applies to the presidency. When we choose a President, we constantly run the risk that his skill and ability will not be adequate to the work that falls to him. For this reason we have tried to form clear and fixed guide lines in the character of our Constitution and laws. If he willfully ignores them, we have a clear judge of his transgression. But the guide lines are often indistinct and the President may err, though he is faithful to his oath. The price of the error nevertheless falls upon us. The Constitution and the laws provide a partial limitation on the extent of the damage he can do before the whole apparatus of the government comes to the popular rescue. But the essential limitation on the range of harm lies in the operation of our

The laws of natural selection

system of presidential selection. For though it raises artificial bars against learning and genius, its compensating tendency is this. It has served the cause of limited government by thus far barring the presidency to any of God's angry men.

Our Presidents, in the main, were all men of hope, even when the hope did not pay off very well in their formative years. They may have felt wronged by fate, disappointed in the men they trusted, basely maligned by their opponents. They may have felt that part of the nation was getting too much, and part not enough. But there were no pathological haters among them who were driven in a search for inner peace by a compulsion to lay waste to all about them. In their own lives they had seen the country distribute its rewards so widely that they could not claim for themselves—despite any intermediate defeats—that they had been cheated. Nor could they excite a sense of injustice among the people to support a policy of desperation; their own careers could be turned against them to prove that patience paid off. To a man, all affirmed that society was essentially good. With some changes here and there, it could be even better.

We take them from among ourselves, men of like passions as we are. This is the essential constitutional point. There have always been angry and bitter men in our midst. But they have never commanded an audience that could form a political majority across the nation. Right or wrong, a majority of our people have continued to feel that the game was not too strongly rigged against them; that if things were tough right now, they would not always be that way; that with a combination of hard work and a little luck and a fair-minded leader at the top, things would get better. It is this belief that has produced Presidents whose supreme talent is a heroic hope for the future, based on a Christian sense of fraternity. And many of our Presidents, in turn, have made important contributions to keeping that hope alive in a historical epoch when other people have raised an elite whose talent is bitterness and bestiality. In the future, as in the past, each time we pick a President, it might be well to remember that we also pass judgment on the character of our own passions.

III

THE OFFICE

11

Manager of social justice and prosperity

IIIIIIIIIIIᴑIIIIIIIIIIIᴑIIIIIIIIIIIᴑIIIIIIIIIIIᴑIIIIIIIIIIIᴑIIIIIIIIIIIᴑIIIIIIIIIIIᴑIIIIIIIIIIᴐ

The constitutional division between the political and the economic order – Industrialization erases the dividing line – Question of who was to do the regulating in the public interest – The rise of the independent regulatory agencies – Problems they create for the President – Proposed solutions – The emergence of the President as the chief engineer for general and lasting prosperity – Reflected in Cabinet expansions – Our consequent political organization along mixed federalist and syndicalist lines – The strain on the President that results – Yet the Employment Act of 1945 holds him responsible for social justice and for prosperity – The rise of the President as the chief insurance agent and banker – Political consequences of use of public credit – Restoration of dividing line between political and economic order lies with the free enterprise system itself – Suggested use of new form of Congressional veto to keep executive discretionary power in check.

The history of the Constitutional Convention has been written largely in terms of its conflicts. We hear of the disputes about monarchy and aristocracy, about republics and democracies, about the need for order and the need for liberty, about strong central governments and strong states.

[239]

But there were agreements, ever present, which softly shaped the final synthesis. The delegates were not prepared to lodge the rule of society in public opinion alone. They knew that opinion was a quick and volatile thing. What it needed was a frame of law, to steady it until the voice of an afterthought was heard. At the same time, the delegates were limitists in their view of the controlling organ. Not one of them said that unjust force was the core of politics, or that the road to an eternal life could be decreed by an absolute state. As constitutionalists, all agreed not only that secular power should be bound by law, but that the law itself should stop short of all matters that bore on the link between a man and his God.

In three more particulars, these men were far wiser than the one-eyed children of light who came after them. The language of the Declaration of Independence said in effect that all power tends to corrupt, while absolute power tends to corrupt absolutely. But their life under the Articles of Confederation had brought home to them a converse truth. It was that a lack of power also tends to corrupt, while an absolute lack tends to corrupt absolutely. Moreover, in observing the conduct of state legislatures, they learned that power is not abused solely by single persons. Committees or a majority could be as despotic as the conventional one-man tyrant. "Give all power to the many, they will oppress the few," Alexander Hamilton warned the Convention. "Give all power to the few, they will oppress the many. Both therefore ought to have power that each may defend itself against the other." Finally, the delegates did not confine their concept of power to its political (in this sense, lawmaking) aspect. They saw it as a family affair. Its diverse members—political, economic, religious, military and social—had to be so arranged that no one could override the others.

Their views were sealed inside the Constitution. By indirection, the delegates set religious power aside on a plane of its own. Then they hemmed in the scope of social power by making all offices elective or appointive instead of hereditary; by prohibiting any grant of a title of nobility by the United States; by prohibiting any office holder from accepting gifts and grants of any sort from a foreign power except by the consent of the Congress; and by an explicit directive to the Federal government to guarantee a republican form of government in each state of the Union.

At the same time, the delegates distributed political and military power *in space* between the Federal and the state governments. In the Federal organ, they sought the mean between too much and too little power by creating what appeared to be a single Executive, a plural Legislature and a plural Judiciary. Moreover, they bound one to the other as the separate fingers of a single hand. Thus the Executive intruded on the legislature by recommending bills to the Congress and by signing or vetoing measures it enacted. The Congress shared in the executive process by organizing executive departments; by auditing, approving and paying their expenses; in the case of the Senate, by approving or rejecting all executive appointments to the major posts in the civil service and all military and diplomatic officers, by approving or rejecting treaties; and in every executive act originating in the exercise of the legislative rights—such as the collection of taxes, the raising of armies, the declaration of war—granted to the Congress by Section 8, Article I, of the Constitution. Finally, the President and the Congress

shared in the judicial process through the appointment and
confirmation of judges, while the Judiciary shared the work
of the other branches in the special sense that it reviewed all
cases and controversies arising from their acts.

The most meaningful detail in this formula for a balanced
power arrangement lay outside the Constitution. Except in
its references to taxes, the public credit, the regulation of
foreign and interstate commerce, the regulation of weights
and measures, and the coinage of money, the Constitution
did not specify how economic power was to be distributed.
But this crucial omission was no oversight. Paradoxically,
the omission expressed what the delegates believed to be a
main support for the interior balance of the Constitution
proper. Whether they wanted the future to be ruled by commercial and industrial interests or by small farmers, they all
agreed that the private person and not the state was to
organize production and distribution.

For the common lesson learned under the mercantile
system had been this: When the political and the economic
order were indivisible; when the government through royal
monopolies, licenses and sumptuary legislation assumed the
economic function, the individual lay open to all the other
arbitrary pressures of government. He could be his own law-
giver in an organic sense only when he was his own bread-
giver. The conclusion necessarily followed that a Constitution under which people were to make their own laws had
to find its cornerstone support in men who could use their
own wits and will to organize the production and distribution of bread, free of any political prescriptions.

The Civil War wrote a bloody finale to this outlook as it
applied to a predominantly agrarian society. By force of

arms, it was decided that the political order centered in the Federal government could intrude on the economic order located in the states to exclude human lives from the definition of private property, and to declare illegal any contracts which dealt with the buying, selling and use of involuntary human labor.

Toward the end of the nineteenth century, a speed-up in industrialization revived this old conflict about Federal-state relations; it also pushed to the fore the friction-laden issue of the proper scope of executive power within the Federal system. Both disputes originated in a single fact. In the America of that day, the organization of production and distribution had ceased to be an individual project, aimed for a local market. It had become a giant concert of hands, serving a national and international market through complicated communications.

In the flashing impact of this change, it was noticed that a constitutional formula that protected the individual from strong-arm government did not shield him from strong-arm concentrations of private economic force. It was also noticed that the well-being of any man depended not on the wisdom he showed as an individual producer or consumer, but on the interaction of all forces at work in the economic community. From these and kindred discoveries, a concept of the "public interest" presently arose as a sort of holy, if vague ghost. Dressed in moral robes, it proceeded to intrude on the old dividing lines between public and private spheres of activity and to speak out in the language of regulation, permission and prohibition in the economic order. The inevitable sequel was that it also intruded on the dividing lines between the Executive, the Congress and the Judiciary.

The point of penetration was the question of who was to do the regulating. Economic policy could be defined in broad terms by the Congress. But the Congress could not foresee all contingencies. Nor could it meet to legislate for every case arising under its broad rules. Someone, somewhere, had to be entrusted not only with police powers, but also with judicial and legislative powers adequate to the new circumstances. It made good sense to locate these functions in a high officer who could answer to the Courts in his legal character, and to the Congress and the people in his political character. But if the officer were the President, he would tend to take on the traits of a parliament and a judge, in a way not contemplated by the Founders. Conversely, if the regulatory agent were someone other than the President, to the extent that he acted as an executive, he would imperil the constitutional concept of executive power centered in the presidency.

The historical record shows a range of hit and miss answers to this enormously complex problem. In particular cases, the answer simply registered a congressional attitude toward an incumbent President, or toward the head of a particular executive arm and the character of his work; or the degree of permanence Congress wished to give to a regulatory function; or the attitude of the President to his own principal aides.

The precedent for placing regulatory functions outside the presidency dates from the Civil Service Commission created in 1883 on the wave of a popular reaction to Garfield's assassination by a disappointed office seeker. In the climate of the hour, it was feared that if the commission were under the President, the pressures of office seekers and spoilsmen

Manager of social justice and prosperity

would be concentrated all the more strongly on his person. Besides, though the presidency was then almost a century old, there was no Office of the President, as distinct from a Cabinet. (Nor was any such office formed until 1939.) In the absence of a visual image of a President served by a congressionally authorized personal staff, the Congress had nothing to remind it that the commission by its nature *was* a staff agency; that it existed to serve all departments through the person of the President; that the rules it enforced could be issued only by him—or revoked by him through a stroke of his pen.

Consequently, the commission was made independent of the executive power of the President, a step that cleared the ground for a similar and more important move six years later. In 1889, the Interstate Commerce Commission, after a two-year residence in the Department of Interior, was sent into the world on an independent career. The pattern was repeated when the Federal Reserve Board was created in 1913, and a year later, the Federal Trade Commission. In more recent years, a combination of factors such as wars, technical developments, depressions and changing social attitudes led to a widening number of independent regulatory creations. They included the United States Maritime Commission, the Federal Communications Commission, the Securities and Exchange Commission, the Federal Power Commission, the Civil Aeronautics Board, and the National Labor Relations Board. As their titles suggest, of the total, three regulate carriers; two regulate finance; two regulate utilities; and two regulate practices in special fields which affect industry generally. In what they police and in what they promote, they intrude directly on private activities such

as labor; transportation whether by rail, truck, pipeline, ship
or airplane; credit and banking; securities both on and off
the stock exchange; trade practices; communications including radio, television, telegraph and telephone; the development, sale and distribution of electric power, together with
the financing of these and other enterprises.

In constitutional terms, the net effect of the foregoing was
a profound change in the traditional aspect of executive
power as it had been exercised for more than a century. The
President and the Executive were no longer mutually in-
clusive, though the people conceived of them as identical. In
point of fact, three magnets of executive power had come
into being. One continued to be centered in the presidency.
The second, represented by some of the regulatory agencies,
adhered to the Congress; while the third, represented by
still other regulatory agencies, adhered to the President and
the Congress simultaneously. Meanwhile, however, strong
and authoritative voices were raised—and are still being
raised—to question the constitutionality of any allocation of
executive functions to parties other than the President. Thus
in his testimony before a congressional committee which
considered the reorganization proposals bearing his name,
former President Herbert Hoover, who could not be suspected of a bias toward "executive aggrandizement of
power," was among those who spoke in the fashion just mentioned. Yet the case was not clear.

To the extent that there was an explicit constitutional
theory behind these independent creations, it seemed to rest
on three main assertions. The first was that the President's
executive power was not the *only* executive power known to
the Constitution. Thus, when the Constitution declared that

Manager of social justice and prosperity

"The executive Power shall be vested in a President of the United States," what it designated was simply an office with powers enumerated in the further passages of Article II. And even some of those enumerated powers were shared in by the legislature. The second assertion was in the form of an addition to the phrase that the President shall "take Care that the Laws be faithfully executed." The addition was, "executed by *others.*" The third assertion also was in the form of an addition. In this case, it was the italicized part of the proposition that the Congress can "make all Laws which shall be necessary and proper for carrying into Execution"— *its own constitutional powers.*

To sum up: In the exercise of its own powers, the Congress could create its own executive arms apart from the presidency. When it did this from within the scope of its granted constitutional rights, far from violating the Constitution's description of executive power, the Congress merely registered a disinclination to let the increased use of its own powers serve as a source for an enlargement of presidential authority.

The loose way the Constitution identified executive power makes it possible for one to agree or disagree with this conclusion. And, from the same cause, there is a strong hint that the Founders deliberately invited a continuous argument on the subject, with the solution in any particular case entrusted to the exigencies of the hour. Where the independent regulatory agencies are involved, however, it is worth noting that even Herbert Hoover, in his proposals for reform, subordinated the constitutional issue to the practical administrative and political difficulties these agencies create for the President, if not the whole governmental order. In this, his approach duplicated that of the 1937 President's Committee on Administrative Management, though his specific remedies were far less sweeping than those endorsed by the 1937 committee.

The findings and recommendations of this body can be briefly reconstructed as follows: In the way some of the independent agencies interpreted their governing laws within the four corners of what was permissible, they became the captives or the special pleaders of the forces they were meant to regulate. Others, though bi-partisan in composition to insure their independence, surrendered their freedom of decision not to the Congress as a whole, but to its special committees or even to single individuals on the committees. Still others branched into purely executive functions which were wholly divorced from any regulatory functions, while some agencies were so wholly absorbed with the details of regulation that they had no time to consider the larger question of planning their public policies. Then, too, within the agencies themselves, there often was no center of administrative responsibility. Authority was either divided to an extreme degree, or was exercised in a willy-nilly fashion over a rudderless staff.

The Congress, meanwhile, considered these bodies to be quasi-legislative. The courts considered them to be quasi-judicial. But when the two quasis were summed up, the frequent result was that they acted as units of power with no real focus of *political* responsibility for what they did. In the after effect, however, the President was blamed for their acts, though he had little or no control over them. He could not compel them to move in concert with the announced and approved policies of the government as a whole, though their activities contributed materially to the success or failure of those policies. Moreover, once he appointed the members with Senate consent, he could not force them to execute the laws in a faithful manner. This power presumably resided in the Congress and the Courts, or at least was shared in by them. But the Congress was too diffuse a body to be accused of guilt for what was done by one of its independent agencies; nor, in any event, was it disposed to point the finger of guilt at its own servants.

The courts were better intentioned. They could and did intervene in questions involving the legal use of administrative judgment. But as long as the legal points were in the clear, whether an agency used its legal power in an imprudent way was not a subject for judicial review. The subject fell in the political forum. Yet here again, the Congress as the responsible parent authority would not suffer itself to be accused of negligence. Blame, wandering about like a displaced person, inevitably settled on the President since it had no other place to go. Conditions of this sort, however, tend to set up their own countervailing forces. Since the President was held politically responsible for acts which lay beyond the reach of his legal arm, the condition invited him to win by "influence" what was not permitted to him in a direct use of his legal power.

What, then, was to be done? The 1937 committee by way of a remedy proposed that the regulatory agencies should be split into two parts according to their judicial and legislative functions on the one hand, and their executive functions on the other, each with a separate head. Both, however, would be located within a traditional department of the Executive, and both heads would be subject to the President's discretionary power of removal. The judicial and legislative parts would continue to function as before without responsibility to any higher administrative authority. The executive part would be directly responsible to the head of the department in which it was located and, through him, to the President. It was claimed that the arrangement would provide a direct and simple way for the President to coordinate all the executive operations of the agencies, short of those which have judicial and legislative traits. Furthermore, by clarifying the lines of authority, it would also clarify the true center of political responsibility for acts executive in nature.

Nothing came of these proposals and the argument was suspended for ten years until 1947 when a Hoover task force brought it to the fore once again. It is beyond the scope of these pages to detail all the findings of the new inquiry. Briefly, however, the task force tempered the sweeping accusations of its predecessor. It claimed that the charges of irresponsibility, of conflicts, of the use of "influence" were overdrawn and, in any event, could not be substantiated except in individual cases. It cautioned against a uniform sort of remedial surgery applicable to all the agencies since each, by nature, differed from all the others. Finally, it asserted that the President, the Congress and the Courts had ample means to exercise a reasonably effective control over the agencies. In sequence, they included the power to appoint and the power to budget; the power to confirm, to investigate, to appropriate and to legislate; and, in the case of the Court, the power to review not only activities bearing on statutory grants of authority, but findings of fact underlying agency policies.

Manager of social justice and prosperity

Though the task force gave a strong endorsement to the existence of agency quasi-legislative and quasi-judicial functions on a plane *outside* the existing departments—contrary to the views of the 1937 committee—it did associate itself with the proposals of the latter body as they bore on purely executive functions. Thus the task force, and eventually the Hoover Commission proper, proposed: (1) that the functions of ship construction and the operation, charter, and sale of ships should be transferred from the Maritime Commission to the Department of Commerce; (2) that equipment inspection, and the functions of the Interstate Commerce Commission relating to safety and car service should be transferred from the Interstate Commerce Commission to the Department of Commerce; (3) that the promulgation of rules relating to the safety of aircraft operation, both commercial and noncommercial, including control operations, be transferred from the Civil Aeronautics Board to the Department of Commerce with a right of appeal to the former body from the enactment of, or the refusal to enact, any particular regulation. Besides these proposals, the Hoover Commission suggested a number of ways in which each agency should be reorganized internally. It also suggested needed changes in the role of the chairman, to make of him a center of authority over the operations of his agency and an effective political link between it and the President.

At the time of this writing, some of these proposals have been enacted into law. Whether they adequately serve the need for a union between power and responsibility in the sphere of these novel governmental growths, time alone will tell. The guess is that they will not; that in the modesty of their reforms, they were drafted with an eye to what the

Congress was prepared to enact, rather than to what the facts of the case demanded. The Hoover Commission of 1947 has not said the last word on the subject, nor, in justice to it, is the last word easily come by.

Thus far in these passages, the emphasis has been on the way the presidency is taxed by the emergence of independent regulatory agencies. This, however, is but one corner of a larger phenomenon now to be considered. It is the emergence of the President as the chief engineer of general and lasting prosperity.

Part of this transformation since Washington's day is reflected in the pattern of Cabinet expansions.

1. The three major departments of the government—Treasury, State and War—which were in being in the first presidency, all shared in forming economic policy or in creating conditions favorable to its support. But the main center of this activity was in the Treasury. In 1790, under Alexander Hamilton, the department consisted of seventy people in Philadelphia and less than a thousand in the field. For an infant country, grasping at stability, their tasks must have been stupendous. They managed a public debt in the neighborhood of $70 million. They collected and disbursed revenues which averaged around $5.7 million. They were parties to the sale of public lands. They paid off pension claims. They purchased army rations. They ran the customs service.

Today, in its structural outlines, the Treasury is not too dissimilar from the Treasury of Washington's administration. The difference is in the intensity of activity within the structure. In June, 1952, the Treasury employed close to 100,000 people. Its Coast Guard covered tens of thousands of miles of navigable waters. Its customs service was represented at every major seaport, international highway, railroad and airport leading into the United States and its overseas possessions. It performed police duties through the Secret Service, and it housed mechanical operations such as the Bureau of Engraving and the United States Mint. It collected $62.1 billion in taxes through the Bureau of Internal Revenue, spent $66.1 billion on expenditures and managed a public debt of $255 billion, or a sum exceeding by one-fourth the total of the private debt in the United States. And finally, the Treasury was part of a web of international monetary and credit organizations. The economic implications of all this need not be spelled out.

2. The Post Office originally was part of the Treasury and remained there from Washington's day until 1829 when it gained independent Cabinet status. In 1792, it consisted of nothing more than Postmaster General Timothy Pickering plus an assistant and one clerk, all working in Pickering's home. Together, they supervised 1,875 miles of post roads and 75 post offices, served by postmasters who ranged from adolescent boys to tavernkeepers. For these, an "obliging disposition" and a capacity to get along with the "mercantile interests" was described by Pickering as a peculiar requirement for the work that was involved. "I mention this," he wrote, "because in detail the business seems piddling; all its emoluments arising from trifles; altho the whole is important. Each trifle demands a *patient attention.*"

For the government year ending in June, 1951, the United States Post Office employed over 500,000 people, making it the second largest department in the Executive. Its business—no piddling affair—was conducted by 41,607 post offices, served by 658,587 miles of post routes, with an inspection system as elaborate as its physical plant. In 1951, it issued over 21 billion ordinary stamps, accounted for $2.17 billion in postal savings, and paid out over $2.1 billion in gross expenditures for a deficit of $.6 million in operating expenses. The significant fact to be drawn from this is that the pattern of postal subsidies to which the President is a party now brings within the range of his economic influence the entire communication industry of railroads, airlines, inland waterway carriers, the mail-order houses, the newspapers, the magazines and the book publishing companies. While he cannot spend funds unless they are authorized by the Congress, as a proponent of legislation, he can either request the subsidies and in this way become an advocate for the industry, or he can veto the expenditure of funds that have actually been authorized.

3. Though there was an Attorney General in Washington's administration, not until 1814 was he made a member of the Cabinet. And not until the close of the nineteenth century did he begin to act as an agent of the President in the economic domain. In Washington's day, the Attorney General was regarded simply as a legal advisor to the President and to other department heads. Moreover, on the early theory that the President was empowered to review the constitutionality of legislative acts, the Attorney General also served as a source of legal information and advice to the Congress. Though he was paid a small salary for his services, he was expected to continue his private practice—an arrangement which led to a classical complaint by Edmund Randolph, the first occupant of the post. "I am a sort of mongrel between the State and the U.S.," he wrote, "called

an officer of some rank under the latter, and yet thrust out to get a livelihood in the former—perhaps in a petty mayor's or country court. I cannot say much on this head without pain, which, could I have foreseen it, would have kept me at home to encounter my pecuniary difficulties there, rather than add to them here."

From this pastoral seed, in June, 1951, the ever-present Justice Department, headed by the Attorney General, employed 31,650 people at a public cost of $313.1 million. It continued its traditional function of briefing the President on his legal powers in all areas, including the economic one. It prepared the legal case in defense of his political acts. Through the Solicitor General, it defended the cause of both the Congress and the Executive in cases before the Supreme Court. Through its marshals and attorneys, spread through all the states, it prosecuted the government's case against offenders of Federal law, including those which touched on economic activities. The work of its Federal Bureau of Investigation covered the whole water front, from the apprehension of criminals and espionage agents to the gathering of information bearing on the loyalty of public employees. Its Bureau of Prisons, Board of Parole and Federal Prison Industries dealt with the affairs in Federal penitentiaries, many of which had a distinct economic cast. Its Immigration and Naturalization service guided the movement of an individual from the time he entered America to his oath of citizenship.

The Courts, as usual, had the final say on what was done in any of these undertakings. But in the interval, the chain of executive command gave the President an option to notice, to harass, to forgive, or to ignore. By these means, he could

extend or withhold the prospects of a livelihood from countless Americans. The Justice Department also contained the
Office of Alien Property, which managed and disposed of a
small empire of wealth seized from enemy powers. It could
not be given away to close friends. But the law of the office
still left open a great and unavoidable region where personal
bias and opinion were free to do their preferential work.
There was an equally significant latitude in the work of the
Anti-Trust Division, committed by law to the preservation of
a free competitive market.

4. Some of the functions of the present Interior Department, established in March, 1848, were performed by the
departments in being during Washington's administration.
But the importance of the Interior Department dates from
the twentieth century discovery that we were mining instead
of cultivating our natural resources. In Washington's time,
Patrick Henry spoke to a deaf national ear when he said that
next to the winners of independence, the greatest patriot
was the man who stopped the most gullies. On the agricultural frontier, with a virginal continent before them, the
early Americans either failed to understand or were indif-
ferent to what happened when they upset the balance of
nature, destroyed wild life, and invited torrential rains to do
their destructive work on the naked earth. Thereafter, with
the coming of the railroad age, and with its flowering after
the Civil War, great areas of the public domain were turned
over to private parties to exploit. And the same indifference
to long-run consequences set the tone for the way in which
our minerals and ores were exploited to feed the expansion
of industry.

But with the advent of the conservation movement, the

Department of Interior gradually took on the role of an embattled defender of the national patrimony. For the fiscal year ending in June, 1951, it employed 63,841 people and spent $313.1 million to manage an empire of public lands, to conduct geological surveys, to operate the national parks, to conserve our fish and wildlife, to run the Bureau of Mines, to conserve our oil resources, to oversee our territorial possessions, to administer three great public power complexes and to act as the guardian of Indian affairs. And in addition to all this, it spent $289.5 million to reclaim various lands. A single example of the economic option the course of this work presents to the President speaks for all the others. In the 1952 presidential campaign, the attitude of the rival candidates toward the disposition of tidelands oil materially contributed to the triumph of General Eisenhower in the state of Texas.

5. Our political history from Washington's administration to the Civil War was marked by a deep conflict between those who wanted the future of America entrusted either to agrarian or to commercial and industrial interests. Jefferson's *Notes on the State of Virginia, 1787,* spoke for the first vision; Hamilton's *Report on Manufacturers, December 1791,* spoke for the second. Yet in the whole of the pre-Civil War period, the agricultural interest was entrusted to one clerk in the Patent Office who registered the inventions of farm implements. Farming had no official representative in the executive branch of the government, though, of course, there were countless unofficial ones; and the same was true of commercial and industrial interests. But in May, 1862, upon the initiative of John Sherman of Ohio, Congress at last provided for a separate Commissioner of Agriculture. He

was Isaac Newton, described by Sherman as "a peculiar character, a Quaker of Philadelphia, a gardener rather than a farmer." Sherman agreed, however, that Newton was "an earnest and active officer," who, though his appropriations were very small and his quarters consisted of one room in the Patent Office, managed "to distribute valuable seeds and cuttings which were in great demand and of real service to farmers." A quarter in which they were not in demand deserves notice. When Newton applied for authority to beautify what was then an unsightly waste between 12th and 14th Streets in the capital—and which is now the majestic mall—he was notified that the "use of it was essentially necessary to the War Department as a cattleyard."

In the post-Civil War years, Grange and Populist uprisings were largely instrumental in changing the Commissioner of Agriculture into a Secretary, and in securing a place for him in the President's Cabinet on February 8, 1889. Since that time, the seeds and cutting once distributed by Isaac Newton have grown into a maze of economic, scientific, cultural and social activities which directly influence the lives of 23.2 million people who dwell on 5.8 million farms valued at $46 billion dollars. In the management of its many programs, the Department of Agriculture as of June, 1951, had 81,062 employees of whom 2,254 were stationed outside the continental limits of the United States. In that year, they spent $69.9 million for research programs ranging from agricultural chemistry to human nutrition. They spent an added $178.9 million on the Farmers Home Administration, $71.8 million on the Forest Service, $1.02 billion on the Production and Marketing Administration, $276 million on the Rural Electrification Administration, $53 million on the Soil Conservation Service, and $134 million on other agricultural services.

6. Ironically, one year after the Secretary of Agriculture became a member of the President's Cabinet, the 1890 census contained the startling news that Jefferson's *Notes on the State of Virginia*, praising the special virtues of farming, was outmoded. Hamilton's *Report on Manufacturers* was now the operational guide of the land, though not of its reveries and nostalgias. The frontier had been spanned. A predominantly agricultural mode of life had been superseded by a commercial and industrial one. Thirteen years after this was clearly stated in the 1890 census, executive note of the same fact was reflected in a 1903 act of Congress, creating a Department of Commerce and Labor. But the intensified pace of industrialization, paralleled by the rise of national labor unions, soon placed the single Secretary in an impossible position. What he affirmed with one hand on behalf of commerce, he countermanded with the other on behalf of labor. Eventually, Congress solved the dilemma in 1913 when it split the Secretary down the middle into separate departments for commerce and for labor, whose heads joined the Cabinet.

For the year which ended on June, 1951, the Department of Commerce employed 64,700 people. It spent $164.1 million on scientific research and the supervision of airports, air routes and a rapidly expanding civil air traffic. It spent $438.5 million on public roads, and $108.9 million on maritime activities. Out of an additional $94.9 million, it dealt with transportation problems arising from 227,000 miles of railways, 27,000 miles of improved inland waterways, and 5,000 ocean-going vessels. It operated the Bureau of the

Census the Patent Office, the Weather Bureau, the National Bureau of Standards. It gathered and disseminated information about business operations and business prospects within the nation and around the globe. And through its National Production Authority, it was in the forefront of the rearmament program.

The Department of Labor is an exception to the general pattern of expansion. A labor force of 60 million men and women should have raised the department to a pre-eminent place in the Executive. Yet the department has had to fight hard to hang on to itself at the very time when the role of government in the labor field has been greatly expanded. Since 1910, what has been given to it with one hand has been taken away with the other, so that its functions never seem to remain long in one place. Nevertheless, what remained to the Labor Department in June of 1951 was not inconsiderable. It employed 7,721 people who expended $231 million on various services, including a Bureau of Apprenticeship, Employment Security, Veterans Employment Service, Labor Standards, Labor Statistics, Veterans Re-employment Rights, Wage and Hour and Public Contracts Division, and a Women's Bureau.

7. The Department of Health, Education and Welfare, established in 1953 with Cabinet rank, summarizes the social progress made in the last twenty years. Some of its present activities were formerly lodged in independent administrative bodies or in other departments. Some of them, too, have a long history dating back to Washington's time. Yet in their scope and intensity, they are a phenomenon produced by a change in the social outlook of the last two decades. The department has direct contact with more citizens than even

the tax collector; in budget terms—$1.7 billion for fiscal 1953—it is larger than all other Cabinet departments, save Defense and Treasury.

Through its Social Security Administration, it acts as the custodian of old-age funds for 67 million people, disburses pensions and welfare funds amounting to $4 billion a year, and protects the nation's disabled and needy, whether young or old. Through its Public Health Service, it manages a wide range of research centers and hospitals and engages in an extensive educational program of preventive medicine. Through its Office of Education, it distributes funds to land-grant colleges, administers the teacher-student exchange program with foreign countries, and supervises the nation's largest Negro university. The minutia of its work was best stated in a comment of *Time* Magazine at the time Mrs. Oveta Culp Hobby was appointed the first Secretary of the new department. Mrs. Hobby, said the author of the comment, "is legally concerned with the problem of tapeworm control among Alaskan caribou, with cancer research, and with the attitude of Congress toward fluoridation of children's teeth."

In this catalogue of developments, two growths have been omitted. The first is the rise of the State Department and the military establishment. (This will be considered in passing in the next chapter.) The second is the rise of a host of administrative bodies, non-regulatory in their essential character, but independent of the executive departments of Cabinet rank. In some cases, they are responsible to the President alone, to the Congress alone or to both. They include enormously influential economic agents like the Atomic Energy Commission, the Veterans Administration

and the Tennessee Valley Authority. In concert with other
agencies to be mentioned presently, they managed expenditures of billions of dollars which directly affected the
economy of persons, regions, and indeed the nation.

What can be said about most of them applies with special
force to the present Departments of Agriculture, Commerce and Labor. Each is expected to speak not for the
nation as a whole, but for the private interests for which they
act as public guardians. They are responsible neither to
each other as individuals, nor to the Cabinet as a united
body. Their loyalties are subject to a two-way stretch, running from the President personally to the private combinations whom they represent, as if we were organized politically along mixed federalist and syndicalist lines. By law or
by outright conquest, they are expected to advance the good
of some leading element in the economic community. In
isolation, each seems to be sovereign in its power. But when
two collide in a chase after their private ends, the power of
one can check that of the other and the public business can
be brought to a halt. From afar the clash may seem to be a
petty jurisdictional dispute, but at close range it shows
towering social importance. Since the many arms of the
Executive are now so frequently bound to particular private
combinations, the question of who shall administer what
contains the answer to who shall get more or less of what
there is to be had. And this is doubly true in a period of
military socialism when manpower, goods and resources tend
to be in short supply.

The best the Congress can do, and, as I have already said,
it often does this with great skill, is to see that no private
economic giant will end with his head on a pike, and that no

giant will be uniformly victorious. It often achieves this general stand-off by sacrificing to the warring giants the interests of the millions of Americans who live unorganized in a no man's land. Again, since the Congress is wholly absorbed in the task of merely easing points of tension, it can rarely give attention to the problems of form and internal consistency for the economy of the nation as a whole. Only the President can do that, if he is willing to speak for the general welfare. He alone can break the economic deadlock in his own household or transcend the natural limits of the Congress. If one interest is getting too much, and another too little, he can summon the nation to throw its weight behind the imperiled party. Or he can summon it to conduct a rescue operation for the unorganized who are caught in the crossfire between the giants. Or he can enforce a truce on the giants so that the national interest can go forward. And precisely because he can do these things, he is under constant pressure to do them in this way instead of that.

Though the separate elements that make up the President's role as the chief economic engineer have been present for some time, only recently has the role acquired a unified, explicit and formal statement in the law. It had not been defined even as late as February, 1933, which was three months after a presidential campaign had been fought on the causes and the curses of the depression, and one month before Franklin D. Roosevelt took his oath of office. At that time, the Senate Finance Committee under the chairmanship of the lame duck Senator Reed Smoot of Utah invited five hundred American leaders to suggest ways in which the economy could be revived. Not a single representative of the Executive was included among those who were asked to take

[263]

part in the public hearing. The implication seemed to be that the Executive was simply to imitate the stewards of the doomed *Titanic* who dutifully locked all the doors on the staterooms so that nothing would be stolen when the ship sank off the Newfoundland bank.

In the twelve years of the Roosevelt administration, the programing of economic policies was shifted to the presidency and away from the Senate Finance Committee where it had been centered in the three preceding Republican administrations. Even so, the sanction for this work was drawn from the political atmosphere alone; except for the brief career of the National Resources Board, the legal directive came only after Roosevelt's death, coincident with a deep concern over the political attitudes of returning war veterans. It was felt that having seen how the government organized the productive facilities of the nation to achieve full employment for the prosecution of the war, they would insist on an equal performance for peacetime purposes.

From considerations of this sort, the Congress in late 1945 passed an employment act of vast significance. It rejected the Marxist prophecy of a remorseless cycle of increasingly severe depressions which would destroy capitalism. It also rejected the assumption that the free competitive system contained automatic internal adjustments which could correct the cycle of boom and bust. Affirming the basic attachments of our society to the values of the free enterprise system, the act assigned to the government the role of a compensatory agent in the system. By its variable fiscal, monetary and credit policies, and by its public works program, the government was to keep the economy in full production at all times.

Manager of social justice and prosperity

On a practical plane, the act brought into being a Council of Economic Advisors, housed in the Office of the President. The Council was to maintain a steady surveillance of the economy as a whole, to chart its aches and pains, and to indicate to the President what general actions would be necessary to achieve the aims of the Employment Act. By the same law, the President was charged with a personal duty to submit to the Congress an Annual Economic Report, containing the findings and suggestions of the Council. Lately, there has been some doubt whether the Council works objectively, or whether it simply rationalizes in economic terms what the President would have done anyway had there been no Council. But the solid fact is that the Employment Act now holds the President to a direct responsibility for economic planning undreamed of in Washington's day.

He is expected to turn the spotlight on economic injustices; fortify the strength of the individual Americans; encourage the expansion of commerce, industry and agriculture; control bigness; guarantee a steady flow of low-cost goods; ensure the existence of mass purchasing power; guarantee access to raw materials—but to respect the structural lines of a constitutional instrument built in a different economic climate. Beyond these implications, drawn from the 1945 Employment Act, the National Security Act of 1947 enlarged the planning function still more to suit martial needs. It created a National Security Resources Board and a National Security Council, with one foot in the Office of the President, and another foot in almost every major executive establishment. Though each of the two new bodies has the character of an interdepartmental committee, what the economy as a whole needs or can provide sets the frame for their work.

It should be stressed that the plans the President sends to the Congress under the terms of the Employment Act and the National Security Act have no more force than the Congress chooses to give them. But the President has a broad range of economic options, present in existing governmental bodies, which he can exercise in the form of rules, regulations, orders and interpretations—all of which help shape the economic climate he wants.

Discretionary activities of this sort have always been a part of the presidency; they are in fact, implicit in the President's duty to "take care that the laws be faithfully executed." But the contemporary application has these aspects of novelty: the frequency with which this discretionary power is used, the objects on which it is used, and the broad terms in which Congress describes the circumstances and the objects on which it can be used.

If an allowance for discretionary power is unavoidable in any government, it is, as I have already implied, best lodged in the officer of the highest rank who is directly answerable to the Courts in his legal character, and to the Congress and the people in his political capacity. Yet the dangers cannot be lightly brushed off. Discretionary power increases the chances of encroachment on private rights. It is also an irresistible magnet, inviting private persons to buy or shove their way to its source. It excites chronic strife between the Congress, the Court and the President on the charge that the President is ignoring the general intentions of the Congress. Moreover, by its description of administrative discretion, the Congress can make it impossible for the President to carry out the very policy to which it has ostensibly consented. The people, however, know only that a law is on the statute books. They expect the President to achieve its aims. They do not always know that the law may contain self-defeating administrative provisions. When a fiasco results, it appears to be the fault of bad management by the President, and he and not the Congress is blamed. But the chain reaction does not stop here. The President who fears the political sequel to a failure has a natural temptation to make the law work by side-stepping congressional administrative bars, though he may argue, contrary to the fact, that he is respecting them. One can excuse this in isolated cases by citing the duress of exceptional circumstances. Yet the practice can create an unfortunate psychological atmosphere around the presidency, leading to free-wheeling executive habits.

The remedy lies in the hands of the Congress. If it commits itself to a program in good faith, it ought to take care that the administrative machinery for the law is equal to its objectives. If the Congress does not subscribe to those objectives, it ought to say so in unmistakable terms. It does not promote the cause of orderly government when, in enacting a law, it shifts the burden of responsibility onto the President but denies him the effective means to shoulder that responsibility. The most recent case in point is the way the Congress gutted the price control legislation, yet held President Truman to account for setbacks in the fight on inflation.

In the last years of the Truman administration, one aspect of the Executive's role as the engineer of the economy was brought under klieg lights. It involved the Executive as our chief insurance agent and banker. Since the outbreak of World War I, public credit has gradually become a main source of support for a wide range of private credit demands. During that war and the one that followed, it served as a generative force to expand the industrial plant and to spur agricultural production. In the depression of the 1930's, through the Reconstruction Finance Corporation, it served to bolster creditor institutions like banks, insurance companies and building and loan leagues. In the New Deal years, it was extended in the form of the Federal Deposit Insurance Corporation to protect the savings in the private banking system. It was further extended through the insurance system of the Federal Housing Authority to quicken a revival in the construction industry. In World War II, it appeared in the special form of the V-loans the Federal Reserve System made to business enterprises involved in war production. And throughout the whole of this period, public credit was the linchpin which held the agricultural wheel to the axle of the economy.

In 1947, the Hoover Commission listed some thirty government agencies which acted as bankers and insurance agents. They managed public credit investments and commitments of nearly $20 billion; backed up $85 billion in loans or deposits in the private banks, and managed $40 billion in various forms of government insurance. The expansion since 1947 can be judged from the single fact that the volume of government-backed mortgages on small homes grew from $19 billion on V-J day to approximately $40 billion at the beginning of 1950. The Federal organs involved in this credit work are now located in many places. Some are housed in the major departments of the Executive, as in the case of loans granted to farmers by the Department of Agriculture. Others, like the Reconstruction Finance Corporation and the Housing and Home Finance Agency, are outside the existing departments and report directly to the President or to the Congress. But whether they work in or beyond the range of the President's vision and control, the public holds him responsible for what they do.

The availability of public credit increases the number of people who want to "get to the President" or to those who "have his ear." The hope is that he will use his influence with government banking and insurance agencies to bail out private enterprises, however inefficient, before they go through the capitalist wringer of bankruptcy and liquidation. He is told that the collapse of the enterprises will put men out of work, with damaging political results in a local community. He is told (as in the case of some New England industries) that they are in dire straits because they respect union labor, while new competitors in other areas do not. He is told that the enterprises are needed for national defense. All these claims may be true and legitimate. But if the President succumbs to the combined force of businessmen, labor, political and military leaders—if he obliges them by the use of his influence, he fosters an unnatural competition between enterprises that pay their own way and others in the same field that survive because they have a political underpinning.

As long as the Executive is forced to buy up to one third of the total national product for military use, it will continue to play a banker's role. But the scope of the role could be reduced somewhat if the private banking system fulfilled its true function. Main Street banks are the custodians of local capital and should use it to develop the local community. Instead, they have commonly transferred the effective use of that capital to a handful of major banks at remote points; they choose to make their living on Main Street from the interest paid them by the major banks, the fees for checkbook services, the interest on government securities, and the interest on ventures like housing in which the government assumes almost all the credit risks. Meanwhile, the handful of major banks, sensitive to the views of the giant corporations among their depositors, hesitate to advance loans for new and competitive enterprises in underdeveloped areas such as the South and the West.

As a result of these common tendencies, the President is pulled in two ways. Political spokesmen of the South and the West tug at him with demands that he use his influence to have public credit underwrite the expansion of their regional commerce and industry. He is tugged in an opposite direction by political spokesmen for enterprises which fear new competition in markets they have earmarked for themselves. While this hassle is in progress, the Main Street businessman comes on the scene. Since his local bank cannot or will not advance capital for his new venture, he is inevitably drawn to Washington to search for public credit. The by-product is inevitable. It is the Washington influence peddler. He can be another businessman, a lawyer, a Congressman, a member of the Executive, and so on. But the work of the peddler, based on the mores of a former epoch when private sources of credit financed private enterprise, is to connect the man from Main Street with those in the Executive who have discretionary power to disburse public credit.

When these transactions come to light, as they did in the

closing years of the Truman administration, the nation reacts as though the cold underbelly of a snake had crawled over its face. There are cries of corruption in the Executive. There are demands for a code of ethics. There are proposals for an inspector general who would be attached to the President. The outcry was fully justified. The corrective measures were generally in point. But in the course of an exhaustive and salutary public discussion of the problem, it was the rare voice that announced or saw any sort of connection between the "moral crisis of the presidency" and the defaults of the private banking system.

In the final analysis, the reduction of the President's role in the economy, and the re-establishment of a fairly clear line between the political and the economic order, depend on one thing. It is the performance of the free competitive system as it governs itself by its own reflexes. If the system of its own accord could guarantee markets, funds for new developments, insurance against all risks, full employment, limitations on the abusive use of private economic power, the supply of needed defense material, a real security against runaway inflations or recurrent depressions, and so on, then it would be possible to take the government as a whole, and the President in particular "out of business."

On the assumption that the system cannot do these things, is there any measure of security against the constant danger that the President may misuse his influence over executive agents or abuse the discretionary powers he holds in his own hands? Part of the answer, of course, is a strong Judiciary which will not blanch if the need arises to cite the President as a lawbreaker. Another part of the answer is a sober and responsible use by the Congress of its investigatory powers.

Yet another part seems to lie in a form of veto power the Congress now enjoys and which it has used to good effect on numerous recent occasions. In the enactment of any law that lodges new discretionary powers in the Executive or in any of its statutory arms, it can insert a clause providing that the power can be withdrawn by a concurrent resolution of the Congress. The benefit of this device is that a concurrent resolution does not require the President's signature; nor is it subject to his veto. Thus, if the President should misuse his power in a way that does not involve a breach of the law cognizable by the Courts, the power could be taken away from him without encountering the obstacle of his consent. The Congress, of course, would then have the duty to provide for effective supervision of the independent agent in whom it may choose to place the same discretionary power—assuming it wishes to keep it in being.

12

Manager of war and peace

‖▫‖‖‖‖‖‖‖‖‖‖‖▫‖‖‖‖‖‖‖‖‖‖▫‖‖‖‖‖‖‖‖‖‖▫‖‖‖‖‖‖‖‖‖‖▫‖‖‖‖‖‖‖‖‖‖▫‖‖‖‖‖‖‖‖‖‖▫‖‖‖‖‖‖‖‖‖‖▫‖‖‖‖‖‖‖‖

The need for a controlled military impulse – Circumstances which underlay the constitutional formula – The character of the formula – Technological factors which strain it – Added strain due to change in our world position – The constitutional formula for the conduct of foreign affairs – Hamilton and Madison state the classic argument over the rights of the Congress or the President in this field – History decides in favor of Hamilton – President not only formulates foreign policy but forms it – President's power to make war has virtually swallowed the right of the Congress to declare war – Congress not structurally built to exert full authority in management of war and peace – It is fully justified in defending its constitutional rights in cases such as troops for the North Atlantic Pact – But it does a disservice when it seeks to elevate the military impulse over the diplomatic one – Or when it renders the military independent of the President – Remarks about the National Security Council – Seizure of steel industry by President Truman summarizes all military, diplomatic and economic tension of our time – Supreme Court tackles question of acts beyond the law – No real decision – The prophecy of Justice Robert A. Jackson.

A fanciful story, of Renaissance origin, is told about the people of Siena, Italy, who once hired a mercenary captain to wage war on a nearby town. When the news was brought back that the captain had won a great triumph, the Siennes

[273]

debated what they could do for a benefactor who could now conquer his employers. No plan joining thanks to prudence seemed quite right until someone came forward with the inspired proposal that the captain should be killed and then worshiped as Siena's patron saint. No time was lost in putting the plan into effect.

If this solution was perhaps too drastic, the problem of which it was a part has worried republican people over the ages. The earliest evidence is in the Bible, whose priests and prophets by divinations and exhortations sought to arouse warriors and to control them. The next evidence is lodged in the Athenian and Roman constitutions, which created a military impulse for the defense of the civil order, while taking care that the impulse would not in the end prove too strong and subvert what it was meant to protect.

In the full tide of history, our own Constitutional Convention was brought abreast of this same need and this same challenge. The unique solution provided by the delegates bore the imprint of their experiences under colonial rule, during the Revolution, and in their life under the Articles of Confederation.

The American colonists had named the principle of civilian supremacy as a leading cause of their rebellion from England. The language of the Declaration of Independence was explicit on this point, charging that George III had tyrannically "affected to render the Military independent of and superior to the Civil Power." Yet during the Revolution itself and at its close, the doctrine of civilian supremacy was preserved by the very slender margin of Washington's self-discipline.

At one moment, the Continental Congress would appoint

generals, not for their skill, but because they came from political quarters that had to be humored. Then, in a sudden swelling of its own sense of authority, it would issue orders to Washington, though withholding the means of carrying them out. There were those in the Congress who plotted to have Washington removed from his command. And there were those, also, who entrusted him with almost plenary powers. So hectic was the atmosphere that even the Virginia legislature, the Southern cradle of the Revolution, lost sight of what had been written in the Declaration of Independence. It twice considered a resolution for the appointment of a dictator. On the second occasion, to the enormous disgust of Thomas Jefferson, the proposal came within two votes of passage.

The sight of victory in no way stilled the call for a military dictator. The transparent fact of civil weakness kept it alive. Yet throughout this period when the government was little more than a junta, or perhaps just a plot, Washington nevertheless scrupulously bent his role as Commander in Chief to the rule of the civil authority as expressed by the Continental Congress. When the Congress twice voted him extensive powers, he returned them intact. He resisted the plan for the creation of a monarchy, with himself as king and with the Order of Cincinnatus, formed of the Revolutionary War officers, as the new nobility. He flared in anger when the suggestion was made that he set up an outright military dictatorship. Even when the army was in the process of being disbanded, Washington's constitutional sense remained as strong as ever. In the Circular Letter he sent to the colonial governors at that time, he felt the need to write: "If in treating with political points, a greater latitude than usual has been taken in the course of this address, the importance of the crisis, and the magnitude of the objects under discussion, must be my apology." The whole of the Circular Letter, in fact, is a plea to end the grievances and abuses which, if left unsolved by the regular constitutional process, would be solved by a military dictatorship.

The plea went unheeded. And from this, a chain of events was set in motion which soon made it clear that all the colonists had won was the American War. The American Revolution still hung in the balance. Instead of the hoped-for new race of men and a new nation, there was Shays' Rebellion. The poverty-stricken debtors gathered around Shays had heard a great deal during the war years about individual conscience, liberty, and the natural rights of self-help. They had been spurred to break the law in the name of a return to the old forms of English legality violated by George III. But after the break was made, war-born habits of civil disobedience did not give way to a more decorous behavior. Men like Shays, foreclosed on their farms for non-payment of debts, had good reason to hesitate before they accepted a new version of justice backed by powers of coercion.

The league of states formed to wage the war had not become a unified people. It remained "the United States in Congress Assembled." The people had no direct voice in the Continental Congress. Nor were they directly embraced by its law. The states alone, each with one vote, spoke for them in the Congress. And though that body nominally combined all executive, legislative and judicial functions, none of its decisions had any more force than any state wished to give them. One great law, the Northwest Ordinance, did emerge from the Congress. Yet the Ordinance expressed little more than a heroic hope that if the Northwest Territory could be pried away from the English who still dominated it and from the Indians who still menaced it, its internal form would follow the line of the law. How to secure that territory merged with all the other unanswered questions of the day which piled up like black clouds before a storm. To win diplomatic recognition from foreign powers—to gain access to their markets—to restrain the states from provoking foreign powers—to arrest frontier depredations which set the Indians on the warpath as in the Carolinas and Georgia—to regulate interstate commerce—to settle the debts of the Revolution—to pay discharged war veterans—to check the torrent of paper money—to open the Mississippi River for American navigation—all these called for concerted action on a continental scale. But the form of the Confederacy was such it could not create powers adequate to these needs. Its powers were restricted to those enumerated in the Articles of Confederation.

The Constitution is star-studded with phrases reflecting the needs unanswered under the Confederacy: "insure domestic Tranquility"—"execute the Laws of the Union"—"suppress Insurrections"—"repel invasion"—"guarantee to every State . . . a Republican Form of Government"—"the common defence"—"the Blessings of Liberty." Yet the military impulse suited to these purposes had to be proportioned to the ends in view. Otherwise either liberty would be left defenseless, or the people would be crushed between standing armies and perpetual taxes. Union itself appeared to be one of the chief ways to mitigate the latter dangers. Union would foster policies that would remove the causes of internal disorder, and thereby reduce the need for a large

[277]

army. The size of the Union would be an obstacle to those in the central government who dreamed of backing personal ambitions by arms. Union would exhibit America as a more formidable obstacle to foreign ambitions. And lastly, the favorable geographical position of the Union would reduce the need for a costly military establishment. Thus a five-point formula was agreed upon.

1. It provided for a Federal force, always at the disposal of the central government. But the main reliance was placed on well-regulated state militias. While they would remove the need for large standing armies, they would also provide the several states with the means of defending themselves "against the enterprises of ambitious rulers in the national councils."

2. The Federal Congress was granted the right to call the state militia into the service of the United States, and to organize, arm, discipline and govern them when they were in that service. The appointment of militia officers, however, was reserved to the states, as was the training of militiamen according to the discipline prescribed by the Congress. In its intent, this part of the military formula struck at the Revolutionary War practice whereby state governors had made their militia independent of the Continental Congress in virtually all matters.

3. The sketchy sense of fiscal responsibility for military operations shown during the Revolutionary War also left its countermark on the formula. As if for emphasis, the fiscal powers and duties of the Congress in this area were stated twice in the Constitution. Congress was granted the power to pay the debts and provide for the common defense. It was also empowered to raise and support armies, and to provide

for and maintain a navy. But to check any possibility that the forces created would remain in being forever, it was provided that congressional appropriations for the common defense should be limited to two-year periods.

4. As a further control on the military impulse, it was explicitly stated that Congress alone should have the power to declare war. It is worth noting, however, that the Constitutional Convention drew a distinction between the power to "declare" and the power to "make" war. In the draft of the Constitution submitted on August 6, 1787, Congress was granted the right to "make" war. But two weeks later, after a debate, the verb "make" was struck out and the verb "declare" was substituted. Madison explained in his notes that the change was made for the purpose of "leaving the Executive the power to repel sudden attacks."

Inferential support for this same construction appears in the twenty-fifth number of *The Federalist*. There, Alexander Hamilton paid his derisive respects to the proposition that the raising of armies in time of peace should be prohibited. If that prohibition were adopted, said Hamilton, "the United States would then exhibit the most extraordinary spectacle which the world has yet seen,—that of a nation incapacitated by its Constitution to prepare for defense before it was actually invaded." Then he added, sarcastically:

As the ceremony of a formal denunciation of war has of late fallen into disuse, the presence of an enemy within our territories must be waited for, as the legal warrant to the government to begin its levies of men for the protection of the State. We must receive the blow, before we could even prepare to return it. All that kind of policy by which nations anticipate distant danger, and meet the gathering storm, must be abstained from, as contrary to the genuine maxims of free government. We must expose our property and liberty to the mercy of foreign invaders, and invite them by our weakness to seize the naked and defenseless prey, because we are afraid that rulers, created by our choice, dependent on our will, might endanger that liberty, by an abuse of the means necessary to its preservation.

Wise politicians, Hamilton concluded, will be cautious about hemming in the government with restrictions that cannot be observed, because they know that every violation of law, though dictated by necessity, "impairs that sacred reverence which ought to be maintained in the breast of rulers toward the constitution of a country, and forms a precedent for other breaches where the same plea of necessity does not exist at all, or is less urgent and palpable."

5. While the military establishment was to be created and controlled in this way, it still needed an executive head, missing under the Articles of Confederation. And so, with an almost insouciant air, the fifth detail of the formula provided that the President would be commander in chief of the army and navy of the United States; and of the militia of the several states when called into actual service of the United States. "The propriety of this provision," Hamilton observed in the seventy-fourth number of *The Federalist,* "was so evident in itself, and at the same time, so consonant with the precedents of state Constitutions in general [where the military authority was concentrated in the hands of the governor] that little need be said to explain or enforce it." And in fact, while *The Federalist* papers probed every word and comma in the Constitution and showed what they meant in a wide range of historical contingencies, the dark continent of the "Commander in Chief" clause was barely touched.

Hamilton's attitude found its counterpart in the Constitutional Convention and in the ratifying conventions held by the states. What seemed to have concerned them most was the propriety of allowing the President to command in person. In a plan Hamilton himself framed and showed privately to a few friends, the President would have the direction of the war when it started, but could not take command in the field without the consent of both houses of Congress. In the Patterson plan laid before the Convention, the Executive was given the direction of all military operations, but was barred from commanding troops either as a general or in any other capacity.

This proposal, however, was not adopted. We can only assume that when the military powers of the President were being considered, the Convention looked to the figure of George Washington, the architect of the recent victory against England. The members probably saw no reason why they should foreclose the right to use his military talents, if, as the President of the new Union, he might again be faced with a need to take the field.[1]

In the original view, the power the President could exercise under the title of commander in chief apparently was limited to purely military objects. He was the top general and the top admiral, and there were no officers over him. In that high state, he was "authorized to direct the movement of naval and military forces placed by law at his command, and to employ them in a manner he may deem most effectual

---

[1] Today, the limitations a President faces in conducting a campaign in person are more political and practical than legal. From the evidence of past precedent, there is nothing to stop him from taking the field in person. Indeed, by vesting in the President the sole right to determine when an atomic bomb can be dropped, the law now gives him a power of direct command undreamed of in a former day when President Andrew Jackson and Zachary Taylor threatened to ride out and hang a few rebels.

to harass and conquer and subdue the enemy." But this was all he could do in the conduct of military operations. Despite his high-ranking title, the President could not wield any powers presumably assigned to the legislative order. It is in point to remark here that this view underwent a sharp change with the outbreak of the Civil War. The commander in chief who had formerly looked forward to the battle line alone was equipped at that time with a second pair of eyes, fixed on the whole zone of the interior which supported the skirmishes between armed formations. Of necessity, Lincoln so interpreted his role as a commander in chief that it became a source of "inherent powers," divorced from the legislature, and virtually unlimited in scope to meet the domestic aspects of a war emergency. And it was these Civil War precedents that were amplified by Woodrow Wilson and Franklin D. Roosevelt for the conduct of total war against foreign powers in the twentieth century.

The pioneer view, however, appeared tenable so long as a fairly clear line existed between the volunteers and mercenaries who formed the army, and the civil population. The standing army in George Washington's presidency never exceeded more than five thousand men—or one third the size of a modern infantry division. And Washington was always on hand with reminders of this sort: "Every officer and soldier will constantly bear in mind that he comes to support the laws and that it would be peculiarly unbecoming in him to be in any way the infractor of them"; that the dispensation of "justice belongs to the civil Magistrate and let it ever be our pride and our glory to leave the sacred deposit there unviolated." And again: "Officers ought to be careful, not to give orders, which may lead the agents into the infractions of the law"; that "disputes be avoided, as much as possible, and be adjusted as quickly as may be"; that "the whole country is not to be considered as within the limits of the camp."

The War Department, as organized by Washington, had few functions beyond the maintenance and use of the armed forces, and the regulation of peaceful relations with the Indians. In its earliest personnel, the department consisted of Secretary Henry Knox, the "furious Federalist" and one clerk—whose temperament is unknown. Until two disasters at the hands of the Indians in 1790 and 1791 led to short-lived reforms, there was no system for procuring, issuing and accounting for regular army supplies. The fate of any force in the field was generally in the hands of private individuals who had contracted to supply its needs. Neither was there any systematic way in which officers were chosen, trained and promoted for professional competence. In this age of the amateur, influence and connection were all important.

By 1796, the affairs of the War Department had become sufficiently complicated to double its size. In addition to a new Secretary, James McHenry, it boasted two clerks instead of one. But from contemporary records, it appears that the two clerks managed to get along on their own. Not long after McHenry's appointment, he was called upon by a French officer who promptly left an account of the event for the amusement of the future. The visitor writes that he found no sentinel at the door. All the rooms, the walls of which were covered with maps, were open, "and in the midst of the solitude" he found two clerks each sitting at his own table engaged in writing. When the officer inquired after the Secretary he was told that he had gone out for a shave. "Mr.

McHenry's name figures in the State Budget for $2,000," the officer concluded, "a salary quite sufficient in a country where the Secretary of War goes in the morning to his neighbor, the barber, at the corner to get shaved." [2]

A Navy Department did not come into being until 1798. Its advent on the eve of a naval war against France was preceded by a hot political fight between the advocates of "unification" and the advocates of "independence" for the component arms of the military establishment. The War Department had just completed three of the six vessels originally commissioned to deal with the Algerian pirates. To supervise their use, the Federalist argued the need of a separate department. Speaking for this view, Harrison Gray Otis insisted that "it was a thing impossible for one man to undertake the business of the War and Navy Department.

[2] If the same officer had returned ten years later, the text of a letter on the desk of Secretary of War Henry Dearborn would have deepened his wonder about the character of the American military establishment. The writer of the letter, the militia-elected General Andrew Jackson, had a few things to say about the Secretary's weird performance when the Aaron Burr conspiracy shook the West. "You stand convicted of the most notorious and criminal acts of dishonor, dishonesty, want of candour and justice," the general informed the Secretary. "I care not where, when or how he shall undertake to resent this language." Six years later, in the opening months of the War of 1812, the French visitor would have had an equally surprising turn. He might have found the Secretary of War busily engaged in sawing off a leg, the Secretary at the time being a Revolutionary War surgeon, Dr. William Eustis. And two years after that, had the same visitor asked for the Secretary of War in the late summer of 1814, he would have been directed to the three-in-one figure of James Monroe. In addition to the War portfolio he held, Monroe was also the Secretary of State, the military commander of the Washington district, and the officer in charge of several artillery pieces on the heights outside the capital. This outdid the best Alexander Hamilton had to offer in 1794 when, as Secretary of the Treasury, he took over the direction of the War Department and rode at the head of troops to confront the Whisky rebels in Western Pennsylvania—an operation which today would be entrusted to a few young lawyers in the Treasury's Internal Revenue Bureau.

As well might a merchant be set to do the business of a lawyer; a lawyer that of a physician; a carpenter that of a bricklayer; or a bricklayer that of a carpenter."

In their arguments for "unification," the Republicans advanced the benefits of economy to be gained. Also, they ridiculed the notion that a specialist in shipbuilding or naval matters was needed at the head of the navy. "Could it be said," asked Edward Livingston, "that the Secretary of War had a perfect knowledge of everything under his direction, except what related to the Navy? Certainly not. To be so, he must not only be a perfect engineer, but be acquainted with the construction of arms. To carry this idea to this full extent, it would not only be necessary to have separate departments, but also a great variety of commissioners: they must have commissioners of gun-barrels and ram-rods."

Livington's view, however, lost out by a margin of six votes in the House. A Navy Department, independent of War, was presently established, not without giving some concern to William Smith, then our minister at Lisbon. When the news reached him that the separation was to be made, Smith wrote to Secretary of War McHenry: "I don't know which way your propensity inclines, whether to the Army or Navy; as you are to be subdivided into two parts, I wish to know with which part the Soul remains, with the Navy part or the Army part? are you to be Mars or Neptune? are you to wield the Truncheon or the Trident? God prosper you in whatever capacity; you have an arduous task and sad Devils to deal with."

In our growth to power from these very modest origins, more than the President's role as a commander in chief has undergone a radical change. The whole of our early consti-

tutional formula for a controlled military impulse has been
strained to the near breaking point. The cause, in part, is
due to technological revolutions in military science. In part,
it is due to a change in our political position among the
nations.

Consider first the consequences of the technological
revolution. In the industrial regimentation military power
now requires in the preparation for war or in the waging of
war, materials and morale alike have been totalized. Property
rights, hinged to the "due process clause," and personal
rights, hinged to the Bill of Rights, have had to make painful adjustments to the overriding claims of factories, mines,
raw materials, food, fuel, transportation, communications
and so on. In the sequel, the President who was once limited
to the supreme command of military and naval forces engaged against an enemy has become a concert master, co-
ordinating and making provision for the intricate elements
that constitute the war potential. The President who was
once barred from exercising powers presumably lodged in
the legislature has of necessity undertaken to prepare for
wars or to fight wars by means of the administrative regulation, directive and order.

Meanwhile, long-range striking arms that can move
swiftly to a target have pierced the geographical barrier
behind which we once could slowly gather our forces. The
oceans have been drained and now seem no wider than the
English channel. From the same technological causes, warfare now calls for a highly trained soldier instead of the
frontiersman armed with a squirrel rifle. A huge standing
army has come into being, answerable directly to the central
government and superseding the militia as the main in-

gredient of effective and swift military action. With the huge standing army has come a permanent class of professional soldiers who alone know how to direct the delicately meshed parts of the whole military apparatus.

Our expenditures on past and current military activities consume over three fourths of the annual budget. The civilian personnel involved are more than one half of all on the executive payroll. With the development of non-conventional weapons employing atomic energy, only a handful of legislators know what they are voting for when they allocate funds for military use. The Congress as a whole moves blindly when it provides for the common defense and pays the debts incurred in the process. Moreover, the length of time required to build some of the principal military weapons frequently stretches far beyond the two years to which Congressional appropriations were limited. In the interval, construction goes on with the lump sums or under authorities granted at the outset, though conditions in the third or fourth year may be so different from conditions in the year of the original appropriation as to justify an end or modification of the project.

These strains, originating in a changed military technology, are now compounded by those which originate in our changed world position. In the eighteenth and nineteenth centuries, we either could do without allies, or could limit alliances to the length of a war. The aim in either case was to pick our enemies and friends by the measure of the land they held or could help us get on or near the American continent. Even when the center of American action moved from a continental to an oceanic diplomacy toward the close of the nineteenth century, most of our external strife was with people much like ourselves. As victors or vanquished, as friends or enemies, the English, French, Spanish, and even the Germans of World War I, held to no social ideas that were fundamentally hostile to our own. All alike subscribed in some degree to Judaic-Christian religious concepts, to the economic concepts formalized by Adam Smith, and to the political concepts dating from the French Revolution. Our greatest fear of other powers was that they might reduce or block our access to the physical assets we wanted. We could be reasonably sure that, whatever the issue, our internal social order would remain relatively unchanged.

For this reason, perhaps, we could concentrate now on foreign, now on domestic affairs. If we erred in one place, the result tended to be self-sealing. Fate, having its own purposes in mind, gave us two oceans, a virginal continent, and a margin of years when, free of outside influence, by trial and error we could store up a treasure house of moods, ideas, moral stamina and sheer physical might. It was as though we were allowed all this so that we could better serve the Western tradition at the moment when it was most seriously menaced.

That moment came with the advent of the Russian Revolution, and its offshoots, the Fascist and the Nazi Revolutions. Without let-up since then, except for the period of our withdrawal in the twenties, the goods we stored up for a century and one half have been drawn on heavily to seal repeated break-throughs in Europe and in Asia by forces hostile to all forms of constitutional government. No other Western power thus far has had the means to provide the staying hand. And it is precisely because we are in the forefront of the fight as the supreme representative of a constitutional republic that our old capacity to concentrate on foreign or on domestic affairs, one at a time, has come to an end. The two preoccupations are now indivisible.

Alliances that were once limited to the beginning, middle and end of actual wars have been changed to permanent alliances without a terminal point. Some of them are designed to prevent the outbreak of war. Others are designed to shore up a country's domestic affairs so as to reduce the prospect that they will be conquered by internal subversion. Still others are designed to win a conventional style of war if it comes. In all of them, "land," the old aim of our diplomacy, has been replaced by "interests"—moral, social, political, religious, economic and strategic—common to most members who belong to the complex system of federations that revolve around the central federation of the United States—and around the American President. In our name, he is expected to preserve the peace of the world. But he is also expected to prepare the world to win a war if one should break out.

Two questions are thus shoved to the fore: Is the President constitutionally equipped to manage the cause of peace for free nations, and to make them ready to fight to victory in any war? How did the Constitution actually distribute power for the management of foreign affairs?

Taking these questions in reverse order, the first point we come upon is that the Constitution *is not* the germinal legal source of power the United States exercises in the foreign field. The external rights of the United States are based on the inherent powers of sovereignty that the United States exercises as a collective entity in international law. The second point is that the Constitution is vague on the question of who shall have authority to determine the course of the United States as a sovereign body in the foreign field. Nor do *The Federalist* papers deal with the subject any more clearly.

In the sixty-fourth number, John Jay detailed the benefits of *secrecy, despatch, continuity* and *accessibility* to be gained by assigning the President a role in the negotiation of treaties. But is the right to negotiate treaties the same as the right to make them? Is the right to *formulate* foreign policy the same as the right to *form* it? Is the President the sole organ of foreign relations in the sense that of himself he can commit the nation to projects it will have to back up? Or is he the sole organ in the sense that he alone may address foreign powers and receive communications from them? Are the discretionary powers of the President in the foreign field limited to the determination of matters of fact? Or do they encompass an initiative to create and to prefer a state of fact?

Jay gave no answer to these questions. The part he assigned to the President in the conduct of foreign affairs is amplified and supported solely on these grounds:

They who have turned their attention to the affairs of men, must have perceived that there are tides in them; tides very irregular in their duration, strength, and direction, and seldom found to run twice exactly in the same manner or measure. To discern and to profit by these tides in national affairs is the business of those who preside over them; and they who have had much experience on this head inform us, that there frequently are occasions when days, nay, even when hours, are precious. The loss of a battle, the death of a prince, the removal of a minister, or other circumstances intervening to change the present posture and aspect of affairs, may turn the most favorable tide into a course opposite to our wishes. As in the field, so in the cabinet, there are moments to be seized as they pass, and they who preside in either should be left in capacity to improve them. So often and so essentially have we heretofore suffered from the want of secrecy and despatch, that the Constitution would have been inexcusably defective, if no attention had been paid to these objects. Those matters which in negotiations usually require the most secrecy and the most despatch, are those preparatory and auxiliary measures which are not otherwise important in a national view, than as they tend to facilitate the attainment of the objects of the negotiation.

The emphasis is a pragmatic one. And so, apparently, is the constitutional emphasis. It divided the conduct of foreign affairs between the President, the Senate and the Congress as a whole. But it left for future events to decide who would have the final and authoritative voice in the actual direction of foreign policy. Once this open-end invitation to strife was turned over to the Washington administration, it presently shook the country to its roots, led inexorably to the suppression of civil liberties, and materially fostered the rise of political parties.

One aside, however, is in point. In reading the story of this tumult, it is difficult but necessary to bear in mind that the State Department at the outset consisted of Secretary of State Thomas Jefferson, who ran what amounted to a one-man show. The six clerks who sat with him were assigned nothing except routine paper work. Nor was the State Department's foreign apparatus more elaborate. In 1791, it was limited to ministers or chargé d'affaires at Paris, London, Lisbon, the Hague and Madrid, all geared to the pace of communications which were then available. One of them at least, William Carmichael, the minister at Madrid, seems to have slowed down to the tempo of a Spanish siesta, unmatched in its duration. Two years passed in which he sent no direct word to Secretary of State Jefferson. When the Secretary felt the situation deserved notice, his reaction too, had a deep anesthetic quality. "Your letter of May 6, 1789, is still the last received," Jefferson wrote Carmichael in March, 1791, "and that is now two years old. A full explanation of the causes of this suspension of all information from you, is expected in answer to my letter of Aug. 6 [1790]. It will be waited for yet a reasonable time, & in the meanwhile a final opinion is suspended."

The conflict over the direction of foreign policy came to a head in 1793 in Washington's so-called "Proclamation of Neutrality." It declared the intention of the United States to pursue a course friendly and impartial to England and France, and it enjoined all citizens to observe the same upon the pain of prosecution. The moment this was made public, the Anti-Federalists, French in their sympathies, attacked the proclamation as an act which lay beyond the President's constitutional powers. A pamphlet war followed in which arguments were raised that persist to this day.

Alexander Hamilton, writing under the pseudonym "Pacificus," launched the defense of Washington's act by contending that the Constitution gave a direct grant of power to the President, detailed in its objects in Article II. By implication, the Constitution also empowered the President to interpret how he was to bear himself toward those objects. Since the direction of foreign policy was inherently an "executive" function, in the absence of any express constitutional language to the contrary, the right of interpretation—and hence, the right of initiative—lay with the President. Hamilton acknowledged that this might enable the President

[292]

to present the Congress with *fait accompli* in the diplomatic field which could force it to declare war. What formed the check on this risk? In the exercise of its own concurrent or co-ordinate powers, the Congress could refuse to back up the President.

At the request of Thomas Jefferson, James Madison undertook "to select the most striking" of Hamilton's "heresies and cut him to pieces in the face of the public." Writing under the pseudonym "Helvidus," Madison charged Hamilton with claiming for the President the royal prerogative of the British Crown to declare war and to make treaties. He argued, furthermore, that the right to determine foreign policy was not autonomous in nature. It was rooted in the antecedent power to declare war. And this power the Constitution lodged in the Congress. What, then, was the power of the President in the diplomatic sphere? He was simply an instrument to carry out the intentions of the Congress. The discretionary powers he exercised in the process did not go beyond the right to determine "matters of fact." To argue otherwise would place in his hands a warmaking power, contrary to the express declaration of the Constitution.

History has generally rendered its verdict on Hamilton's side of the case, without too close attention to the Constitutional issues. To preserve the existence of the United States as a sovereign entity at international law—to keep the peace or to prepare for victory in case of war—the presidential prerogative in the foreign field has been steadily enlarged. Presidents not only *formulate* foreign policy; they have come to *form* it. This is so much the case that the character of a foreign policy has often depended on the character of a President. Again, the enlargement of the President's diplo-

[293]

matic prerogative, when joined to his role as a chief executive and as a commander in chief, has as Hamilton admitted it might, placed in his hands a capacity to bring on a state of war that the Congress has been forced to acknowledge. The danger here, as in the action of President James K. Polk on the eve of the Mexican War, has always been great. But in the present epoch of cold wars, half wars, and undeclared wars, it has appeared at times that the President's power to "make war" has virtually swallowed the Congressional right to "declare war."

We are, as a result, caught in an acute opposition between our need for constitutional controls over the President, and our demand that he move swiftly and effectively to quell any danger or to seize any opportunity of advantage to us. The reconciliation between these two needs defies any easy solution. For even if Madison was right in insisting that the Congress was the proper originating organ for foreign affairs because it alone could declare war, the pragmatic note struck by John Jay in the sixty-fourth number of *The Federalist* has been amplified to a shriek by the conditions of the time. When our friends and enemies come to us in bulk lots; when the tides of diplomacy make unexpected shifts; when threats and opportunities suddenly loom up and just as suddenly recede; when our generals command foreign troops, and our own troops are under foreign command; when we sit at the head of a complicated set of military, diplomatic and economic alliances; when all people who stand with us are battered by a sustained Communist assault; when these things and more like them are our daily lot, how can the Congress provide the leadership that is wanted, not alone for America, but for a *concert of allied powers?*

It is not structually organized to exert that leadership. It has no means by which it can assess on a day-to-day basis the opportunities and dangers which spring up in remote places. It has no means to relate a happening in one part of the globe to another one ten thousand miles away. It has no ambassadors and no military officers of its own. It is not in continuous contact with foreign leaders everywhere. It does not send or receive communications from them, except under special circumstances. It does not negotiate with them. The President alone is in a position to appraise, formulate and propose what ought to be done and how it should be done so that all parties in the alliance can move forward toward the goals they have in common. In the very nature of things, therefore, the President cannot wait until the Congress tells him what he should do. He must exercise his own discretion—in matters of timing in particular—as he responds to swiftly moving events. For it is he to whom Americans and free people everywhere look for management of peace or war.

The Congress has a right to protest at the way historical events have reduced it in this field from a concurrent and co-ordinate partner with the President to a second who must find the material means to make good what he does. Indeed, if the Congress did not protest, its silence might reflect a dangerous relaxation of its constitutional sensibilities. Most recently, for example, the Congress was on solid ground when it insisted on a chance to register its sentiments before President Truman committed any troops to the North Atlantic Defense Pact. It was immaterial for the Executive to argue that the President had the right to "dispose" of or to deploy the military forces in being without congressional consent. In a strict view, the President, as commander in chief probably has that right. He uses it every day when his authorized agents do as much as post a single Marine on sentry duty before an American embassy abroad. Yet in practical terms, there is a difference between a Marine on sentry duty and several hundred thousand men stationed in Europe and ready for battle. Their presence there clearly forecasts the use of the warmaking power. It clearly involves the capacity to raise, support and maintain armies. All these touch on the powers the Constitution vests in the Congress. And the Congress would have been guilty of negligence if it had not stoutly defended them.

But if this case was clear, a segment of Congress was not without fault in the way it tried to control other expressions of the diplomatic and military impulse. The aim here may have been short run. It may have been inspired solely by the desire of certain Republican spokesmen to create a climate favorable to the victory of their party in the 1952 presidential elections. But if the aim was to safeguard constitutional government—and this was the object claimed for it— then the means used imperiled rather than served that aim. It is important to stress again that neither the Congress nor the Republican party as a collective body was at fault. Nor in some cases, was there lacking a fair ground of objection to the course of the Truman administration. What I have in particular mind, however, as destructive of the constitutional balance, was the way a strong faction of the Congress reached into the presidency and tried to raise the military impulse over the diplomatic one.

One method was a sustained and indiscriminate attack on the loyalty of numerous civilians involved in diplomatic activity. Few of our diplomatic officials, it is true, were driven bodily from the scene, though the number of civilians who refused to accept appointments because of the corrosive atmosphere can never be known. Yet the air was such that President Truman drew increasingly on military figures to fill foreign policy posts that our former tradition assigned to civilians. The motive here admittedly may have been mixed. It may have originated in part in President Truman's private inclinations, divorced from external pressures. Yet the leading element in these selections was the hope that the uniform of the military men in diplomatic stations would fend off a charge that they were pro-Communist. (It is to be remembered that Franklin D. Roosevelt resorted to the same device in the closing days of the New Deal when he appointed military men to stormy jobs related to his economic recovery program.)

The effects of the attacks were not limited to single individuals, whether justly or unjustly accused of pro-Communist sympathies. They pierced the sources of diplomatic intelligence. If the men in the field were to write full, frank and critical reports, they had to be reasonably certain that they were writing in confidence for the eyes of their superiors alone. That confidence was shaken when supposedly confidential reports were broadcast after congressional hearings, when simple statements of fact were wrenched out of context and used to support demands for a loyalty investigation. Even when individuals were cleared months later, the stigma of an investigation still clung to them, with a consequent loss in their utility and effectiveness. Would it not have been reasonable for the President to expect others to guard themselves by qualifying, balancing and diluting their reports so that what they said meant nothing or anything? And since intelligence of this sort is not only useless but dangerous to the national security, would it not have been reasonable for him to assign still more military men to diplomatic missions, counting on their aura of patriotism and respectability to protect them?

Yet this was the least of the ways in which a faction of Congress contributed to the ascendancy of the military. Each time a State Department view was said to conflict with a recommendation of the military, there were those in Congress who insisted that the military one should prevail. (In point of fact, the State Department view often was the one incorrectly attributed to the military, or the other way around.) The necessary sequel was that the operational freedom of the military was enlarged, while a psychological strait jacket was put on civilians involved in the formation of diplomatic policy.

Parallel with all this, some members of the Congress attempted to reach into the presidency, and to detach the military from *his* control. This, of course, is nothing new. From the very outset of our national life, members of the Congress have used various military figures as weapons with which to strike at the President. They encouraged these men to violate orders they received from him. They promised them aid and comfort in their violations. They encouraged interservice rivalries, destructive of military discipline. They tried to arrange things so that military men could report directly to the Congress, thereby circumventing the President's constitutional role as commander in chief.

In a previous era the effects could be absorbed without too much danger. In the age of the amateur soldier, the character of the military establishment and the scope of warfare alike tended to confine the shock to the United States alone. But now that military policy is closely geared to diplomatic policy—and now that both policies are geared to a network of international organizations—and now that our military establishment is spread over the most remote parts of the globe, attempts to detach the military from the effective control of the President can lead to world-wide tremors. Yet, toward the close of the Truman administration, there were those in the Congress who played the old game as if the stakes were the same as in 1818.

It is to the glory of our military that in a time of great danger it produced figures like Generals George C. Marshall, Omar Bradley and Dwight D. Eisenhower, all of whom shared George Washington's firm constitutional discipline. Indeed, one of the few sources of comfort in the past few years was the sight of these men reminding the Congress again and again that the civil authority was supreme. Yet a faction in the Congress still insisted that President Truman should bow to the will of his professional military advisors. A minute later, the same men insisted that the President had "sold out" to those advisors. Then they insisted that his advisors were mere puppets who echoed views that he had reached by a kind of Hitlerian intuition. After that they insisted that one set of advisors should be dismissed and a second set put in their place; that *their* views should bind the President.

Nothing could have more seriously imperiled the traditional American ideal of a skilled military leadership, untouched by, and not of itself touching domestic politics. The Joint Chiefs of Staff, representing the chiefs of the army, air force and naval operations, plus a non-voting chairman, became a central issue in domestic politics. The advice it gave, the plans it proposed, were kicked around as political footballs, with an untold cost in military discipline, confusion, misunderstanding, and in the excitement of doubts among our allies about our political stability. Far from contributing to the principle of civilian supremacy over the military, behavior of this sort can encourage military men to undertake the shaping of public policy by themselves.

The unavoidable strains on our concept of a controlled military impulse define an urgent need to defend all the more vigorously the integrity of the President's role as the commander in chief. Because he is the civil as well as the military head of the armed forces, he is the only person the nation can remove without dragging the whole military apparatus into the market place of domestic politics. This is not to say that the President has no need for professional advisors or for assistance in co-ordinating the work of the government as it bears on the problems of war and peace. Through the recent reorganization of the Defense Department, the Joint Chiefs of Staff, and in any prospective new use of the National Security Council, the aforementioned needs may be more effectively met than they have been up to now. But the leading constitutional fact is that the President is under no obligation to act upon the advice he receives from these quarters.

Few among us have not felt uneasy at times because the President has a latitude to ignore even the best of advice. Yet the Constitution vests in him a primary responsibility for what is done by the Executive. He alone is the commander in chief. He cannot evade or divide the burdens of the part.

Nor in any showdown would we allow him to. His task would be easy, and we would rest comfortably if all he had to know was the body of laws, interpretations of the law, the customs which ruled the behavior of his predecessors, and the opinions of men trusted for their wisdom and devotion to the common interest. But what is he to do in the face of emergencies for which the past provides no rule of action, and the opinions of the present are mixed?

The question rules the atmosphere of our time. Yet it was raised in part by Thomas Jefferson two years after he retired from the presidency and seven years after the Louisiana Purchase. Jefferson observed at the outset that the question was "easy of solution in principle, but sometimes embarrassing in practice." A strict observance of the written laws, he continued, "is doubtless one of the highest duties of a good citizen, but not the highest." In his view, the higher law was the law of necessity, of self-preservation, of saving our country when it was in danger. "To lose our country by a scrupulous adherence to the written law, would be to lose the law itself, with life, liberty, property and all those who are enjoying them with us; thus absurdly sacrificing the end to the means."

Jefferson then put a hypothetical case which was really the Louisiana Purchase thinly veiled. He assumed a situation where the Executive knew that Florida lands could be gained for a reasonable sum; that the sum had not beforehand been appropriated by law, but that Congress would meet within three weeks and then on the first or second day of the session would authorize the necessary money. Ought the President, "for so great an advantage to his country, to have risked himself by transcending the law and making the purchase?"

Jefferson asked. "The public advantage offered, in this supposed case, was indeed immense; but a reverence for the law, and the probability that the advantage might still be *legally* accomplished by a delay of only three weeks, were powerful reasons against hazarding the act."

He continued: But suppose the President could foresee that someone like John Randolph would protract congressional proceedings on the measure until the ensuing spring, by which time new circumstances would change the mind that wanted to sell Florida. "Ought the Executive, in that case, and with that foreknowledge, to have secured the good to his country, and to have trusted to their justice for the transgression of the law?"

The reply was a double affirmative. "I think he ought, and that the act would have been approved." At the same time Jefferson warned against overstepping the law for trifling reasons or in ordinary circumstances. The cases he had in mind where this was permissible were those involving self-preservation that "rendered the *salus populi* supreme over the written law." The officer who is called to act on this superior ground, he said, may risk himself "on the justice of the controlling powers of the Constitution." But those who accept great charges have a duty "to risk themselves on great occasions, when the safety of the nation or some of its very high interests are at stake."

An officer [he concluded] is bound to obey orders; yet he would be a bad one who should do it in cases for which they were not intended, and which involved the most important consequences. The line of discrimination between cases may be difficult; but the good officer is bound to draw it at his own peril, and throw himself on the justice of his country and the rectitude of his motives.

The Jefferson who wrote these words was not thinking primarily of the office and the powers of a President. He had in view the institution of the presidency and what was expected of the man who had its temporary custody. Forty-one years later it was the institution of the presidency that Lincoln also had in mind when he asked his leading question: "Are all the laws but one to go unexecuted and the government itself to go to pieces lest that one be violated?" And three years after that, in 1864, he answered:

My oath to preserve the Constitution imposed on me the duty of preserving by every indispensable means that government, that nation, of which the Constitution was the organic law. Was it possible to lose the nation and yet preserve the Constitution? By general law, life and limb must be protected, yet often a limb must be amputated to save a life, but a life is never wisely given to save a limb. I felt that measures, otherwise unconstitutional, might become lawful by becoming indispensable to the preservation of the Constitution through the preservation of the nation. Right or wrong, I assumed this ground and now assert it. I could not feel that to the best of my ability, I have ever tried to preserve the Constitution, if to save slavery or any minor matter, I should permit the wreck of the government, country, and the Constitution altogether.

The results a Jefferson or a Lincoln produced were excuse for the means they used. And more than that. The Union owes its strength and its life to their acts beyond the letter of the law. Yet we instinctively and rightfully recoil from the notion that one man among us who happens to be the President may have the power to decide what constitutes a crisis for the nation; that one man can decide wherein the greater good of the country lies; that he can decide what law shall be respected; that he can say that existing orders were not intended to rule the circumstances directly before the nation. Our instinct tells us it is not enough to say that when the President makes decisions of this sort he does so at his own peril, and that the country can judge the rectitude of his motives. When we consider but one invention—the atomic bomb—and when we recall that the President has the sole authority over its use, it is plain that he no longer imperils only himself by his decisions. If his decisions are wrong, he can imperil all of humanity, and no one might be left to judge him.

Lately, the Supreme Court attempted to nail down one aspect of this threat when it decided that President Truman's seizure of the steel industry was unconstitutional. The case summarizes all the diplomatic, military and economic forces that shape our times—and for which the internal balance of the Constitution provides no safeguards. We were fighting an international war in Korea, though no formal declaration of war had been made. We had declared a national emergency in the United States, though the war powers granted to President Roosevelt had not been granted to President Truman. We were committed to a build-up of the North Atlantic defense forces. We were committed to supply England with raw steel, to relieve the drain on its economy. Meanwhile, giant labor bargained with giant steel for a new contract. There was a deadlock, and the efforts of executive officers to mediate the dispute failed. The Secretary of Defense at once certified to the President that if there was to be a prolonged strike, the military establishment would be crippled in its defense preparations. Whether the certification expressed a true appraisal of the facts may be debatable; nevertheless, the source of the judgment commanded respect for his opinion.

President Truman, on whom all these pressures converged, thereupon seized the steel industry. The union men went back to work, and the steel companies took the case to the courts. Presently, the Supreme Court rendered a judgment. But what did it actually decide? Three Justices—Fred M. Vinson, Sherman Minton and Stanley Reed—upheld the President. They recognized that his action was extraordinary. But they observed that the times were also extraordinary; that in seizing the steel industry, the President was doing nothing more than ensuring the means by which he could faithfully execute the laws Congress had recently enacted affecting our diplomatic and military efforts.

Six justices—Hugo L. Black, Felix Frankfurter, William O. Douglas, Robert H. Jackson, Harold H. Burton and Tom C. Clark—held against the President. Yet their dictums suggest a broad range of constitutional attitudes.

Mr. Justice Black: The President's power, if any, to issue the order must stem either from an act of Congress or from the Constitution itself. There is no statute that expressly authorizes the President to take possession of property as he did here. Nor is there any act of Congress to which our attention has been directed from which such a power can be fairly implied.

Mr. Justice Frankfurter: The issue before us can be met, and therefore should be, without attempting to define the President's powers comprehensively. I shall not attempt to delineate what belongs to him by virtue of his office beyond the power even of Congress to contract; what authority belongs to him until Congress acts; what kind of problems may be dealt with either by the Congress or by the President or by both . . . what power must be exercised by the Congress and cannot be delegated to the President.

Mr. Justice Douglas: The emergency did not create power; it merely marked an occasion when power should be exercised. And the fact that it was necessary that measures be taken to keep steel in production does not mean that the President, rather than the Congress has the constitutional authority to act. The Congress, as well as the President, is trustee of the national welfare. . . . If we sanctioned the present exercise of power by the President, we would be expanding Article II of the Constitution and rewriting it to suit the political convenience of the present emergency. . . . Today a kindly President uses the seizure power to effect a wage increase and to keep the steel furnaces in production. Yet tomorrow another President might use the same power to prevent a wage increase, to curb trade unions, to regiment labor as oppressively as industry thinks it has been regimented by this seizure.

Mr. Justice Jackson: That comprehensive and undefined presidential powers hold both practical advantages and grave dangers for the country will impress anyone who has served as legal advisor to a President in time of transition and public anxiety. We should not use this occasion to circumscribe, much less to contract, the lawful role of the President as Commander-in-chief. I should indulge the widest latitude of interpretation to sustain his exclusive function to command the instruments of national force, at least when turned against the outer world for the security of our society. But, when it is turned inward, not because of rebellion but because of a lawful economic struggle between industry and labor, it should have no such indulgence.

Mr. Justice Burton: The present situation is not comparable to that of an imminent invasion or threatened attack. We do not face the issue of what might be the President's constitutional power to meet such catastrophic situations. Nor is it claimed that the current seizure is in the nature of a military command ad-

[*306*]

dressed by the President, as Commander in Chief, to a mobilized nation waging, or imminently threatened with, total war. The controlling fact here is that the Congress, within its constitutionally delegated power, has prescribed for the President specific procedures, exclusive of seizure, for his use in meeting the present type emergency.

Mr. Justice Clark: I conclude that where Congress has laid down specific procedures to deal with the type of crisis confronting the President, he must follow those procedures in meeting the crisis; but that in the absence of such action by Congress, the President's independent power to act depends upon the gravity of the situation confronting the country.

Detailed examination of the opinions would show that only Justices Black and Douglas attempted to circumscribe the powers of the President. The four other Justices who concurred in the majority opinion held that the President was specifically directed by the Congress to use the Taft-Hartley Law in the dispute, and this he failed to do. But none of these four, any more than the three who dissented from the majority, attempted to fix the presidential course in a future international emergency. If the membership of the Court is viewed as a whole, a seven to two majority acknowledged the wisdom of allowing events to decide the merits of any further cases which might arise. This, and not a hard and fast denial of the President's inherent powers to deal with a grave emergency, is, I believe, what gives this case its "historic importance."

The question which worried Jefferson remains unanswered by the Court. Our constitutional rules and our pressing physical needs are still in a state of conflict. What we expect the President to do under the law continues to encounter the opposite pull of what we expect of the presidential institution. How can the tension be reduced? It can be reduced if the Congress does its *legislative* part in meeting national and international expectations. If it fails to do what it is competent to do, then the people, in their search for pragmatic solutions, will enlarge the presidency to a dangerous point where it might become an autonomous source of action, indiscriminate in its objects, and beyond the immediate and effective reach of the other organs of the government.

The opinion of Mr. Justice Jackson in the steel case contains an eloquent passage which bears on this point.

I have no illusion [he said] that any decision by this Court can keep power in the hands of Congress if it is not wise and timely in meeting its problems. A crisis that challenges the President equally, or perhaps primarily, challenges Congress. If not good law, there was worldly wisdom in the maxim attributed to Napoleon that "The tools belong to the man who can use them." We may say that power to legislate for emergencies belongs in the hands of Congress, but only Congress itself can prevent power from slipping through its fingers.

13

Reorganization of the Executive

IIIIOIIIIIIIIIIIIIOIIIIIIIIIIIIOIIIIIIIIIIIIOIIIIIIIIIIIIOIIIIIIIIIIIIOIIIIIIIIIIIIOIIIIIIIIIIIIOIIIIIII

Jefferson's warning about Washington's merits – Amplified into theory about modern presidency – its doubtful historical basis – Hamilton on the subject of executive energy – Negative effects on presidency if Vice President shared the executive work – If Cabinet members were held to collective responsibility – If English-style Cabinet Secretariat was formed – If Cabinet members had the right to share in congressional debate – If Council of Elder Statesmen was attached to the presidency – Or if Legislative Council was attached – Warning against legislature with great powers and few responsibilities – Solution in management of Constitution lies in strengthening all arms – Experience in strengthening the President as a manager – But administration is no substitute for social policy – Congress must play its part.

Not long after the draft of the new Constitution reached Thomas Jefferson at his Paris post in late 1787, he made it known that he was deeply concerned over the absence of a Bill of Rights, and the presence of an invitation to a President to succeed himself for life. "Our jealousy," he wrote, as he warned about the second defect, "is only put to sleep by the unlimited confidence we all repose in the person to whom we all look as our President. After him inferior characters may perhaps succeed and awaken us into the danger [Washington's] merit has led us into."

[*309*]

Though an agreement on a Bill of Rights was reached without great difficulty, only three states showed any desire to seal off the open end provision on executive tenure. Nor was it sealed off until 164 years later with the enactment of the Twenty-second Amendment in February, 1951.

In the meantime, Jefferson's warning about Washington's merits moved far beyond the point of re-eligibility to which it was originally limited. It is now a full-blown theory which presumes to explain the main strains of the modern presidency and to sanction various reforms in its nature. Briefly, this theory asserts that the Founders, knowing that Washington would be the first President, scaled all the powers and duties of the office to his size. But when he passed on, what had been formed at Philadelphia in 1787 as if for a single life span remained fixed in the Constitution as a legal mandate for a greatness that can never be repeated. The deep fracture in the modern presidency, therefore, is due to the upward hoist of the law, and the downward pull of limited men, whose talents are inadequate to the occasion. How can the breach be closed? Only by scaling down the presidential role so that it can fit the lesser men who came after the first giant.

Of the specific remedies advanced, six are here presented: (1) The Vice President should share more fully in the work of the presidency. (2) Cabinet members should be held to a collective responsibility for policy and administration. (3) A Cabinet secretariat on the English mold should be formed to co-ordinate all executive departments, define what needs a decision, and then oversee how those decisions are put into effect. (4) Cabinet members should have the right to sit on the floor of the Congress and share in a debate. (5) A Coun-

[*310*]

cil of Elder Statesmen, above party and ambition should be formed as an advisory group to the President. (6) A Legislative Council, formed of the Cabinet, party leaders in Congress, and Elder Statesmen, should be joined to the presidency, to bridge the gap between Executive and the legislative policy-making efforts.

It is argued that the adoption of these proposals would ease the physical wear and tear on the President. It would reduce the number of decisions he has to make in person. Through a division of labor, moreover, each problem would get a careful but swift study by the person to whom it was entrusted. And, finally, with more persons actively engaged in the work of the presidency, the danger of executive dictatorship would be reduced, and republican principles would be better safeguarded.

The argument sounds plausible. But before looking into its merits, suppose we first ask if its two underlying historical assumptions are true. Do the *functions* and *character* of the presidency as described in the Constitution actually owe their presence to the figure of Washington? And have his successors actually fallen below the mark he set?

The record of the Constitutional Convention answers the first question in the negative. To the extent that Washington was the model for the work done there, he was the type symbol in whose name certain restrictive proposals were omitted from the constitutional text. But his physical existence did not visibly enter into the *positive* grant of functions and duties to the President, as they are actually set forth in the Constitution. The lines of the grant were abstracted from the experiences under the Articles of Confederation, from the model of governorships in Massachusetts and New York,

[*311*]

and from the English Crown. Above all, they were abstracted from the other parts of the constitutional system within which the Executive was to function.

This is not to say that Washington had no influence at all over the presidency. The influence was enormous. But it came *after* he took his first oath of office. He was acutely aware that he stood on virginal ground; that all his acts might pass over into precedent; that it would be far better to make correct and sound first decisions than to attempt to remedy initial errors at a later date. Indeed, the proof of his genius is in the fact that the presidency today still adheres to the organic decisions he made more than a century and one half ago. Besides the deep mark he left on legal precedents, Washington lent the moral force of his person as a rule for imitation by his successors. It was he, more than any other man, who asserted and defended the basic view that the civil impulse shall be superior to the military impulse. It was he, too, who proved that there could be a transfer of power in the Executive without the political tumults or the interruption in administration known to the other governments of the day. Yet this does not say that the actual words in the Constitution were tailored to his form.

The second question was whether Washington's successors have actually fallen below the mark he set. One must admit that in the history of the presidency faltering men have been elevated to the post, though significantly, since the opening of the twentieth century, strength has followed more frequently on the heel of strength. But on balance, the appraisal Abraham Lincoln made of his fifteen predecessors on the day of his inauguration seems a fair one for his sixteen successors as well. "They have conducted [the nation] through many perils," Lincoln said, "and generally with great success." In fact, it is this "general" success which has steadily enlarged what the people expect of the presidential institution.

One of the great events of the Jackson years, for example, was the fight over the National Bank charter. And the part played by Jackson has given a heroic cast to his whole administration. Yet in 1935, when the Roosevelt administration put through a banking measure with political and economic overtones at least as great as those which rang out from Jackson's effort, the event was lost in the other achievements and expectancies of the hour. President Truman initiated an extraordinary number of new programs in the field of foreign affairs. Yet he was attacked for being indecisive and timid in standing up to the dangers of the day. Thus, while Roosevelt's Lend-Lease program is viewed as a great imaginative achievement, Truman was demoted in status—though the bold scope of what he actually inaugurated far overshadowed Lend-Lease. General Eisenhower, similarly, will be strained by this subtle process in which the mark set for a President is progressively raised above the one to which his predecessor was held.

The historical record, then, denies the assumptions underlying the six proposed reforms mentioned at the outset. Nevertheless, the reforms should be examined on their own merits, particularly since they have been advocated by presidential candidates, authorities on constitutional law, experts on public administration, and eminent journalists. Proceeding in this way, we find, however, that their supporting argument is challenged by the men who sat in the Constitutional Convention. If the latter could now speak, they would say that they had considered all the proposed reforms in one or another way and had rejected them. They would also say that the reforms would change the presidency into a Cabinet form of government without changing the Congress into an English parliament. And from this they would say that the reforms would produce a sharp, if not fatal, cleavage between power and responsibility.

All this, in fact, is clearly stated in the seventieth number of *The Federalist*, written by Alexander Hamilton. The compass of that paper was narrowed to one point, namely, the unity which is a leading ingredient of executive energy. This unity, Hamilton said, could be destroyed by vesting the Executive in two or more men of equal dignity and authority; or by vesting it ostensibly in one man, subject in whole or in part to the control and co-operation of others in the capacity of counselors to him. When two men are clothed with equal dignity and authority, he argued, a natural ground for personal emulation and even animosity is staked out. Their bitter dissensions can lessen their respectability, weaken their authority, and distract their plans and operations in critical emergencies. Moreover, the dissensions radiating outward can split the community into violent and irreconcilable factions, adhering to the different individuals who compose the Executive.

Even when the Executive is vested in one man, but subject to the partial or complete control and co-operation of others, the arrangement deprives the people of the two greatest securities they can have for the faithful exercise of any delegated power. These, said Hamilton, are the power to censure and the power to punish. Both would lose their force, because blame would be shifted from one person to another with so much dexterity, and so plausibly that it would be impossible to determine on whom the punishment for a pernicious measure ought to fall.

The further refinements of the Hamiltonian argument can be waived. But the truth of the part just cited has its proof in the experience of the contemporary presidency. What splits the energy of the President—what causes bottlenecks in the White House—what contributes to a confusion of policy—what fosters bitter dissensions—what slackens the force of public opinion in censuring and punishing misdeeds—all have a common cause. It is that the presidency is shared, divided and crippled by a multiplicity of hands in the executive department proper, by a corps of independent agencies, and by that element of the Congress which chooses to act as if it were the President, while it defaults on its proper legislative duties. Part of this disorder is unavoidable; part of it may even provide long-run Constitutional safety valves. But would matters be helped if any of the proposed reforms were adopted?

1. Consider, first, the reforms aimed at enlarging the importance of the Vice Presidency. What duties can the Vice President lawfully share with the President? Can he be the chief administrator? The commander in chief of the armed forces? The chief organ of foreign affairs? The Constitution lodges all these functions and many others in the President. If he delegated them, he would define the basis for his own impeachment. And this would be quite apart from the compounded chaos any such delegation would produce through the whole executive order.

Nor would matters be helped any if the Vice President were put in charge of an independent agency or board. Our experience with such an arrangement in the case of Vice President Henry Wallace during World War II posts a warning of what this leads to. It neither relieves the work load of the presidency, nor fosters administrative efficiency. The Vice President at the head of an agency or board is just another administrator. The President may want to change, abolish, censure or supersede the board by something else. If called upon to judge between its claims and those of a rival body, he is not free to do what he thinks is best. He knows that if he decides against the Vice President, the nation does not see that the Vice President is simply one more administrator who has to take his chances in the normal scuffling that goes on inside the administrative order. The nation sees that the man who stands second in the land is cast aside in favor of someone in a far inferior station. Under the circumstances, the President would be inclined to tolerate inadequacies in a vice presidential performance that he would not hesitate to correct if they showed up in a lesser person. Conversely, if the President censured the Vice President, the personal humiliation, strain and messy political complications for all parties would be intense.

Much the same sort of danger arises when the President surveys the non-legal functions inherent in the presidency. He cannot readily ask the Vice President to assume the role of party leader, since the Vice President generally represents a different party viewpoint; in fact, they often represent opposite wings of a party. If the President turned over the direction of the party apparatus to the Vice President, he would place a powerful legislative lever in the hands of his party rivals, while he completely disarmed himself. As things now stand, the vice presidency is not so weak as some people say. Though the Vice President sits in the Cabinet only by invitation, the caution some Presidents have shown in extending that invitation underscores one leading fact. The Vice President may lack the power to hang any private citizen. But he can at least try to hang the President by betraying Cabinet confidences, and by misrepresenting the attitudes of the President to the Senate, or the other way around. But if he is faithful in his role as a communication link, and if he is discreet in the power of warning he wields, he can materially assist both the President and the Senate in their working relationships.

Nor is this all. As the presiding officer of the Senate, the Vice President receives communications affecting the public business which reach him directly, without first passing through the President's hands. A 1951 example was the important communication Vice President Alben Barkley received from the Council of Europe, requesting the presence of a United States congressional delegation at Strassburg to discuss crucial aspects of European federation. He can pigeonhole messages of this sort and few men in the Senate will be any the wiser. Or he can transmit the messages to the Senate at a time most favorable to the results he wants. To all this activity there should of course be added the vote he casts in case of a tie and his parliamentary ruling, which can shape the whole course of legislation.

But of the President's work which might be increasingly shared by the Vice President without compounding the ground for strain, only one area holds some promise—the purely ceremonial functions. In England, the whole Royal House shares the ceremonial burden. Even so, the English press has come to say that the work still left to the sovereign subjects him to an inhuman strain. How much more, then, is the strain on the President, who must bear the whole ceremonial burden by himself, in addition to all his bread and butter duties. The Vice President's share in the ceremonial burden might be enlarged and at the same time carried off with more grace if he was furnished with an official residence of his own. Perhaps Blair House might do. Beyond this, it is difficult to see any further areas where the Vice President can be safely employed.

2. What is true of the Vice President is equally true of the Cabinet. The work of each Cabinet officer, as *a department head,* is specified by the laws of the Congress and is kept under examination by the special committees of the Congress and by the courts. But the President, I repeat, has a constitutional responsibility for what the executive branch of the government does. He cannot divorce himself from it. Nor can he entrust to his Cabinet members, individually or collectively, any primary responsibility for formulating executive policy. In an organic sense, the President must be his own Secretary of State, his own Secretary for Defense, his own Secretary of the Treasury, etc.—subject, of course, to the laws.

Furthermore, the President must have the right, limited only by law, to use his Cabinet in any way he feels will best advance the national interest. Specifically, he must have the right to invite anyone to a Cabinet meeting; to hold meetings at his pleasure; to impose a strict limit on what is discussed; to throw the discussion open to all voices on all subjects, or to ignore any advice he gets. He will suffer in the long run if he does not or cannot surround himself with men who because of their ability and integrity rightfully deserve his confidence. And he will also suffer if he has gifted men about him whose sound advice he ignores. But for good or ill, nothing in the law demands that he bind himself by the advice he receives. As John Adams said in his *Letters to a Boston Patriot:*

> In all great and essential measures the President is bound by honor and his conscience, by his oath to the Constitution, as well as his responsibility to the public opinion of the nation, to act his own mature and unbiased judgment, though unfortunately, it may be in direct contradiction to the advice of all his ministers.

If the President surrendered any part of his primary policy-making functions either to Cabinet members individually, or the Cabinet as a collegiate body, one or all of three things would probably occur. Dissension within the Cabinet would be multiplied. Again, the nation would not know on whom praise or blame should be fixed. The President would find that he was the captive of the men he had appointed and he would have to work twice as hard to restore his authority over them.

3. A Cabinet secretariat, formed of permanent civil servants on the English model, meets the same objection. It is doubtful if the high reputation for effective actions this sort of secretariat enjoys even in its native home is fully justified. But this aside, if a secretariat were brought into being in an American frame, the great danger would lie *in* its effectiveness. Because of its permanency, it might draw rights to itself through a process of squatter sovereignty, and in this position would be a wedge between the President and the Cabinet members. On the other hand, it is altogether possible that Cabinet officers would be tempted to use the secretariat's bureaucratic trappings of minutes and agendas

as a straight jacket to restrict the President's freedom of action. The strain on the President, unavoidable in any event because of the way Cabinets are formed, would be increased instead of diminished. The intra co-ordination of Cabinet work must come from the *President's* personal staff, and not from one that serves the Cabinet as a collective body. It can come from an assistant to the President. It can come from the Bureau of the Budget. Also, it can come from inter-departmental *ad hoc* committees, formed for a special pur-pose and dissolved when the purpose is served. The latter device was effectively used by President Roosevelt in World War II, and invites continued imitation.

4. Would the public business be handled better if Cabinet officers were allowed to sit on the floor of the Congress and take part in its debates? The answer is no.

To begin with, simply as a means to get at the facts, this proposal offers nothing equal to what comes out of com-mittee hearings. A basis of comparison was provided in 1951 when Secretary of State Dean Acheson spoke to the Con-gress in the auditorium of the Library of Congress in re-sponse to a general protest that the Congress was kept in the dark about the course of our foreign policy. After reviewing the main trends in our diplomacy, Secretary Acheson invited questions from the floor. Judged in the most favorable light, this experiment in Cabinet government produced nothing more than a formless press conference. The general feeling of those present was that the affair was a waste of time. But if the same Secretary appeared before a Congressional com-mittee, he would be taken apart cell by cell. Not all of them would be put back in the same place when the committee members were through with him.

Reorganization of the Executive

The more serious objection to the plan is that we have none of the constitutional traits that give buoyancy to the arrangement in England. Our Cabinet officers do not rise exclusively from the legislature. Those that do, do not hold their seats in the legislature while they serve in the Cabinet. The fate of rank and file party members in power is not indivisibly linked to the Cabinet by party discipline. We do not have group responsibility in the Cabinet for what all do. Above all, the Executive does not hold a constitutional mandate to provide a legislative impulse from on top. Here, the legislative impulse is designed to come from below, from the individual members of the Congress.

If our conscious aim is to produce a profound revolution in our whole constitutional system, then a grant to Cabinet members of a right to share in congressional debate would materially advance it. But if that is not our aim; if our aim is to preserve the present constitutional balance, then we run great danger of upsetting it by extending the right of debate to Cabinet members. The full and, I believe, unanswerable argument to this effect was set forth by the late Professor Harold J. Laski in his book, *The American Presidency.* I quote two of the most pertinent passages:

If the cabinet is to sit in the Congress, the President must choose its members from those who are likely to be influential with it. This at once narrows his choice. It makes him think of the men who already have some standing in its eyes, and some direct knowledge of its complicated procedure. But this means putting a premium on the experienced members of either house as cabinet material. It means, further, that the more successful they are upon the floor of Congress, the more independent they are likely to be vis-a-vis the President. They will develop a status of their own as they become known as the men who are able to make Congress take their views about the bills they promote. They are likely, in fact, to become rivals of the President himself for influence with Congress. The problem, in this situation, of maintaining cabinet unity would necessarily become a difficult matter. Congress might easily tend to weaken the administration by playing off the cabinet, or some part of it, against the President and some other part. The loyalty of the cabinet officer would be divided.

And again:

Would not the position of a President like Lincoln, whose hold on his own colleagues was small when he assumed power, become virtually untenable if Congress were in a position to play them off against him? Is there not, indeed, the danger of a powerful cabal of cabinet officers becoming the effective mediator between the President and Congress with a vital shift, as a consequence, in the present delicate balance of power? Would it not, further, be likely that a tendency would rapidly develop for any cabinet officer who became outstandingly influential with Congress to become the rival of the President himself, and where the latter was weak, in actual fact his master?

In short, the effect of the arrangement would be to transform the President into a person more akin to the President of France than to the President of the United States. The Congress, meanwhile, would not be changed into an English parliament. It would assume the character of the Continental Congress. It could effectively overthrow the policies of the President without overthrowing itself at the same time.

5. What would be the effect of a Council of Elder Statesmen, organized on a formal basis, and attached to the presidency? The probabilities are these. It would be drawn into a rivalry with the existing Cabinet; and the President, caught in the middle, would be pulled apart. If rivalry was avoided,

the Council could still be a source of strain. If the President acted contrary to their advice on any point, it would be charged that he willfully ignored the views of selfless men who had nothing except the interest of the country at heart. Few would see that the President alone is responsible to the electorate; that in making a decision in any one area, he must weigh its effects on all the other areas for which he alone is personally accountable.

This does not mean that we can do without the service and advice of our elder statesmen, or that we have no need for advisory groups formed of private parties. We need both. Yet the elder statesmen can better serve the President and the nation when they are employed in these ways: to head private groups *outside* the government set up to clarify opinion or to suggest solutions to important public problems; to head presidential commissions appointed to study particular problems falling within the scope of their expert knowledge; to advise the President in private and at his request; and finally to act as advisors to the *Congress,* not alone before congressional committees, but at the grass roots level of congressional districts.

6. A presidential council formed of legislative leaders, members of the present Cabinet and elder statesmen, could prove the most destructive of all plans to "help the President." In the legislators, the public would see a body of men who had actually been elected to posts of authority. And because they are so closely identified with the lawmaking process, if they gave the President advice and he ignored it, there would be a great outcry that the President had willfully violated orders. Moreover, many of these men, being ambitious for the presidency in their own right—whether

they are of the President's party or of the opposition—would not hesitate to betray private confidences and to make political capital out of any discussion that suited their purposes.

In the end, either the President would never solicit the opinions of the council, in which case, there would be no point to its existence; or he would find that his role as an Executive had been usurped by the leaders of the Congress. If he had to contend with a group of advisors he couldn't fire but who took away his power of decision, yet held him responsible for what *they* had decided, not only the President's position but our entire constitutional order would be unsettled.

There is a great and serious gap in our constitutional system between the President as a policy maker, and the Congress as a policy maker. Both hold constitutional mandates which merit them that role. But it makes no more sense to subordinate the President's mandate to that of the Congress than it does to turn the order of subordination around. As things now stand, it is difficult enough for the President to find a congenial group of party leaders in the House and Senate who can act as his representatives on the floor of the Congress. These men have their own home districts to worry about while they are acting the part of majority leaders. They will not lightheartedly run home-town risks in the name of the national interest. Moreover, they are not elected to the post of majority leader by Americans as a whole. They are elected by the dominant party faction inside the Congress; and this faction can be hostile to the President. As it is, the President must strain to the limits all the gentle arts of political seduction when he tries to swing a majority leader to his cause. The present formula is bad. Why worsen it, by saddling the President with institutionalized political advisors?

Beyond these six proposed innovations, there are numerous others, all designed in some way to crop the existing size of the presidency. In defense of the innovators, it can be said that they have a right to propose any change that suits their fancy. We are not bound until eternity to be ruled from the grave of the constitutional fathers. Yet the by-stander also has a right to demand that the innovators accept one of two alternatives. If the functions shorn from the President are transferred to the Congress, the transfer must be accompanied by a new constitutional formula which would make the legislature responsible and accountable for the way it used its new powers and met its new duties. Otherwise, the weakness of the amputated Executive would serve as ground for enlarging the license of the legislature.[1] If this idea is rejected, the only other alternative is that no part of the government shall assume the functions shorn from the President. They would revert to the people. And the people would have themselves to blame if they then suffered from causes the organs of the government had neither the power nor the duty to check.

[1] It can be observed in this connection that American political literature contains exhaustive and exhausting debates about the respective merits of the American presidency and the English prime ministership. In a sense, the whole discussion is pointless. The two can be compared in their isolated details and judged for the strength and weakness they show in specific situations. But the basic fact is that they do not function in isolated detail. They function within integrated and wholly different constitutional formulas for responsible power. And any attempt to graft a special trait of the prime ministership onto the presidency, without regard to the whole system it serves, could produce as great a distortion of line as if the grafting process was reversed from the presidency onto the prime ministership.

Some innovators are prepared to take the logical step of tying responsibility to a new gravitational center of power. But others are not. In the name of checking the danger of "executive aggrandizements," what they really want is a legislature with great powers and few responsibilities, and an Executive with few powers and great responsibilities. The real name for this is the no-government of the Articles of Confederation. It is made to order for free-booters in the political, military, economic and social community, who could then raid the legislature for subsidies, offices, emoluments, prestige, immunities and privileges, to the detriment of the people as a whole. The real authors of the mischief would be lost in the crowd as the people tried vainly to determine on whom to fix the blame and finally turned their accusing glance on the clear and solitary figure of the President.

What in the long run would be the result of a tendency to hold the President responsible for whatever happened at the hands of a powerful but irresponsible legislature? In all probability the tendency would set forces in motion which would reverse the current of danger and then quicken it. For it would become apparent that, contrary to expectations, the troubles that beset the nation had not vanished when the President was cut down. Bit by it, the notion could take hold that legislative skullduggery was at the bottom of the evil. Then, just as the people had formerly viewed the triumph of the legislature over the Executive as the guarantor of all good, now in a turnabout, they would seek the guarantee in the triumph of the Executive over the legislature; and they would be strongly disposed to support all proposals to enlarge the autonomous powers of the President. And so, in this sequence, the innovators who aimed at an all-powerful but irresponsible legislature would advance their own undoing. They would foster the rise of one-man rule, beginning perhaps, in the golden haze of Augustus, but ending in the blood bath of a Nero.

We are, of course, not immune to such dangers even though the paper powers of the Executive seemed to keep pace with his mounting responsibilities. The political climate could still be such that the President might be denied the authority to use the legal powers vested in him. He might be forced to rely wholly on moral persuasion and on gentlemen's agreements to achieve the public results for which he was responsible. But the rival elements in society who had nothing to fear except a tongue-lashing would have no real inducement to be gentlemen. As they continued to tear at each other, they could also tear about the whole of the society they had earlier paralyzed. Thus far, our constitutional order, except at the time of the Civil War, has managed to foster a healthy power rivalry while holding all forms of power in check. The Constitution, in short, has helped create the sort of social and political conditions favorable to its own existence.

Its continued functioning in this way does not lie in the direction of a Congress raised *over* the President or a President raised over the Congress. Along with the Court, each must be strong in its own right. Each must be equipped to do the work that falls to it as a legislature, or as an executive, or as a court.

Recently, we have come to recognize that the presidency has needed strengthening *within itself* as an Executive. Until 1939, Presidents had nothing except a random clerical and secretarial staff to serve them directly. Clerks were either paid by the President himself, or they were loaned to him by various departments. Even presidential secretaries until the turn of the twentieth century were generally male members of the President's family; but in any identity, their salaries came from the President's own pocket. It was in the days of Theodore Roosevelt that Congress for the first time appropriated funds for a single presidential secretary. But it saw no reason to provide for any more than one until the days of Herbert Hoover. The number was then increased to three, a fact that won the acid compliment of Franklin D. Roosevelt, who said it was the finest accomplishment of the Hoover administration.

The mushroom growth of executive operations in the course of the depression led to the appointment in 1937 of the President's Committee on Administrative Management. Its job was to examine and suggest how the whole engine for executive energy could be made to run more efficiently. Briefly, the Committee called for an expansion and continuous reorganization of the President's personal staff; for the re-establishment of the President's control over the executive branch of the government; for a new system of consultation; and for a continuous regrouping of executive functions into a manageable number of major departments and agencies. All this strengthening at the top was to be an intermediate stage leading—in a seeming paradox—to the decentralization of executive operations on a regional basis. That is, with the President in firm control over all his arms, their center of gravity could be shifted out of Washington and closer to the people they touched. Here they would be more responsive to local conditions with a consequent reduction in bureaucratic rigidity.

The effort to turn these recommendations into law was defeated by a combination of forces. Among them, Roosevelt's plan to reorganize the Federal Courts had produced a political climate in which the word "reorganization" rang out as a synonym for "dictatorship." Fortunately for the management of the war that lay just over the horizon, a reorganization act was finally approved in April, 1939. But the forces that had opposed the plan proved successful at least in preserving the fugitive chastity of the independent agencies. These were expressly exempted from the President's touch. However, subject to the right of veto vested in the Congress, the President was empowered to regroup, transfer or reassign the functions of a host of lesser executive agencies.

The major achievement of the 1939 Act was the provision it made for an Executive Office of the President, the first in history. Forming it at first were the White House Office itself; the Bureau of the Budget, which had been transferred from the Treasury Department; the Office of Government Reports; the National Resources Board; and the Office of Emergency Management. At the time of this writing, the White House Office, representing the President's personal staff, consists of three secretaries, one assistant to the President, six administrative assistants, one special counsel to the President, an executive clerk, a physician and military aides from the three service branches. The Executive Office as a whole consists of the Council of Economic Advisors, the Bureau of the Budget, the National Security Council and the National Security Resources Board.

The events of World War II and the continuing defense

program which followed it set the stage for the Hoover Commission, authorized in 1947. Its work at the time represented the most thoroughgoing inspection of the executive machinery that had ever been made in our history. Its recommendations differed in scope and details from those made by the 1937 Committee, but the general aim of the Commission was along the lines laid down by its immediate predecessor. Though the old forces of negation and suspicion in the Congress, the Civil Service, the agency spokesmen for pressure groups, etc., are as strong as ever, some progress has been made in enacting its proposals. In this, the Commission has had an advantage which its 1937 forerunner did not have. An increasing part of the public has come to see the problems of administrative management as something more than a dry-as-dust issue. Without an effective and continuous answer to this problem, the presidency can flounder, and with it the nation and its Western friends. It is this new awareness, apparently, which underlies the successful adoption of a number of recommendations proposed by the special committee President Eisenhow appointed to streamline the Executive.

This committee, or any of its successors, should be backed up by a *permanent* reorganization law, enacted by the Congress. Since the operations of the presidency are now subject to so many sudden expansions and contractions, it is of essential importance that the work of executive reorganization should go on continuously. There should be no limitation on the period in which the President is free to submit plans to the Congress. He should always have that right. Moreover, the plans should go into automatic effect if the Congress does not choose within a stated time to exercise its veto by a concurrent resolution.

But it is well worth remembering that administration efficiency does not by itself guarantee a better presidential performance, any more than the introduction of the Civil Service in 1883 proved an automatic guarantee of good government. The simple and regrettable fact is that administration is no substitute for social policy. It is simply the means by which a policy can be attained. Indeed, it would be far better to have bad administration and good policy than it would to be have good administration and bad policy. The proof of this lies in the unsurpassed excellence the Nazi administrators showed in the management of their concentration camps and gas chambers.

It is equally important to note that if administrative reorganization is to achieve its maximum aims, it must be paralleled by modifications in the congressional performance. No matter how well the Executive is ordered as a working machine, that machine is still geared in the main to the administration of laws enacted by Congress. The Congress does not fulfill all its Constitutional duties when it merely posts a strict guard on what the President does, any more than the President fulfills his when he calls the nation's attention to what the Congress failed to do. They are meant to wrangle; if they did not, we would have reason to be suspicious. But they are also meant to rule so that the nation's business can go forward.

That business is not well served when the Congress shuns its own responsibility as a legislature when it is confronted by hard decisions. It is not well served when the Congress, in violation of its own rules, adds pernicious legislative riders which defeat the very purposes for which a measure is enacted. It is not well served when the Congress votes pork barrel appropriations, while it calls for economy in government. It is not well served in any detail when the Congress loads the President with responsibilities but denies him the means for discharging them. By methods of this sort, the Congress can bring the most perfect administrative machine to a halt. It can heighten the evils of bureaucratic rigidity and forever delay consideration of how power can be decentralized once the President's authority is reasserted over the executive branch. It can force the President to resort to devious and circuitous means to meet the needs of the hour. It can contribute to the formation of habits where the law is ignored in all cases.

If we cannot stiffen the will of the Congress to act the part of a legislature in all cases, we can at least equip the President with a defensive instrument when the Congress shows signs of placing him in an impossible position. That instrument is the right of item veto. The Confederate Constitution armed Jefferson Davis with it. Three fourths of our states have similarly armed their governors. Its use would enable the President to pinpoint the pernicious details of legislation and appropriations, and to veto them while he signed what remained. At present he has to throw the baby out with the bath water, or to drink the bath water in order to embrace the baby. The Congress could override the President's veto if it wished. But the people would know who was the responsible agent for any mishap that resulted later.

As the President is entitled to this defensive instrument, so is the Congress entitled to equip itself with the full staff it needs to scrutinize every penny the Executive requests for its operations. The Congress, at present, has only the sketchiest means for examining the requests for money it receives from the Executive. And to this extent, it forfeits its authority over the spending power which the Constitution correctly vests in the Congress alone. Perhaps the Congress could employ the General Accounting Office as its screening agent, in addition to the Appropriations Committees which now attempt to do this work. If the General Accounting Office, which is an agent of the Congress, proves an inadequate instrument, the Congress might consider setting up a joint budget bureau of its own, as a countercheck on the enormously influential Bureau of the Budget which serves the President. Through the wise use of its power over the purse, the Congress could materially reduce the danger of Executive irresponsibility in those matters where the President of necessity now holds the power of initiative.

But if all these things need pointing out, only a man with the soul of a slave can fail to marvel at the way these two arms of the government have generally met all the shocks and murmurs the nation has encountered since its infancy. We are told by James Madison that on the last day of the Constitutional Convention, as the members were signing the product of their debates, Benjamin Franklin looked toward the President's chair, at the back of which a rising sun happened to be painted. Then he observed to a few members near him that painters had found it difficult to distinguish in their art a rising from a setting sun. "I have," said Franklin, "often and often in the course of the session, and the vicissitudes of my hopes and fears as to its issue, looked at that behind the president without being able to tell whether it was rising or setting. But now at length I have the happiness to know that it is a rising and not a setting sun." No chance remark by any man has won so stupendous a confirmation at the hands of history.

Index

[335]

Index

Index

Index

Index

Kitchen Cabinet, 97–98
Know-Nothings, 141
Knox, Henry, 283
Korean War, 37, 228, 304

Labor Department, 259–60, 262
Labor leaders, 229–31
Labor Standards Bureau, 260
Labor unions, 229–31
Labour party, English, 179, 230
La Follette, Robert M., 44, 154, 202
La Follette Progressive movement, 42
Lamar, Mirabeau Buonaparte, 93
Landon, Alfred, 185–86
Laski, Harold J., 321–22
Leadership, political parties, 40–42, 83–84
Legal talent, natural selection, 224–25
Legislative Council, 311, 323–26
Lend-Lease program, 313
Letters to a Boston Patriot, Adams, 319
Liberal political party, 177–82
Lincoln, Abraham, 24–25, 26, 65–66, 67–68, 79, 83, 84, 107, 180, 184–85, 204, 211, 222, 223, 224, 282, 312–13
Lincoln, Mary Todd, 198
Literary Digest poll, 185
Livingston, Edward, 285
Loco-Focos, 141
Longevity, presidential, 187–88
Longstreet, James, 25 fn.
Louisiana Purchase, 36, 69–72, 301–303

MacArthur, Douglas, 211
Machiavelli, 92–93, 97, 208
Madison, Dolly, 197
Madison, James, 3, 72, 76–79, 81, 85, 105, 107, 119, 121, 124–25, 131, 132, 184, 211, 221, 225, 279, 293, 333
Mangum, W.P., 145
Maritime Commission, 245
Marshall, George C., 299

Martial talent, natural selection, 210–17
Martyred presidents, 83
Mason, George, 119
McCarthyism, 210
McClellan, George Brinton, 184
McClellan, John, 211
McHenry, James, 283–84, 285
McKinley, Ida Saxton, 197
McKinley, William, 26, 37, 66, 83, 176, 185, 211, 222
McLean, John, 140, 145
Mercantile system, 242
Mexican War, 212, 294
Military powers of president, 280–83
Military technology, 286–88
Militia, state, 278
Mint, U.S., 253
Minton, Sherman, 305
Monroe, Eliza, 197
Monroe, James, 66, 79, 123, 131, 132, 140, 211, 221, 284 fn.
Morris, Gouverneur, 119
Moses, George H., 44
Mussolini, Benito, 217

National Bank charter, 313
National Bureau of Standards, 260
National Labor Relations Board, 245
National primary election, 160–66
National Production Authority, 260
National Republican political party, 139, 141, 144
National Resources Board, 264, 329
National Security Act of 1947, 265
National Security Council, 265–66, 300, 329
National Security Resources Board, 265–66
Natural aristocracy, 111–16, 183–84, 200, 221
Naturalization Service, 255
Natural selection, laws, 183–236
Navy Department, 284–85
Nazi Revolution, 288
Newton, Isaac, 258
New York *Herald*, 68

Index

[*340*]

Index

Index